The Economist
Intelligence Unit

Making Quality Work:
Lessons from Europe's Leading Companies

By GEORGE BINNEY

Special Report No. P655

The Economist Intelligence Unit
A member of the Economist Group
40 Duke Street, London W1A
United Kingdom

Ashridge

MANAGEMENT GUIDES

LONDON
The Economist Intelligence Unit
40 Duke Street
London W1A 1DW
United Kingdom
Telephone: (071) 493 6711; Telex: 266353 EIU G; Fax (071) 499 9767

NEW YORK
The Economist Intelligence Unit
215 Park Avenue South
New York
NY 10003
USA
Telephone: (1 212) 460 0600; Telex: 175567; Fax: (1 212) 995 8837

HONG KONG
The Economist Intelligence Unit
10th Floor, Luk Kwok Centre
72 Gloucester Road
Wanchai
Hong Kong
Telephone: (852) 529 0833; Telex: 74364; Fax: (852) 865 1554

© The Economist Intelligence Unit, October 1992

ISBN 0 85058 685 2

The authors are selected from a wide range of professional and academic disciplines. All the information in the reports is verified to the best of the authors' and the publisher's ability, but they do not accept responsibility for loss arising from decisions based on them. Where opinion is expressed, it is that of the authors, which does not necessarily coincide with the editorial view of The Economist Intelligence Unit or *The Economist* newspaper.

THE ECONOMIST INTELLIGENCE UNIT

The Economist Intelligence Unit is a research, publishing and advisory firm established to help companies initiate and manage operations across national borders. For 45 years it has been a source of information and know-how on worldwide business developments, economic and political trends, government regulations and corporate practice.

In 1986, the Economist Intelligence Unit merged with Business International, a well-established publisher and adviser with a strong connection to multinational companies. Business International built a reputation for providing senior managers with the highest quality of information, analysis and advice on the critical issues affecting their business across borders. In 1992 the EIU and BI began to publish under a single brand name: the Economist Intelligence Unit. The EIU also has divisions for conferences and consulting. The combined firm is a wholly owned subsidiary of The Economist Group.

Contents

List of Figures

Executive Summary

WHO NEEDS TOTAL QUALITY?

Total Quality (TQ) needs rethinking. In the way it has been tackled by most companies, TQ has failed to deliver the hoped for results. It has been internally focused, lacking a clear link to customers or business results. At best, it has led to incremental improvements; at worst, it has made it more difficult for organisations to increase their competitiveness.

However, TQ is working in some companies in Europe and producing results. Continuous improvement, customer delight and people empowerment are a reality in these companies, not management consultants' buzz-words. There are no inherent cultural reasons why Europeans should not apply TQ, provided they go about implementing it in the right way.

What marks out the successful companies is that they have consistently applied the TQ principles. In their hands TQ is not a programme or a strategy but a philosophy, the set of operating principles needed if a company is to continuously improve. For companies in internationally competitive markets, application of the TQ ideas has become a precondition of survival: not a panacea but part of what companies must do to stay in business.

Quality pays. Based on data on over 3,000 business units in Europe and North America held by PIMS Associates, every two per cent improvement in the rating by your customers of your quality is associated with a one per cent increase in its return on investment.

WHAT DO THE LEADING COMPANIES MEAN BY TOTAL QUALITY?

The companies agree that TQ is concerned with continuous improvement in performance, aimed at delighting customers: it is much more than the incremental improvement or problem-solving tools and techniques with which it is sometimes associated. To achieve continuous improvement, companies need a holistic approach to change: focusing on customers *and* practising fact-based management *and* creating an environment in which people bring to work the same energy, ability and commitment that they display in their life outside work. For most organisations, this means a step change in approach and culture.

HOW DO YOU START TO IMPLEMENT TQ?

The Total Quality principles are easy to say but very difficult to do. They are a most uncommon sense. TQ involves a radical rethinking of management and of organisations and a shift of power from shareholders to customers and employees/suppliers. Top management must have a gut commitment to quality and an instinctive belief in people's potential. Implementation is hard work, requiring dedication and patience.

Total Quality programmes – top-down, company-wide, training led, add-ons to existing jobs – do not work. They are ineffective and can "inoculate" organisations against real change.

They do not work because change is being imposed from above: the exact opposite of the TQ thinking.

Many of the companies which have gone furthest in applying the TQ principles do not have identifiable TQ initiatives. They have made continuous improvement part of their philosophy and strategy.

Successful implementation starts at the top. Senior management need to take responsibility for quality and not seek to delegate it as they so often do at present. They should begin by understanding the TQ principles, assessing where their organisation is and where it wants to be and then deciding what place TQ can or should have in their philosophy and strategy.

TQ is not for everyone. If the values implicit in TQ do not fit your company's it is better to leave TQ alone; you will fall flat on your face if you try to implement it.

The route to quality of each organisation should be "home grown", developed and "owned" by its own people. Companies need to be objective but also to value the things they inherit from the past which may differentiate them in the future. For this self-assessment to be effective, a company needs to benchmark its performance against world class best practice and to listen carefully to customers and employees.

For most organisations the ISO 9000 (BS5750) standards are not the best place to start Total Quality. The quality systems which they codify are important but only part of TQ. Starting TQ with ISO 9000 is beginning a process of change with the bureaucracy of quality: it puts the cart before the horse.

WHAT GUIDELINES SHOULD A COMPANY FOLLOW IN IMPLEMENTATION?

Forthright, listening leadership

Implementation requires leadership of a new type: forthright and willing to go out on a limb as to objectives, but listening and responding when it comes to the "how". What is needed is persistence and consistency in putting quality first, combined with a willingness to learn, not charisma or great intellect.

The necessary leadership exists when top managers have powerful reasons to change, a clear vision of how they want the organisation to be and the personal confidence to lead at the same time as listening to others.

Provoking but not imposing change

The TQ process of change must mirror the principles of empowerment it seeks to implement. People must be involved early so that they take ownership of change. Senior managers must resist the temptation to push through ready made answers drawn from their previous experience. They need to "let go" controls, giving people room and encouragement to change, without being able to monitor and measure every aspect of what happens.

Leaders need to create a "market for change" in their organisations, sharing sensitive information about the challenge the company faces and painting a simple and compelling vision of the organisation it needs to become. It is not a case of persuading people to change; they will motivate themselves if they understand the challenge and the vision. Top management should recognise that change is an uneven and frustrating process, and focus support and training on those most receptive to change; it is their early successes that will begin to persuade others.

The top managements of multinationals need to be sensitive to differences in local and national cultures. They should not seek to impose one process of improvement but instead provoke change that fits the local patterns of behaviour and belief.

Integrating quality into the fabric of the business

The process of change should be tied closely to business needs and results. The vision for the business needs to be translated into clear, measurable objectives. Short-term results should be required as well as progress towards longer-term objectives.

Quality needs to be integrated into the management process. Management teams must take responsibility for quality, not a specialist quality function. In their reviews of business and individual performance, management must give full weight to indicators of customer perceived quality.

"Keep it simple" should be the abiding motto of change agents. Communication, appraisal, reward and recognition, training and recruitment do not need endless new initiatives or highly paid specialists; they need new thinking, simply implemented.

Learning by doing

The successful quality companies see a sustained and heavy investment in training and development as a precondition of business success. They recognise that real learning comes from doing and therefore provide training on a "just-in-time" basis, avoiding mass training programmes and delivering skills and knowledge at the moment when they can be applied.

People learn new patterns of behaviour by doing (not by sitting in culture change workshops); they should be given responsibilities where they can experiment with new ways of doing things and where they have room to make mistakes, to review and to learn.

Consultants can help with specific services such as training and as enablers but companies should be wary. Ironically, companies are frustrated by the poor quality of much of what consultants in the quality field offer. Companies should not look to the consultants for ready made answers; they need to work out their own pathway to change.

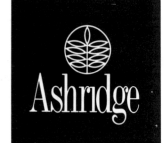

Introduction and Route Map to the Report

THIS REPORT IS ORGANISED AROUND THE ANSWERS TO
FOUR QUESTIONS

1. Who needs Total Quality?

Chapter 1 reviews the clear evidence provided by PIMS Associates and others that quality (that is, quality of products and services as perceived by customers and relative to that of competitors) pays. Indeed quality emerges as the most effective way of developing a sustainable competitive advantage.

Chapter 2 looks at the research that has been done on the links between Total Quality initiatives and quality. The evidence is mixed: a study by the US government suggests that TQ initiatives do lead to quality and to business results; other work by consultancy firms shows disappointing results. However, what is clear is that application of the TQ principles – often as opposed to a TQ programme or initiative – does produce results; indeed in internationally competitive markets it is essential to survival.

2. What do the leading companies mean by Total Quality?

Chapter 3 deals with the principles of TQ (the "what" of TQ, as opposed to the "how" examined later in the report). The researchers were impressed by the degree to which the more experienced companies agree on their definition of TQ; that it is "broad" quality they are now aiming at, the changes necessary to develop systematic continuous improvement. They were also continually surprised by the extent to which senior managers in less experienced companies are ignorant of the quality principles. The greatest barrier to implementation of TQ is often said to be one of a lack of management commitment. The researchers disagree: the first barrier is the lack of understanding. Very many managers identify TQ with quality assurance or ISO 9000 (which is only one part of the picture) and/or they fail to see the challenge from organisations which are continuously improving and have mobilised people commitment and fact based management to serve customers.

3. How do you start to implement TQ?

Chapter 4 analyses the shift in fundamental (and often unconscious) assumptions about organisations and management that TQ requires. The first step in implementation should be a serious effort to get to grips with the change in thinking TQ involves.

Chapter 5 deals with what typically goes wrong when companies seek to implement TQ. The dangers of TQ programmes – top-down, training led, company-wide, add-ons to existing work – are described. To be successful, TQ should be seen as a process of change and managers need to take account of the lessons which have been learnt about how to lead a process of change.

TQ should start at the top of an organisation. Chapter 6 deals with the issues for the board: how to fit quality into vision, strategy and objectives. Senior management must take responsibility and not seek to delegate it to more junior staff, as they often do at present.

Chapter 7 is concerned with ISO 9000 (BS 5750) and its relationship to TQ. Handled correctly, ISO 9000 can play a valuable role. However, it is not the best place to start quality work if an organisation has a choice (because of pressure from customers, many companies do not and are obliged to seek certification).

4. What guidelines should a company follow in implementation?

Chapters 8–11 deal with the clear themes observed in the companies successfully applying TQ. Together they represent a radical rethink of how to implement TQ.

Chapter 8 describes the distinctive style of leadership encountered: forthright and listening, assertive about objectives and standards but responsive to the views of others on how change should occur. The personal qualities necessary for such leadership and the behaviour and approach the leaders exhibit are analysed. An explanation is given of why this style of leadership is very different from conventional thinking that stresses charisma and intellect. In the case study companies, consistency and determination were the attributes most valued.

Chapter 9 examines how to provoke but not impose change: engaging with staff early to understand the challenges that face the organisation and drawing them in to decide how to respond. Change develops organically: the job of senior managers is to encourage champions of change, to foster successful developments and experiments that convince by example (not to seek – and fail – to impose change evenly across organisations).

Chapter 10 deals with integrating quality into the fabric of an organisation from the start, particularly in measurement, in management processes and in organisation structures. TQ is concerned with long-term development but there also needs to be a concern for short-term action and results.

The last of the four implementation themes – learning by doing – is analysed in Chapter 11. A heavy and sustained investment in education and training is essential, as well as new roles and responsibilities for people which give them an opportunity to learn new skills and ways of doing things.

Chapter 12 deals with the value and possible pitfalls of using outside consultants. Companies which have relied on consultants have failed to achieve real change; on the other hand using consultants as partners in learning pays dividends.

Research Approach and Acknowledgements

This report is based on original research conducted between July 1991 and July 1992 by a team at Ashridge, working closely with the Economist Intelligence Unit. Case studies were compiled on the experience of six very different companies across Europe which have sought, for more than five years, to apply Total Quality (TQ).

- Grundfos is an international company, based in Denmark, which holds half of the world market in domestic water pumps.
- Nissan Motors UK is the company's manufacturing plant in Sunderland, UK.
- Club Med is the international holiday and leisure company, based in France.
- Ciba-Geigy, Italy, handles the marketing, sales and distribution of all the group's products in the country.
- Federal Express UK is the local operation of the worldwide parcels transportation business.
- ICL Product Distribution is the unit in Stevenage, UK, responsible for the storage and distribution of the company's hardware, software and literature around the world.

We were as interested to see what difficulties these companies had encountered, and how they had tried to overcome them, as in their successes. We wanted to get below the surface, to find out what the real experience of Total Quality implementation had been. Few areas of business activity suffer from as much hype, exaggeration and confusion as TQ. We wanted to strip this away in order to learn from those who have tried long and hard to apply TQ.

To this end we talked to people at all levels in the case study organisations, both individually and in groups, and had discussions with staff without managers present. We interviewed customers, read published material and reviewed findings with senior managers.

Our purpose in undertaking the research was constructive: to see what could be learnt from the real-life experience of TQ. It was clear to us from the first that it would be easy to produce a damning report, pointing to the gap between aspiration and reality in many companies with TQ initiatives; to say that as an approach to change it is all so much mechanistic and simplistic nonsense.

This would be wrong in our view for three reasons.

- TQ has matured. As espoused by the leading companies, it is no longer concerned only with process improvement or problem solving tools and techniques. To a degree that surprised us, the experienced companies see TQ as concerned with the broad organisational and cultural change needed to achieve continuous improvement in performance.
- Companies in Europe urgently need to discover how to achieve systematic, continuous improvement. As is often remarked, the competitive challenge from Japan and other Pacific Rim countries grows ever more intense. Customers become more demanding and their needs and wants develop ever faster. Continuous improvement, bringing together real customer focus, fact based management and the unlocking of people potential, is becoming a condition of survival in internationally competitive markets.

- There is a rich vein of experience in the companies which have worked with TQ. Over ten years increasing numbers of companies in Europe have struggled to implement the TQ thinking. Millions of Ecus and thousands of hours of management time have been devoted to TQ in an effort to improve the competitive position of companies. Here is an experience from which others can learn.

In addition to the case studies we have interviewed the 40 other companies whose names are listed (most of whom have three years' or more experience of implementing TQ) and tested our conclusions with a broad range of consultants and academics.

I am indebted to Colin Williams of Ashridge for his support, ideas and encouragement throughout the project; to Andrew Campbell of the Ashridge Strategic Management Centre for the inspiration which led us to start the project; also to Virginia Merritt and Alex Knight of Ashridge who were instrumental in securing the necessary support and resources for the work.

Eight Ashridge consultants, tutors and researchers carried out the research: apart from Colin Williams, Alex Knight and me, there was Martyn Brown, Kathryn Evans, Kathryn Leishman, Anthony Mitchell and Jan Rabbetts. Colin and Anthony in particular organised and wrote three of the case studies and helped me with the main text. Helen Gibb masterminded the administration of the project (after Pat Furzland started us off) and Deborah Barrow and Andrea Jackman assisted.

Robin Ladkin, Kate Charlton and Bill Critchley reviewed the draft report as it emerged and provided incisive and insightful comment.

Outside Ashridge, David Jackson at the Centre for Service Excellence, Sue West and Libby Raper at IDV, and Jonathan Smilansky, former general manager at VISA International, read the report and gave very helpful feedback. Responsibility for the contents of the report remains, of course, with the Ashridge team.

George Binney
Ashridge Consulting Group
October 1992

STAYING AHEAD
DEPENDS ON
WORKING TOGETHER

Success in the tough, demanding world of motor racing requires teamwork of the highest order. Designers, mechanics and driver each have vital skills to contribute. And to win they must work together with flawless efficiency, however great the pressure.

It's much the same in business. The people, management and systems that drive your organisation must operate together as effectively and efficiently as possible. Only by doing so can they deliver products or services which delight your customers and keep you ahead of your competitors.

Gilbert Europe can help you gain this winning edge. We provide consultancy, training and auditing of the very highest standard in a wide range of specialist management disciplines. Our experienced consultants can identify the complex, inter-related processes on which your business depends and help you reshape them to attain optimum performance.

For example, we can work with you to implement and develop the Total Quality, Quality Systems and Business Process Management initiatives which will enable your organisation to achieve continuous improvement; or help you structure your Health and Safety policies to eliminate avoidable losses. And we offer more besides. So why not contact us for detailed information about our services?

You'll find that we can provide all the fine tuning you need to take the lead, and stay there.

Companies Interviewed

Case studies

Ciba-Geigy, Italy

Club Med, France

Federal Express, UK

Grundfos, Denmark

ICL, UK

Nissan, UK

Others

3M

AEG

Air Products

Anchor Foods

AT&T Bell Labs

Avon Industrial Polymers

Baxi Service

BT

CMB Packaging Technology

Courtaulds

Daintyfit

Electrolux

Exxon Research & Engineering

Ford

Forte

Hewlett Packard

IBM

ICI

IDV

Ilford Films

KLM

Kodak

London Underground

Lubrizol

Lucas

Manpower

Mardon Flexible Packaging

Mercury Communications

Milliken

Mitsubishi, UK

Motorola

Post Office

Rank Xerox

Shell UK Oil

Sollac

Sony

VISA International

Wedgewood

Wellcome Foundation

West Midlands Employment Service

Part 1

Who Needs Total Quality?

1 Quality Pays

As a rule of thumb, every two per cent improvement in the rating of your quality by customers is associated with a one per cent increase in return on investment.

PIMS Associates

QUALITY IS LINKED TO PROFITABILITY

The most authoritative study of the link between quality and business results has been done by PIMS Associates using its unique database on over 3,000 businesses in Europe and North America (see box). The database is remarkable in that it:

- contains price, quality, financial and market information (over 200 data points on each business) which is not publicly available;
- includes data by business unit, not legal entity;
- provides at least fives years' data on each business;
- covers all types of businesses.

Data are supplied by firms which are members of PIMS on a confidential basis; in return they are able to draw on the database.

The PIMS Research

The PIMS work looks at "relative customer perceived quality" – the perception of quality by customers, relative to the offerings of competitors – and therefore goes beyond the "conforming to requirements" definition used in quality assurance. The measure is dynamic: as the company and its competitors improve their offerings, the customer's assessment will change. It takes account of all the issues which are important to customers: image and service, for example, as well as product quality. This external perspective puts it at the heart of the debate about business strategy.

The process for assessment is as follows.

- A multi-function team of managers and staff specialists is asked to identify the key non-price criteria on which customers base their purchase decisions; these will include both product and service attributes.
- The team weights these criteria according to their importance to customers.
- The team rates the performance of the company in question and of its competitors in meeting the criteria.
- From this information the program calculates an index for the relative quality of each company in a given market segment.

PIMS says that in 90 per cent of cases the assessments by managers are tested against the opinions of customers recorded in surveys and where necessary the assessment changed to reflect the actual views of customers.

Figure 1.1 shows the first key finding from looking at this enormous pool of information. There is a clear positive correlation between quality and profit, which applies as much in Europe as in North America. The higher the relative quality, the higher both the average return on investment and return on sales.

Figure 1.1   Relative quality boosts rates of return

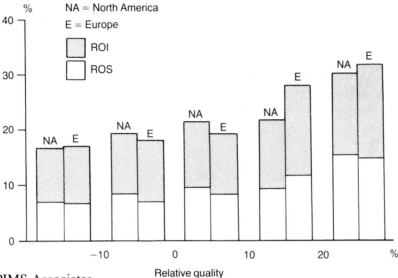

Source: PIMS Associates

However, it is important to keep in mind that this is a statistical relationship only. It does not say that quality guarantees superior profitability nor that improved returns can only be obtained by those with higher quality. There are certainly businesses which achieve good returns without high quality and high quality businesses which have not turned in a good profit record.

What the PIMS work does show is that you are more likely to have a good financial performance if you have superior quality working for you. For Figure 1.2 the PIMS businesses

Figure 1.2   Quality increases the odds of earning a high return

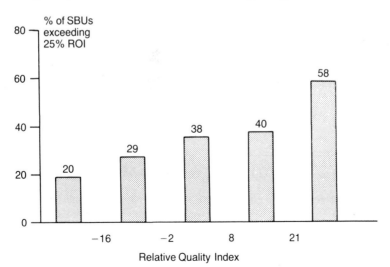

Source: PIMS Associates

3

were divided into groups of 600 according to quality. Of the group with low relative quality, only one fifth achieved a return of investment of more than 25 per cent; while of the high quality scoring group, over half achieved this rate of return.

The relationship between quality and profitability is clear and strong. The next question is why.

Figure 1.3 summarises the PIMS evidence on how quality drives profitability and growth. If you do a better job than competitors in serving the needs of customers, you have a choice of two ways of cashing in on this advantage (see Figure 1.4). One route is by charging higher prices than competitors (because of the higher quality you can do this without losing volume); the other is not to charge more but offer your customers better value. Customers typically respond well to this, rewarding you with more market share which in turn can mean lower relative costs.

The evidence is that the main link to profitability is through this increase in market share and consequent leveraging of indirect costs. Indeed firms offering better value need to spend less on sales and marketing than companies offering low value and are more successful at retaining and increasing market share. PIMS Associates estimates that the use of better value to gain share is about twice as important an effect in leading to higher profits as using quality to justify increased prices.

The right hand side of Figure 1.3 shows the important, but subordinate, role that reducing the cost of quality also plays. Making it right first time can feed through to the bottom line by reducing relative costs.

Figure 1.3   How quality drives profitability and growth

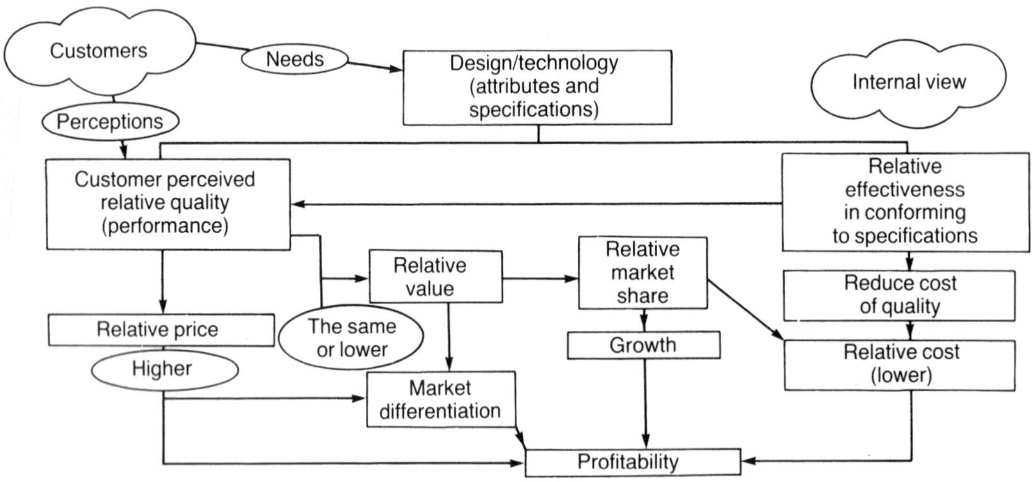

Source: PIMS Associates

QUALITY AS THE MOST EFFECTIVE STRATEGIC WEAPON

The conclusions to be drawn from the PIMS work go beyond saying that customer perceived quality is one factor to consider in formulating business strategy. They say that quality is the most effective strategic weapon.

In the long run, the most important factor affecting a business unit's performance is the quality of its products and services, relative to those of competitors.[1]

Figure 1.4   Poor value means poor results

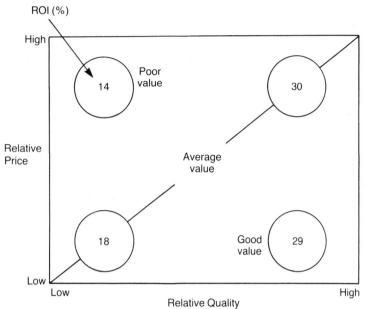

Source: PIMS Associates

By contrast, strategies which focus on cost reduction alone have not led to improvements in competitive position.

> In one industry after another where cost reduction strategies have prevailed, prices have fallen but no clear winners (other, of course, than customers) have emerged. Cost reduction has begot price reduction, a phenomenon aggravated by investments in highly automated equipment which have not just reduced cost but, because of their efficiency, actually increased industry capacity when overcapacity was the major cause of collapsing prices in the first instance.[2]

INCREASING PROFITS BY KEEPING CUSTOMERS LONGER

A related but different approach to making the link between quality and profitability comes from the work done by Bain & Company on improving customer retention. It has focused on the customer retention rate (defined simply as the percentage of customers at the beginning of the year who remain customers at the end of the year) as a measure of customer satisfaction. The more satisfied the customers, Bain argues, the higher the retention rate.

Increasing the retention rate means that customers remain loyal for longer. A retention rate of 80 per cent, for example, implies that customers remain for an average of five years. As the average "life" of a customer increases so dramatically does profitability of that customer to the firm.

Long-term relationships are more profitable because they reduce costs, add to revenue and prices and protect market share.

● The cost of acquiring a new customer can be substantial; a higher retention rate means fewer new customers are needed and they can be gained more cheaply; established customers place frequent, consistent orders and therefore usually cost less to serve.

● Existing customers tend to buy more and often refer new customers to the supplier at virtually no cost.

● Satisfied customers are often willing to pay premium prices to a supplier they know and trust.

● Retaining customers makes market entry or share gain more difficult for competitors.

Overall profitability increases dramatically as the retention rate improves (see Figure 1.5). More and more companies are now focusing on increasing customer retention as a key lever to increase profitability.

Figure 1.5   Profit impact of a five percent retention rate increase on customer value

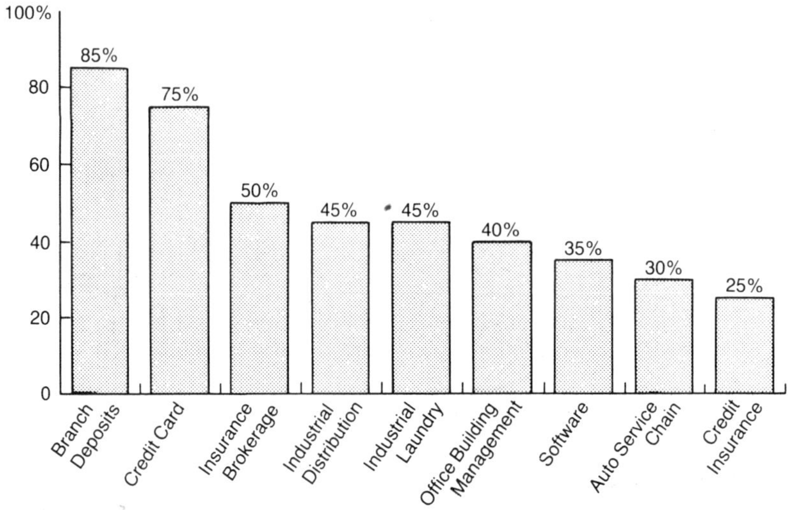

The vertical axis shows the percent increase in present value of pretax profits over a customer's lifetime (15% discount rate).

Source: Bain & Company

AVOIDING "ME TOO" STRATEGIES

There is one more twist to the relationship between quality and profitability. The companies which have the highest returns do not just have superior customer perceived quality; they

Figure 1.6   Companies need to combine differtiation with relative quality to obtain highest returns

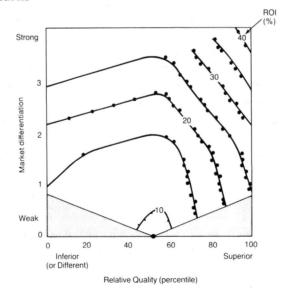

Source: PIMS Associates

combine it with a high degree of differentiation, that is, they compete on different attributes from other companies.

The evidence from the PIMS data is shown in Figure 1.6: market differentiation is the extent to which all participants in a market differ from one another. Those companies which can encourage this market differentiation by themselves competing on a different basis from that of other companies, will reap large rewards.

Companies which see their products or services as commodities are challenged to see whether they can differentiate their offerings; organisations which already compete on quality see how they can maximise differentiation. "Me too" strategies which aim to develop those aspects of quality which everyone else in an industry is seeking are not likely to lead to an improvement in relative quality nor to market differentiation.

The need to differentiate your approach is also considered in the discussion of quality strategy formulation in Chapter 6.

SUMMARY

1. Quality – as defined by the customer, relative to the offerings of competitors – is associated with high profitability; in the long run it is the single most important factor affecting the performance of a business.
2. With higher customer perceived quality, a company can choose how to reap the rewards: higher prices and/or improved value (leading to increased market share and lower costs).
3. Companies are increasingly focusing on quality in order to retain customers for longer and realise the lower costs and higher prices this leads to.
4. The highest returns go to those companies who not only delight their customers but do so in a different way from those of their competitors.

References

[1] *The PIMS Principles*, Robert D. Buzzell and Bradley T. Gale.
[2] *Quality as a Strategic Weapon*, Bob Luchs, Director, PIMS Associates.

2　The Value of Total Quality

> *Actually the problem will solve itself. The only survivors will be companies with constancy of purpose for quality, productivity and service.*
>
> Dr Deming

Chapter 1 examined the data which show that quality pays. But how do you ensure that your organisation delivers quality, particularly now that it means continuous improvement? Is Total Quality the answer?

The evidence is mixed. One survey in 1990 of finalists for the Baldrige Quality Award in the USA showed that Total Quality initiatives did lead to improved business performance: lower costs, increased market share and profits. Unfortunately the sample of companies surveyed was too small to be conclusive.

Spectacular success stories from individual companies appear to support the Baldrige survey, although these should always be taken with a large pinch of salt. Total Quality, more than most approaches, has been the subject of absurd public relations hype and it is impossible to know for sure what would have happened to these companies if they had not adopted TQ, nor how durable their success will be. Nevertheless a number of companies – Xerox, Motorola and ICL are three examples – insist that they would not have had the success they have had, or possibly survived at all, without Total Quality.

Studies by consulting firms, including both those sympathetic to and those sceptical about TQ, have leaned the other way: only a minority of the TQ efforts have had a "significant impact" on competitiveness.

Relatively few companies in Europe have gone very far in applying Total Quality. Few yet integrate customer focus, process development and people involvement in the way described in Chapter 3.

From looking at those companies which have made a sustained effort to apply TQ, two conclusions stand out. First, the TQ programmes do not work (the reason why is analysed in Chapter 5). Second, the companies observed which have gone furthest in applying Total Quality have never had a TQ initiative or programme; in them TQ has developed organically.

THE EVIDENCE FOR IMPROVED BUSINESS PERFORMANCE THROUGH TQ

Surprisingly little rigorous research has yet been done to establish the link, if any, between Total Quality initiatives and quality results and business performance. That which has been done is interesting but not conclusive. This is partly because not enough initiatives have been running for long enough to give the approach a full test. One of the central messages of TQ, after all, is that it is a long-term process; 5–10 years is the period often mentioned as needed to achieve a TQ transformation. Yet results – at least in customer satisfaction, if not profits – should begin to show through long before this.

The most extensive review of the impact of TQ initiatives was published by the General Accounting Office of the US government in May 1990. Entitled "Management Practices – US Companies Improve Performance Through Quality Efforts", it looked at the quality programmes in 20 companies, all high scorers in the competition for either the 1988 or 1989 Baldrige Awards. Using a detailed survey and extensive follow-up interviews, the GAO concluded that there was a cause and effect relationship between Total Quality Management practices and corporate performance, as measured by profitability, customer satisfaction, internal efficiencies and employee satisfaction (see Table 2.1).

Table 2.1 Selected results from the GAO study

| Performance indicator | Responding companies (no.) | Direction of indicator | | | Average annual improvement (%) |
		Positive (favourable)	Negative (unfavourable)	No change	
Employee related					
Employee satisfaction	9	8	1	0	1.4
Attendance	11	8	0	3	0.1
Turnover	11	7	3	1	6.0
Safety/ health	14	11	3	0	1.8
Suggestions received	7	5	2	0	16.6
Total	**18**[a]	**39**	**9**	**4**	
Operating					
Reliability	12	12	0	0	11.3
On time delivery	9	8	1	0	4.7
Order processing time	6	6	0	0	12.0
Error or defects	8	7	0	1	10.3
Product lead time	7	6	0	1	5.8
Inventory turnover	9	6	1	2	7.2
Costs of quality	5	5	0	0	9.0
Cost savings	9	9	0	0	...
Total	**20**[a]	**59**	**2**	**4**	
Customer satisfaction					
Overall satisfaction	14	12	0	2	2.5
Customer complaints	6	5	1	0	11.6
Customer retention	10	4	2	4	1.0
Total	**17**[a]	**21**	**3**	**6**	
Financial performance					
Market share	11	9	2	0	13.7
Sales per employee[b]	12	12	0	0	8.6
Return on assets	9	7	2	0	1.3
Return on sales	8	6	2	0	0.4
Total	**15**[a]	**34**	**6**	**0**	

[a] Total number of companies providing data, not total number of responses for all performance indicators.
[b] Unadjusted for inflation.

Source: GAO

Unfortunately the study was not conclusive. It did not use statistical methods, the sample of 20 is very small, and the companies did not answer all the questions. The average response was only nine companies per question.

Examples of individual company successes support the positive conclusion of the Baldrige survey:

- Motorola says that between 1987 and 1991 it saved $700 mn in manufacturing costs as a result of its "6 Sigma" drive to reduce defect rates and was able to increase the reliability of its radio pagers to the point where it has won the largest share of the fiercely competitive Japanese market.
- Xerox says TQ enabled it to survive in the face of Japanese competition by dramatically improving product quality (see box).
- ICL, as reported in the case study on its Product Distribution Division (page 116), has achieved a renaissance in a fiercely competitive industry. It is the only one of Europe's four full-line computer manufacturers to make a significant profit. The company believes it could not have achieved this success without the consistent emphasis it has placed on TQ for the last seven years.

TQ has had a dramatic impact on Xerox's business results . . .

- Product and operations quality: defects per 100 machines improved 10X. Benchmark achieved.
- Production suppliers (US, EC, Pacific): reduced 10X from 5,000 to 500.
- Production line defective parts (PPM): reduced 13X from 4,000 to 300.
- Receiving inspection: reduced to 5 per cent of incoming materials.

. . . and on the competitiveness of Xerox products

Xerox products ranked best in class

Product Class (copies per minute)	1984	1986	1988	1990
95+	Competitor	Competitor	Competitor	XEROX 5090
60-95	Competitor	Competitor	XEROX 1090	XEROX 1090 *
40-60	Competitor	XEROX 1055	XEROX 1065	XEROX 5065 **
30-40	Competitor	XEROX 1045	XEROX 1045	XEROX 5034
15-30	Competitor	Competitor	XEROX 1025	XEROX 5018
8-15	Competitor	Competitor	XEROX 1012	XEROX 5014 ***

◇
Product Class
(copies per minute)

* Buyers Lab – most outstanding High Volume Copier of 1990
** Buyers Lab – Copier of the Year
*** Buyers Lab – most outstanding Very Low Volume Copier of the Year

Source: Rank Xerox

THE EVIDENCE AGAINST IMPROVED BUSINESS PERFORMANCE THROUGH TQ

Surveys undertaken by firms of management consultants all paint a gloomy picture of the effectiveness of TQ initiatives.

Only 20 per cent of respondents to a recent survey by the consulting firm A.T. Kearney and *TQM Magazine* claimed that their Total Quality initiatives had led to "a significant improvement in performance in the last 12 months". (The judgement of what constituted a "significant improvement" was entirely their own.)

The experience of McKinsey & Company is that:

> Two out of three quality management programmes in place for more than a couple of years are stalled; they no longer meet the CEO's expectations for tangible improvement in product or service quality, customer satisfaction, and operating performance.[1]

A survey by Arthur D. Little of 500 US manufacturing and service companies found that only a third felt their TQ programmes were having a "significant impact" on their competitiveness.

FEW COMPANIES HAVE MADE SUSTAINED TQ EFFORT

A review of firms in the UK by the London Business School revealed that many companies are talking about TQ. Among the manufacturing firms questioned 77 per cent were using or planning to adopt a formal TQM programme. There was widespread use of quality assurance based on ISO 9000. Yet when 42 organisations were assessed by managers within them using the Baldrige criteria the conclusion was that "most UK firms are a long way from TQM and finding it difficult to get there ... the managers reported little sustained effort".

When it came to improved quality or service or reduced cost, managers were unable to identify examples of tangible results.

This report confirms these findings. Many companies in Europe have some form of quality initiative. Few have made a sustained effort to implement together the key elements of Total Quality – customer focus, process improvement and people empowerment – aimed at delighting customers (the TQ principles are defined in Chapter 3).

APPLICATION OF THE TQ PRINCIPLES PRODUCES RESULTS

The case study companies which have made most progress in applying TQ are the ones which have not had a TQ programme. In these companies TQ has developed organically. Their business results are impressive.

- The Nissan Motors UK plant in Sunderland is the jewel in Nissan's overseas crown. Quality and productivity match Japanese levels. Colleagues from sister plants in Spain and the USA come to learn. Best of all, the company now exports cars back to Japan.
- Club Med is something of a legend in the holiday industry, and now has villages in the USA and Africa as well as Europe providing a unique holiday experience "away from it all".
- Grundfos has achieved remarkable results. It used a Japanese type of approach to win world leadership in a specific market: clean water pumps. The company has captured 50 per cent of worldwide sales of domestic circulators and has a leading position in commercial and industrial water pumps. It employs 7,000 people in 25 countries and is the acknowledged quality leader in its industry.

THE NEED FOR CONTINUOUS IMPROVEMENT

As explained in Chapter 3, the Total Quality principles define what a company has to do in order to achieve continuous improvement. For companies in internationally competitive markets, continuous improvement has become a necessary condition of survival: it is the entry ticket that ensures you can play the game. It does not ensure that you will win, but if you do not adopt TQ your competitor will and that may put you out of business.

The best researched example of this is the exhaustive work done by a team at MIT on the world car industry, reported in *The Machine That Changed The World*, published in 1990. It found that the new, continuously improving, approach of "lean production", developed originally by Toyota, has transformed the industry. The competitive lead available to companies effectively applying lean production is so great that the old mass production firms are either changing to lean production or going out of business. On average lean production uses "half the human effort in the factory, half the manufacturing space, half the investment in tools, half the engineering hours to develop a new product in half the time. Also it requires keeping far less than half the needed inventory on site, results in far fewer defects, and produces a greater and ever growing variety of products".

How do lean producers achieve this overwhelming competitive superiority? Not through automation alone: some European producers have this and still experience poor productivity. Nor through simpler product lines. The plants with the highest productivity have the highest number of body styles and models under manufacture. The factors which do make the difference are a product development process that brings together all functions as an effective team and ensures manufacturability of new products; and, in the plant, an organisation which "transfers the maximum number of tasks and responsibilities to those workers actually adding value to the car on the line, and has in place a system for detecting defects that quickly traces every problem, once discovered, to its ultimate cause".

The MIT report has a sting in the tail for European manufacturers. It found that they have "not yet begun to close the competitive gap" between themselves and the Japanese lean producers. One German luxury car producer "was expending more effort to fix the problems it had just created than the Japanese plant required to make a nearly perfect car the first time".

SUMMARY

1. While there have been spectacular successes by individual companies, the evidence from the surveys which have examined the impact of Total Quality initiatives on a range of companies is mixed.
2. Few companies in Europe have yet systematically applied the integrated TQ principles.
3. TQ programmes do not work.
4. The companies which have achieved results either have developed TQ organically or have overlaid TQ programmes with other changes.
5. To survive in internationally competitive markets, a company must continuously improve. Application of the TQ principles, not TQ programmes, is the key to this.

Reference:
[1] "When Quality Control Gets In the Way of Quality", Graham Shorman, McKinsey & Co, *Wall Street Journal*, February 25, 1992.

CASE STUDY

NISSAN MOTOR MANUFACTURING (UK) LTD: TQ IN ACTION

In 1984 Nissan, the second largest car maker in Japan (see box), decided to build a manufacturing plant in Sunderland, UK. In its move towards globalisation, it had decided that it not only wished to sell in the European market but also to manufacture and design products there. The Thatcher government had lobbied hard to persuade Nissan to follow other Japanese companies such as Sony and Hitachi which had already come to the UK. The government believed the Nissan influence would benefit the whole British motor manufacturing and components industry and improve the balance of trade with Japan and continental Europe.

It was not an easy decision. The British car industry had an appalling reputation for disputes, low productivity, little flexibility and poor quality. Privately many Nissan managers were doubtful about the project and described it as a "suicide mission". The labour union denounced the plan believing it would mean "exporting" jobs to Europe.

Initially only a tentative step was authorised: £50 mn was to be spent, a flea bite by motor industry standards. An existing model, the Bluebird, would be assembled for sale in Europe.

Eight years later Nissan Motor Manufacturing (UK) Ltd (NMUK) is the jewel in Nissan's overseas crown. Quality and productivity match Japanese levels (see profile). Colleagues from plants in Spain and the USA come to learn. Best of all, the company now exports cars back to Japan.

How has it been done? How has the company been able to establish world class quality in a British car plant? Three themes stand out.

- Quality, defined as the drive to satisfy customers, has genuinely had priority.
- Quality is not seen by NMUK as a separate item but as part of an organic package. Flexibility, teamwork and quality are seen as a whole, a philosophy for the business, each element dependent on, and reinforcing, the others.
- Ownership of the change process in NMUK is with the local team, first the core of ex-Ford and Rover managers who got the plant going, now with all employees. They have had a very clear picture of the organisation they have been seeking to build and very personal reasons for being determined to succeed. This has been a very British achievement.

NISSAN PROFILE

Nissan ranks second to Toyota among the Japanese car producers. It currently has about a quarter of the Japanese market and, with a total international production of 3 mn cars a year, some 6 per cent of the world market. It is aiming for continued rapid growth with sales targeted at 5 mn cars by 2000 and for 40 per cent of production to be outside Japan.

The mid-1980s, when the Sunderland plant was being established, was a period of most unJapanese internal discord. The argument over whether to invest in the UK led to a public row between the company and the union and ultimately to the resignation of the union leader. Meanwhile the company was staggering under the weight of the revaluation of the yen (by 70 per cent in 1985–86 alone) and a sluggish home market. In the first half of 1986 the company reported the first loss in its history.

GENUINE PRIORITY FOR CUSTOMER SATISFACTION

Quality a condition of investment

The Sunderland plant started small but it had the potential to become a major business. From the start there was the possibility of expanding production to 200,000 cars by 1992 with 80 per cent local content and introducing new models. But there was one condition: quality. As Ian Gibson, now managing director, recalls, the Japanese told the British team managing the start-up: "We would much rather not build cars than make ones that do not meet the quality standards." These standards would be the same as those applied in Japan; no concessions would be made for British manufacture.

At each stage of the company's growth the message from Japan has been the same: "Meet the quality (and cost) standards and we will authorise further investment."

THE SUNDERLAND PLANT

The plant is much more than a screwdriver assembly factory. It now includes an engine plant (where engine components from Japan and Europe are machined and assembled), a foundry, a plastic injection and blow moulding plant, a service/parts operation, as well as assembly operations. The plant has the largest body presses (5,000 tons) in Europe. Only the engine blocks and transmission systems are imported from Japan.

The plant produces many variants of two models – Primera and New Micra – and in 1993 the plant is scheduled to produce 270,000 cars. By the end of 1992 over £900 mn will have been invested. The number of employees will rise by more than 50 per cent to 5,000 during 1992.

More than 70 per cent of production is sold outside the UK, principally to mainland Europe. The company says the value of EC content in both models currently produced exceeds 80 per cent.

Design and development takes place in Sunderland and in the group's European Technology Centre at Cranfield in southern England. Marketing is the responsibility of the European HQ in Amsterdam.

Quality first

The objective, set at the beginning, was to "build profitably the highest quality car sold in Europe". Initially quality alone was the absolute. Slow production schedules might be agreed, some trade-off against costs (both internally and those of suppliers) might be accepted: both of these could be tackled later. But quality, once compromised, could never be recovered. Peter Wickens, director of personnel and information systems, explains:

> To achieve real quality everyone at every level in the organisation has to genuinely believe it and act on the belief. Management must mean what it says. As soon as a senior manager allows a car to go through which is not at the right quality level "because I have to meet the schedule" the battle is lost.
>
> Everything you hear about the Japanese attitude to quality is true. Commitment to a zero defect product is absolute throughout the company. Assembly workers take a pride in building the perfect product, and they insist that the components they receive are of the same high standard. They totally fail to understand the attitude prevalent in the West that quality is someone else's business.

Thus everyone in Sunderland is responsible for his or her own quality. Self inspection is the key and the final rectification area is deliberately small. There are no repair areas. There is training and more training to ensure that workers have the skills to do the job right first time. There are close partnerships with suppliers so that they understand and apply the quality standards.

A purchasing manager comments:

> In the early days particularly it would have been easy to compromise on supplier quality but we did not. If necessary we took the pain short-term in extra cost.

One other message the British managers absorbed from the Japanese was the driving questioning to get the facts and establish root causes. The purchasing manager again:

> I remember my anger when a Japanese colleague challenged me over what I thought was a stupid detail: he wanted to know why the windscreen washer hose was a different colour in the UK. I didn't know and I couldn't see it mattered. He went away and found out the answer. The hose was of a different plastic with a lower melting point. For sales to hot countries it would matter. We ended up buying a different hose which cost 1p per car more but wouldn't melt under any conceivable conditions.
>
> At management meetings the quality measures are the ones that count – people soon get the message.

Kaizen: continuous improvement is part of the normal job

Customers' expectations rise as technology develops and competitors' offerings improve. To satisfy its customers NMUK recognised that it had to build in a process of continuously increasing the value of its products and services and reducing its costs. For this process the British team (against the advice of its Japanese advisers) adopted the name *Kaizen*.

Kaizen means "continuous improvement" in Japanese. It focuses on small-step incremental improvement which can be achieved without major investment. It proposes that everybody can improve the way they do their jobs, adding value, reducing cost or just making the work easier and that the small steps can add up over a period to provide as least as much improvement as the major innovation the West stresses.

From the start NMUK decided that *Kaizen* was to be part of everyone's normal job. There are thousands of suggestions each year for improvement but no suggestions scheme and no awards (or monetary rewards) for suggestions. There are no separate quality circles; instead every team is charged with continuous improvement and supervisors are given training in the problem solving techniques required to lead this. Other companies debate whether to enlist volunteers or mandate people to work on continuous improvement; in NMUK, as Peter Wickens explains, "Because we regard it as part of everyone's job to strive to improve continuously, the question of whether the activity is voluntary or compulsory does not really arise". It is the supervisor's "responsibility to ensure continuous improvement".

A determination to achieve continuous improvement is ingrained in all areas. Service parts, finance and personnel have recently had improvement initiatives. But the most obvious work has been done in production. Some examples are as follows.

- Changing the mechanism for assembling axles into the cars which meant the job could be done with one man instead of two.
- Putting in larger carriers for the screws needed at one assembly station which made the job of that person on the line easier.
- Installing a short conveyor line so that the person installing petrol tanks does not have to walk over to collect the tanks.
- Placing new heating strips to speed up the adhesion of protective rubber along the side of the cars; this was safer, cheaper and more effective than the previous process.

All these ideas came from manufacturing staff. In each case they helped develop the proposals as they were examined for effectiveness and practicability. They had the opportunity to try out their proposals in *Kaizen* workshops (special areas in the plant set aside for this purpose).

All NMUK employees are taught to understand the essentials of problem solving, the need to trace back to root causes, often finding a quick fix for the problem but then working on until an effective long-term countermeasure has been found. They also understand the ethic of continuous improvement and the means to do it.

Improvement includes cost reduction as well as increasing the value and reliability of products. In 1991, for example, a cost reduction effort on Primera production led to more than 1,300 ideas being collected from all departments and a threefold reduction in certain costs of production.

Only elementary statistics are used in most areas. Full statistical process control is reserved for selected tasks such as machining of engine blocks.

Benchmarking is used. The company is keenly aware of the need to look at best practice throughout the world and has current work examining selected fields in different companies in Europe and the USA as well as Japan. The Japanese advisers also provide cross-referencing against processes and practices elsewhere: they carry with them very extensive databases on procedures in factories (not just Nissan's) throughout Japan.

HOLISTIC APPROACH TO QUALITY

Not a total quality programme

NMUK's approach to quality has been built in from the start. It is not the result of a Total Quality initiative, added at a later stage, but an integrated element of a strong and cohesive philosophy of business.

That approach was prepared by the start-up team in 1984–86 as they waited for the plant to be built and it is laid out with great clarity in Peter Wickens' book *The Road To Nissan*, written in 1986/87.

The start-up team drew on their own experiences of car manufacturing (mainly in Ford and Rover) and on the expertise of the small group of Japanese managers working with them. They formulated an approach in which quality depended on, and reinforced, the two other themes: flexibility and teamwork.

Flexibility reinforcing quality

As quality is everyone's responsibility it is essential to build in very high levels of flexibility. Factory workers are expected to keep their own work areas clean. They carry out routine maintenance of their machines and help the maintenance staff with the more difficult jobs. Maintenance staff themselves have both electrical and mechanical skills.

There are no job specifications; instead every individual from managing director to factory floor worker agrees his or her own objectives for the year ahead. There is only one union, the AEU, and so there is no question of interunion rivalry or disputes.

Alongside quality, the company has driven for just-in-time processes in the factory, avoiding inventory and work in progress and other forms of waste and exposing process problems. Production is flexible, with the ability to switch quickly from one model variant, and even complete model, to another quickly. Automation is balanced by the need to remain flexible. In some areas this means retaining people on the line and not changing to robots.

Quality allied to teamwork

The effort to break down barriers and develop the teamwork necessary for quality has gone far beyond the better known symbols. There are common canteens for all employees, common terms and conditions of employment, no designated parking spaces for managers and blue overalls for everyone. No one has their own office. The managing director sits in a large open plan area. Everyone is paid a salary (the notices advertising manual jobs with an annual salary were an important public signal that Nissan would be different). All employees have an annual appraisal. Common terms and conditions mean that everyone is offered private health care. No one has to clock in and all are paid when late or sick.

The company works hard to make communication a genuinely two way business, not just from management to employees but from staff upwards. It is handled not in formal monthly briefings nor by company newsheets or videos but face to face, managers and staff, starting with the supervisors and their teams. At the beginning of each day a short time is allowed to review and discuss. Team areas have been created in the plant so that each group has its own territory for team meetings and for breaks.

The demand for continuous improvement makes it clear that the ideas of all staff are welcomed. A strong social and sports club encourages teams to bind together outside working hours.

Cross-functional teamwork

One of the most obvious areas for improvement, and one of the most difficult, in any quality initiative is cross-functional cooperation. NMUK has made gains but still sees this area as an important opportunity for improvement.

At the top management level, Ian Gibson says one of the main things he learnt from Japanese managers was their different approach to departmental responsibilities.

They're very good at sharing things. They stick their noses into everything. It's not good enough to say "that's my function's job". You have to be prepared to justify in detail what you're proposing.

With everyone examining suggestions from a company-wide perspective, this cross-examination is "mutually supportive". "Everyone needs to be good and problems are the focus for the whole team."

Further down the organisation, the company has launched an "internal customer" exercise so that functions can spell out what they need from other areas and get feedback on existing products and services. The company is working to get more rotation of jobs between middle managers and particularly between line and staff functions. As one manager describes it: "We should share more between areas so that best practice is used throughout the company."

Recruiting the best people

Throughout its existence NMUK has had the pick of the local labour force. By carefully nourishing its links to the community and its local reputation as an enlightened, successful and secure employer, it has turned round British prejudices against factory work and manufacturing industry. For the 1,600 jobs currently being recruited, it has received 32,000 applications. Ratios of 25–50:1 applied to its earlier recruitment as well. To gain a job at NMUK has become a matter of admiration in North East England.

The company further enhances its reputation by the thoroughness of its selection process. Manufacturing staff go through a series of written aptitude tests before doing practical skills tests, on line trials and finally two interviews with potential supervisors. Says Peter Wickens:

> We're looking for people with empathy for the way we do business. Attitude is key, once we have established technical aptitude.

Recent work skills are regarded as much less important: almost half of those appointed were unemployed before joining Nissan.

Successful applicants proceed to the induction process: one week off-line, learning about quality, safety and the philosophy of NMUK, a period in the off-line training school, then several weeks assisting on the line before moving to a line station.

For the supervisor jobs the new role and higher salaries attracted many applicants; an exhaustive assessment centre process led to highly qualified young candidates being selected, distinguished by their enthusiasm and willingness to learn.

There is fallout, individuals who do not fit into the teams, do not like the pressures of shift work or fail to be flexible, but usually this happens within three months. After that the workforce is very stable: labour turnover is just 5 per cent.

The following is a typical anecdote from a member of the manufacturing staff.

> Two years ago we employed someone who had come from Vauxhall and who had performed brilliantly in the entrance tests. When he started work he wouldn't sweep the factory floor and didn't fit in. He soon left. At the same time we took on someone who used to pick potatoes and who had never worked in a factory before. He is still with us and has been really successful.

Among the management team there was the same pattern of rigorous selection, an initial sorting out of the team and then great stability. Three managers out of the original start-up team of 15 resigned within 18 months of joining in 1984; since then all the remaining managers have stayed together.

Training as an article of faith

Once employed, manufacturing staff participate in constant training and development. To the visitor it comes across as a matter of faith. Training and education is good. The more education staff receive, the more capable and motivated they will be. The training is concentrated on shopfloor workers; there is no question here of managers receiving the bulk of it.

The statistics are impressive. Every new employee received an average of 61 days' training in 1991; existing employees received an average of nine days. If the salaries of those being trained are included, the company spends 14 per cent of its annual salaries bill on training. Direct expenditure on training equals 4.5 per cent of the salaries bill.

Central to the shopfloor training effort are the ILUD charts displayed in the factory, recording the progress of each member of every team in mastering all the different jobs in their part of the plant.

Training is linked closely to work by two mechanisms. The first is the continuous development plan which each person agrees with his or her supervisor. This may include provision for broader development, for example assertiveness training, more often associated with managers than manual workers, as well as job specific skills. The second is the book of standard operating procedures. These are drawn up and "owned" by each team and are therefore an up to date record of how each job is actually done. As part of their training new recruits read and help to update the standard operating procedures. They help to ensure that everyone in the team is doing the job in the best known way and that training on the job teaches high standards (and is not the copying of bad practices so often found in other companies).

Quotes from manufacturing staff
- "They're trying to develop you all the time."
- "No other company I know can touch the training here."
- "If you want to learn, the company will help you to learn."

The best suppliers

The company has implemented a revolutionary approach to suppliers aimed at securing reliable and consistently improving quality. From the start it saw that quality from suppliers was as important as quality in the work done internally and has been prepared to invest precious management time and engineering skills in improving supplier quality. Genuine partnerships are sought; the old practice of playing one supplier off against another has been abandoned. All supplies, except tyres, are single sourced. And the partnerships are working. NMUK takes great pride in the success of its suppliers in meeting ever tougher quality requirements. Out of 126 UK suppliers chosen for the original Bluebird model, only six were rejected when it came to choosing suppliers for the next model, the Primera.

Partly because of the lack of engineering expertise in many suppliers, NMUK provides free consultancy on process and quality improvements. One manager comments:

We don't tell our suppliers what to do. They have to own the answers so we let them find them for themselves – sometimes with a little encouragement.

In some cases the relationship is so close that NMUK is trusted to work out suppliers' charges for their work. In other cases working practices in the supplier companies have changed to the point that staff compete to work in the "cells" producing items for Nissan, just as they compete to join NMUK itself.

TRANSFER OF OWNERSHIP TO THE LOCAL TEAM

There is a very tangible sense of ownership among the NMUK team. They may or may not have adopted a Japanese formula but it was their decision; they feel passionately, because of their experience, about how to build a world class company; they were involved from the first in drawing up the plans and they have had the responsibility for implementation. They know the company created is their achievement.

Personal reasons for change

From the first Nissan decided that Sunderland was to be a British operation run by a British team. The company had concluded from its experience of setting up a plant in Smyrna, Tennessee, three years earlier that it was essential to localise the plant. Only a local team could get the best from local workers and suppliers. It therefore set out to recruit a team that would within two years take full responsibility for the business.

The first group of managers were bloodied by the failures of the British car industry in the 1960s and 1970s. Peter Wickens, now personnel and information systems director, had spent his early years at Ford working "in the front line of the revolution". Moving from industrial relations to general personnel management, he tried out many of the principles that were to be applied in Nissan, helping to set up a new plant in North Wales for the US company Continental Can. Flexible working, common terms and conditions for all employees, employee involvement, a single union, the abolition of clocking-in for manual workers, simplified job grading and appraisal, changing the role of the supervisor from progress chaser to true leader of manufacturing teams: all these principles were "road tested" in Continental Can.

Ian Gibson, now the managing director of NMUK, was the second manager recruited. After studying physics at university, he had joined Ford and worked his way up the manufacturing function. In his mid-30s he was responsible for the production and development of cars made in Spain, Germany and the UK and saw the comparison between the productivity and quality of the UK plant and of the mainland Europe operations. "The difference was phenomenal," he says. Even though the plants all used the same equipment and technology and the incoming levels of education and training were lower in Spain, the performance of the UK plant was abysmal. The difference had to be in the way the people were organised and led.

The third member of the original core of British managers was John Cushnaghan, now production director of NMUK. He was also an ex-Ford man but this time with most recent experience of the Rover Group.

Talking to these managers and to other members of the core group reveals their missionary zeal to show that "Brits" could run a world class car company. "We were determined to avoid the disaster that was the British car industry in the late 1970s," says Ian Gibson.

Free to choose

The start-up team insist that when they were setting up the plant they were able to pick and choose from Japanese and other ideas according to what seemed practical and sensible in a British context. As Peter Wickens puts it: "The Japanese have no monopoly of wisdom; they can't teach us how to manage people." Because of different Western attitudes to individuals and personal initiative, "people strategies are not transferable". For example:

The Japanese have a much greater sense of status. In Nissan Japan, everyone wears baseball caps and you can see from the number of gold rings on the cap what position someone has. Here that would not be acceptable.

Keith Jones, director of quality assurance, adds:

We were not a transplant. The Japanese did expect some things – quality, for example, and the blue workwear – but on the rest we made up our own minds. We said no to morning exercises. Provided we met the quality standards, we could stand on our own feet.

Ian Gibson says:

The group ethic in Japan and the respect for superiors mean that people there don't have to be managed as they do in the West. If the boss says "jump", staff take that direction as given. The emphasis on group harmony means the team is incredibly effective in deciding how to achieve the objective. In the West neither point is true. Senior managers have to keep selling and they have to support implementation.

Ian Gibson recalls some of the early debates.

They used to drive us up the wall, asking why again and again. Once the Japanese MD drove us to distraction because he couldn't understand that staff would not work during their holidays. In the end we understood that he meant weekends and we were all able to work overtime on Saturdays.

What was of value was that they "challenged our common sense", the accepted ways of doing things.

The objective of the team now is to do better than the Japanese end of the company, to harness the individual initiative, youth and dynamism of the team to achieve superior performance, at least in some areas.

Delegation to operating managers and supervisors

The start-up team decided to transform the authority and responsibility of production management in general and of supervisors in particular. Instead of being the poor relation, with specialist departments steadily eroding its position, production takes centre stage. The job of the functional departments is support and advice. Decision and responsibility rests with production. As Peter Wickens puts it:

It is imperative that there be a sea change in the role of the first line supervisor if British industry is to gain in status and become a sector which the brightest students regard as desirable. There are two main areas in which individual companies can influence this change. First of all the actual role of the supervisors must be considerably enhanced from its present lowly status and following from this their selection and status must be radically different.

As the recruitment advertisements said: "Supervision with Nissan will be different". Supervisors in production areas (and elsewhere):

- select the people who work for them;
- communicate all matters face to face to their team;
- train on the job;
- develop their people;
- balance the work of the team;
- ensure high levels of attendance and timekeeping;
- solve problems and maintain equipment (or help the maintenance people if they cannot do it themselves);
- have total responsibility for quality (there are no inspectors), the team checking its own work and for *Kaizen*.

Instead of the bypassed and undervalued role of past car companies in the UK, the supervisor becomes the leader, guide and mentor of the team. A team is typically 20 strong with two team leaders to assist.

Delegation has not always been easy. One manager describes how the start-up team tried to do too much detailed work and had to be reminded to delegate more effectively. They have worked hard to do this. For example, the statement of corporate philosophy was recently reviewed to ensure that it represented latest thinking and had everyone's commitment. The review was carried out not by the directors but by a diagonal slice of some 150 staff from all functions and levels.

Open and visible management

There are only six job levels in the company (managing director, director, manager, senior supervisor, supervisor, manufacturing staff) and only two job titles among front line staff (manufacturing staff and technician).

NMUK makes extraordinary efforts to communicate, not only through line management as described above but also directly, for example in the managing director's twice yearly briefings to all employees. Sensitive commercial information is often released to all employees.

Sense of empowerment

The word empowerment is much used and often misused. The researchers investigating Nissan for this report were sceptical. They kept checking that what they were hearing and seeing was authentic. Having looked as carefully as possible, their judgement is that NMUK has empowered its employees. The consistency of comments and examples was impressive; there was little of the cynicism to be found in many large organisations when they are studied closely; managers and staff volunteered, without prompting, telling evidence of their ability to shape the way they worked and contribute to development of the company as a whole. They say that managers listen.

The sense of empowerment is rooted in shared purpose and values. People consistently play back the objective of being the best among European car makers in achieving customer satisfaction; they take responsibility for meeting the expectations of quality, flexibility and teamwork. They talk about "being roped together", of depending on each other for success. They have enormous shared pride in their achievements and drive to go on achieving.

Involving people early and informing them fully is another consistent theme. A manager who had come from Ford described how he had learnt to stop telling people what to do. He sees his job now as explaining objectives clearly but not prescribing how something should be done. This the team should discuss openly and he should support and contribute but not feel under an obligation to come up with the answer. Against a background of full information of what is happening in the company and shared objectives, staff can be trusted to act in the best interests of the company.

Ian Gibson describes the painful learning he went through in the early days. Instead of being able to use his position to force decisions through, he had to justify and explain things that before he took for granted. He has to accept much tougher questioning from subordinates. The result is that the decisions and actions are not just his; they are the team's and as such are much more likely to be fully implemented.

The attitude to mistakes is revealing. The views expressed are mixed. One shopfloor worker says that when you make a serious error "you get your back ripped out" by your supervisor and colleagues. Another has a different picture. He says that when you make a mistake it is blamed on the system or on the failure to train properly. Clearly there is enormous peer pressure to perform and a visible atmosphere of strong team support for each other.

Finally, and most intriguingly, there has been some shift to measuring and recognising process rather than results alone. Says Ian Gibson:

You have to measure process and effort as much as achievement ... if you are to demonstrate the necessary people as opposed to task orientation.

Realising self through work

Many staff describe how they personally learnt and changed as a result of working at NMUK and how personal values and objectives coincided with company ones.

- "Nissan is what I have been waiting for for 20 years."
- "Here I don't feel like an employee, I'm part of something I feel proud of."
- "In the shipyards I played cards all day and learnt nothing; Nissan has changed my life."
- "I'm more self-confident since I came to work here."
- "I have learnt more here than in 17 years with my previous company."
- "It feels good to tell people you work at Nissan."
- "Nissan has changed me at home: I can't even wash the car slowly."

Rethinking management

NMUK is an example of the Total Quality principles in action. Managers and staff work to different rules from those that applied in the companies in which they worked before Nissan. NMUK people look like winners: there is tremendous pride in what has been achieved and drive to continue improving. The trick they have pulled off is not one of complex ideas. As one manager comments: "How simple it is – once you're doing it." What they have done is rethink the way they run a business and then determinedly implement it.

CASE STUDY

CLUB MED: TQ IN A SERVICE BUSINESS

Club Mediterranée is something of a legend in the holiday industry. It successfully provides the key ingredients of many traditional holidays (often crudely termed the Ss: sun, sea, sand or snow and sport). It also provides something significantly different from even the best traditional holidays: a unique environment and atmosphere which dissolves the holiday makers' cares and concerns, transporting them to a world of *vitalité, tendresse et nuance*.

For the last 40 years the name Club Med has conjured up images of happy people having a good time "away from it all". It is not, of course, an accident. It is the result of 40 years of concentrated effort in designing, developing and delivering high quality holiday experiences. When Club Med directors say "happiness is our business" it is not a flippant remark. The skilful crafting of this unique atmosphere is the essence of their business. The aim of this case study is to explore how they "manage" this intangible quality.

BACKGROUND

Club Med was created by Gérard Blitz in 1950. A sports enthusiast, he wanted to create a way for others to enjoy sporting holidays at a reasonable cost. The concept of the "club" was conceived to allow members to travel and camp together, to share the chores and the costs of the holiday. Many of the principles formed in those very early days remain at the core of Club Med's philosophy today.

For example, the meal seating arrangements still found in many Club Med villages, with tables of eight people, exist because in those very early days "members" travelled to the holiday location by train in compartments of eight. They struck up friendships during the journey which they wished to pursue during the holiday. This is one of many examples of how one of the early principles of the Club (in this case making new friends) is still evident today. The challenge of retaining the "core" (or "soul", as Richard Segalowitch, Campus Manager, put it) of Club Med and yet developing in line with global changes and evolving customer expectations is a key issue for Club Med.

In 1954 Gilbert Trigano (the current chairman of the board of directors) joined Club Med and the first traditional Polynesian style villages were built. This style, including features such as a spacious, green environment and self-sufficiency was the beginning of Club Med as it is known today. In 1956 the first ski village was built in Switzerland and in 1965 the first permanent village at Agadir in Morocco.

Club Med became a publicly quoted company in 1966 and expansion continued through the 1970s with the opening of villages in the US market and offices in New York and Japan.

The 1980s saw continued expansion, internationalisation, decentralisation and diversification. It was in response to the challenges which these consecutive activities generated that Club Med looked in depth at how it managed and enhanced its service quality. The primary focus of this study is the work undertaken in the late 1980s and its consequences.

KEY PILLARS OF SUCCESS

Les gentils organisateurs

The concept of the *gentil organisateur* (nice organiser) is one of the key pieces in the Club Med jigsaw that has helped to create and maintain its unique atmosphere. From the first Club Med holiday in 1950 until today the GO has never been a "typical" staff member. Although a technician (in sports, administration or child care, for example) he or she shares the same life as the *gentil membre* (as the guests are known at Club Med). Eating, sleeping and relaxing in the same facilities, taking every opportunity to converse with the GMs, the GO controls the emotional tone and the atmosphere of the village.

"The GO spirit is one of availability, creativity and extroversion. Their aim is to convey the impression of not working." They are the guardians, custodians or mediators of village life. How this challenge is met is explored in more detail below.

A unique client relationship

There are no clients or customers at Club Med, there are members and organisers. The nature of both these roles and the relationship between them is something special to Club Med.

"At the service of all, but servile to none." There is an interesting paradox in Club Med's application of this cliché. It is because the GOs genuinely want to go to virtually any lengths to make the GMs' stay as pleasurable as possible, that there is no sense of obligation which would create a feeling of servitude. This enthusiasm to be helpful is appreciated by the GMs who therefore "close the loop" on a virtuous circle of behaviour by responding warmly to the GOs.

This is reinforced in a number of practical ways. For example, when the GO is involved in a show or spectacle in the evening the GM considers him or her as a friend in amateur dramatics rather than a professional entertainer to be criticised. It is common for GMs to seek out GOs in their "day jobs" to congratulate them on the previous evening's performance.

Customer focus: feedback and reaction

One of the main features of Club Med as a company is its ability to obtain and react to customer feedback. As long ago as 1967 the Club established a computer based system to centrally collect and analyse GMs' feedback on the quality of their holiday experience in all of the different locations. Today the "barometer" as it is known evaluates over 250,000 GM responses every year. Where necessary immediate corrective action can be taken in any locality and trends are analysed for future planning and development. This quantitative information is also used to evaluate the performance of a particular team running a given location.

Systematic analysis of all letters received from GMs is undertaken in order to follow up issues which are perhaps more subtle or more personal than those highlighted through the questionnaire analysis.

The commercial director for each market (ie. the GMs' originating country) also formally solicits feedback from three sources on a regular basis; the GOs working in Club Med's own distribtion network (which is responsible for 50 per cent of the sales worldwide); other major distributors (mainly travel agents); and the GMs themselves, through focus group. These conversations are designed to reveal the more subtle perceptions the GMs hold about Club Med.

Customer feedback is also formally solicited during the GMs' stay in a village. The "Round Table" is a type of quality circle run by the village manager to encourage GMs to provide extra feedback.

Apart from these formal mechanisms, the closeness of the GOs to the GMs helps create a rapid reaction to informal feedback picked up during conversations.

Originality of concept

The Club Med concept is inherently simple: provide an attractive location with all the classic ingredients for a good holiday, remove all the hassle for the holiday maker and top it by creating an atmosphere which makes the holiday maker feel superbly at ease with him or herself and everyone else.

It is, however, exceptionally difficult to copy because it is dependent on so many intangible dimensions of quality. To deliver these consistently requires the weaving of many different, interdependent aspects of management from recruitment to leadership and from marketing to operations passing through communication, intercultural sensitivity and an ability to make hard work feel like fun.

Effective market segmentation

Club Med has adopted a number of different approaches to market segmentation. It segments customers by culture or nationality. Not rigidly, because mixing people in the villages is one of the ingredients for success, but sensitively to avoid one nationality dominating another and to help communication. It also provides information to allow potential customers to select with whom they wish to spend their holiday; for example, "in this village you will be in the company of our US members". Languages spoken are indicated in Club Med's brochures as clearly as the sports facilities.

It also segments by type of holiday sought. Different types and grades of village appeal to people with different requirements. It has different brand names for different products, such as Valtur, Clubhotel and Club Med Decouvert, sometimes promoting one brand to a particular segment of the market across a number of countries.

An interesting experiment currently being undertaken is to mix, within the same village, holiday makers and business people in conferences and on seminars. The financial advantages of doing this are obvious, as many resort hotels know. However, the risk of failing to satisfy either or both sets of clients is high. At Opio, just outside Nice on the Côte d'Azur, two years "down the track" Club Med seems to be winning the bet. It probably has something to do with seeing the two products as synergistic rather than incompatible. The oil that makes it work is part of that Club Med atmosphere.

CLUB MED AND TQM

"Club Med has always been a quality organisation," says Michel Perchet, human resources director, expressing a view reinforced by many other managers in Club Med. Since its inception in the 1950s the "Club" has dedicated extraordinary energy to delivering service quality "as the customer defines it".

In many ways it is true that Club Med's way of interacting with both customers and its own people has always exemplified the Total Quality principles. However, during the 1980s, in response to the events outlined above, it became necessary to consider formally the management and improvement of service quality.

In 1985 a process was developed to define exactly what "Quality" meant to the GMs. Using extensive customer feedback the Quality Charter was produced. This initial step was reinforced by taking each aspect of the charter and developing a methodology for delivering that dimension or aspect of quality across the 100 plus villages worldwide.

As Jacques Horowitz, who led the process for Club Med, said:

It became necessary to make explicit the implicit knowledge held by thousands of people within the Club in order to ensure consistency of delivery across an increasingly complex organisation.

1985 CLUB MED QUALITY: "ZERO DEFECT OBJECTIVE"

The dilemma

The success of the Club was indisputable but it was felt that to retain its position as market leader during this continued expansion, action was needed to ensure consistency and development of service quality. This was highlighted by some difficulties in the US market. US customers were more demanding than the Europeans; quicker to complain, they had different expectations which were not always understood by the GOs; cultural differences were creating some problems. The expansion into Asia meant these problems might be repeated or even worse.

Customer expectations everywhere were rising. Club Med was now an international, decentralised business and the feeling of "hands on" control was less sure. The nomadic lifestyle of the GOs, so central to Club Med's success, was becoming more difficult. Local adaptations to the Club formula in different parts of the world made it harder for incoming managers and GOs to assume their responsibilities smoothly.

The response

A first step involved senior managers visiting organisations that were recognised as leaders in delivering quality, such as Disney, IBM and American Airlines in the USA, to discuss their approach to managing quality. Concurrently Club Med ran an in depth analysis, lasting a full year, of customer feedback by geographic area and by individual villages. The overall market trends in terms of changing needs and expectations and individual requirements per village were identified. The travel agents who sold Club Med holidays were extensively consulted as were people working in Club Med's own distribution network. In depth discussions were also held with GOs to obtain "grass roots" feedback on developments in customer expectations.

A commission was formed

Six people formed a tightly knit group to work full time on this project for "as long as it takes". They were drawn from different parts of the organisation to give a balanced view. There were two village managers, a senior catering/purchasing manager, a construction/maintenance manager and the external advisor.

A "war room" type atmosphere was generated where each memeber fought fiercely to ensure that his/her point of view was represented. Each individual member developed a network of 15 other people representing a cross-section of the population who were to implement the quality approach selected.

The commission first produced a Quality Charter, with Objective Zero Defects. This contains ten specific dimensions of quality as the *customer* perceives it. This list (see below) of "bottom up" generated criteria was personally validated and agreed by Gilbert Trigano, the company chairman.

Quality is exceeding the GM's expectations. These are:

- to arrive (at the village) and live without worry or risk;
- an attractive location;
- to be paid attention, receive generosity and imagination;
- to be able to use the village's facilities easily;
- everything works and is clean;
- freedom of choice;
- to eat and drink what, when and as much as the GM wants;
- to meet people easily;
- to learn new skills;
- for the contract to be honestly respected.

These quality statements were felt to cover the range of expectations GMs had of a Club Med holiday.

The next task was to translate these into much more detailed standards which, if respected, would deliver the desired experience to the GM.

Developing service standards

The commission looked at each statement of the Quality Charter in relation to each activity within the villages to measure its importance in relation to delivering the charter. In developing the service standards a number of factors were taken into consideration.

- What the customer feedback had indicated was required/desired.
- What market trends suggested would become increasingly important.
- Current practice.
- What the GOs who specialised in that particular field felt was important.

Standards were developed for each activity using a three part framework.
- What is the standard (expressed from the clients' viewpoint)?
- What task must the GO undertake to deliver this standard?
- How is this task to be carried out?

The standards applied equally to tangible dimensions of quality, such as the appearance of a buffet or availability of sports material, and to intangible dimensions such as the ease with which a GM's problem is solved or the quality of the attention GMs receive.

Several hundred standards were developed in total; an example is shown in the box below.

A CLUB MED STANDARD

QUOI: la tâche

Le GO surprend le GM par son imagination et son sens créatif.

COMMENT la faire

Le GO innove pour répondre au style, aux gouts et aux modes du moment.

- Il organise avec son équipe des réunions de créativité.
- Il organise et réalise tout ce qui peut être monté dans un bon rapport qualité, prix, créativité.
- Il sait utiliser tous les effets techniques.
- Il est curieux et international.
- Il passe en intersaison voir ses responsables et prend connaissance des événements nouveaux qui "marchent".
- Il va voir les nouveaux spectacles.
- Il visionne les vidéo-cassettes du club.
- Il écoute les nouveaux disques. Etc.

Standard: le résultat

De l'imagination. Le GM veut être surpris par la créativité et l'imagination de l'équipe d'animation.

Involving the staff

Many organisations have service standards, so why are Club Med's any different? And would they be accepted by the staff?

The importance of the people who were going to use the standards achieving ownership of them had been recognised as crucial at the outset of this process. During the development of the standards the commission team had deliberately sought to involve a wider audience both to benefit from their input and to begin the process of sharing ownership.

The next step was to involve the village managers, whose role resembles that of the captain of a ship. They are often found in far flung corners of the world with ultimate and immediate responsibility for making that village successful during their time in charge of it. They are a very powerful figurehead for both the GOs and the GMs. Their support for the standards initiative was vital.

All the village managers were invited to spend one week at a seminar, presided over by Gilbert Trigano, which was designed to share with them the rationale behind the standards and the way in which they should be used. The managers quickly saw the standards as a vehicle for helping them in their job not as a straitjacket or policing operation. What they saw was a formalisation of many of the processes with which they were familiar, but which had never been formally identified and documented.

A number of immediate positive uses for the standards were recognised by the village managers:

- to assess the current situation when moving in/taking over a new village, to identify what and how to prioritise;
- as a training aid for GOs;
- as a training aid during induction of new GOs;
- as a system of benchmarking for ongoing performance measurement;
- as a way of improving consistency of performance across the villages.

Managers also saw that they would have a degree of flexibility in developing standards specific to their village.

A number of GOs were trained to run seminars like the one the village managers had experienced. Every GO then attended a five day seminar introducing the standards.

Did the standards work?

From the ongoing feedback received from GMs on their holiday experience it was possible to identify, the following year, an improvement in some key dimensions of quality. For example, there was a five per cent improvement in the customer perceived ratings for the restaurant, the mini club and the baby club.

Why did the standards work?

Quick positive action. The information being received and analysed from customer feedback was indicating a need for some changes in the type of service or the way in which it was being delivered. If standards were to be implemented which related to customers' expressed preferences, then investment decisions needed to be made.

During the five month period in which the commission was working on standards they had weekly meetings with the chief executive, Serge Trigano, who took vital decisions on the spot as to what could be done and how soon. For example, it became apparent that the standard Club Med formula of everybody eating in tables of eight was no longer pleasing all the GMs. They wanted more flexibility to sit in large or small groups. (This was part of a more general trend away from "everyone does everything with everybody".) The chief executive was able to make an informed decision (based on costs of restaurant modifications, staff costs of changing the delivery system, etc.) and say, yes, we will offer greater flexibility in this area and to state when and where the required modifications would take place.

Forthright, clear leadership. There was never any doubt about the senior management commitment to this exercise. They instigated it, remained personally in contact with it on a weekly basis and allocated the resources needed to implement the recommended changes. These powerful actions communicated more about commitment than the many words of support which were also frequently used.

Straightforwardness. The approach taken by Club Med is both delightfully and deceptively simple.

Delightfully because it is so logical, so uncluttered, so practical, a way of working which typifies the Club's approach to many things. If it is straightforward, get on and do it, and do it exceptionally well. Do not create unnecessary complications.

Deceptively because successful implementation is due to the carefully crafted culture of the Club and the thought that went into the question "What do we need to do in parallel with developing the standards if they are to be really successful?". The answers included things like special task forces to pursue problematic issues, reviewing recruitment and induction programmes, and seeking better ways of handling cultural differences between GMs in the same location.

Viewing from the customer's perspective. The standards were developed from customer research and written in a way that expresses the customer's perspective. This reinforces Club Med's core ethic of being completely customer focused.

Ownership and training. Careful thought was put into how to develop ownership of the standards by the key stakeholders, the staff. This was linked to training in how to implement the standards and how to use them as a training aid in themselves. Each O received eight days' training in the new standards. They were all trained in problem solving techniques such as brainstorming, pareto analysis and fishbone diagrams.

Standard, task and process. A characteristic of the standards is that they are much more than standards. The Quality Charter provides ten key principles expressed as customer expectations. These are easy to remember and reinforce focus. The standards detail the component elements of the ten principles and importantly they explain what task is necessary to hit each standard, and the process (the "how" as it is called) to complete the task. It is this aspect of the standards which makes them live and which is used in training.

Innovation and ongoing development. There are risks in setting standards of any sort. They can become the minimum and the maximum levels. Dr Deming firmly believes that people perform down to standards. They can also become "set in concrete".

Club Med has sought to avoid these pitfalls by ensuring that the standards are seen only as a minimum on which the GOs build. "The GOs invent the Club every day," says Michel Perchet. Innovating on and around the standards is part of this. Club Med's whole approach to quality also provides some autonomy for managers to adopt and modify some of the standards in each village.

The ability to innovate and a willingness to take risks go hand in hand. Club Med support innovation in a practical sense by supporting people who have taken a risk which has not proved successful. This was exemplified by Gilbert Trigano in his speech to shareholders at the annual general meeting in April 1992. He began by referring to a project involving two airline companies. "I spoke a year ago of how hopeful I was about our involvement with Minerve and Air Liberté. I was mistaken. I do not usually look for excuses and I shall not now. I have been unable to unite these companies, neither their management, nor their shareholders." Such openness about mistakes at the top of Club Med sends a powerful signal to those within the organisation.

If customer feedback shows that problems are arising in spite of villages working to the standards, special task forces are set up to investigate and recommend solutions. The output from these groups is incorporated into the standards. The special recipes for salad that are used in the USA are an example of this.

Other standards are targeted

As a consequence of undertaking the Quality Zero Defects work the management of Club Med were able to target some specific actions above and beyond the service standards. An example is in the areas of recruitment, induction and training of the GOs. The next section explores these developments and the role of the GOs.

CLUB MED IS PEOPLE

Les gentils organisateurs are people

The GOs are fundamental to the Club Med concept. Developments in customer expectations and the increasingly international nature of the Club meant that the role of GOs was subtly (but significantly) changing. The standards research highlighted in particular a need to look at their recruitment, induction and training.

Recruitment

Two concurrent developments drove the need to review recruitment of GOs. One was the increasing internationalisation of the customer base. This led to a policy of recruiting more widely resulting in the recruitment of 70 per cent non-French nationals as GOs since 1988.

The other was the increasing sophistication of some villages. This has meant that the people chosen to be GOs are no longer the stereotyped "fun loving teenager out for a good time". Although they do need to like a "good time" and tend to be in their 20s, they also have to be skilled professionals in their chosen discipline. For example, a golf monitor must have a handicap of 12 or less.

Provided the potential GO has the correct professional qualifications and speaks at least two (usually three) languages, the other selection criteria are:

- willingness to participate;
- team spirit;
- flexibility;
- adaptability;
- service orientation; and
- ability to communicate.

They are also evaluated against two of the basic principles of GO life: vitality and a nomadic lifestyle. GOs must be able to learn, help others to learn and "do" and "invent" all the time. Given these varied and demanding criteria, it is perhaps not surprising that fewer than 3 per cent of all applicants are finally accepted as GOs.

GOs change location every six months. This deliberate policy has a number of advantages.

- A sharing of experience. Staff rotate between "villages" learning new ideas.
- A willingness to question themselves. Will this work here? Why might it not? What assumptions am I making which may be inappropriate?
- New challenges: different jobs, different people, different cultures.
- Interest: variety of work.
- Development of cultural sensitivity through experiencing several different cultures.
- Personal development.
- Reinforcement and sharing of the "Club Med" way of doing things (with local sensitivities) rather than 100 different ways of doing things in 100 different villages.
- Creation of a common bond between GOs wherever they find themselves in the world. Everyone has the same lifestyle which facilitates movement of employees.
- Ease of establishing norms of performance and standards across and between villages.

Training

Once selected GOs undergo a period of five days' training at head office which imbues them with the Club's values, concepts and principles. Following this they are posted to a village for six months.

Regular ongoing training of GOs takes place either in the village or back at head office for specific courses. All promotions are accompanied by appropriate training before moving into a new post. For example, a village manager receives 102 days' training primarily focused on leadership and communication skills before taking up his or her position.

There is a rolling series of programmes about customer and cultural awareness aimed at sensitising the GOs to some of the dos and don'ts of different cultures to help them strike up relationships quickly with GMs from other cultures without giving offence.

Mentoring

On arrival in a village, a new GO is assigned to a more experienced one for a few weeks. They work in tandem while the new GO familiarises him or herself with the role, including understanding and implementing the service standards.

This is an area in which Club Med has identified the need to improve. Because there are a relatively high number of new joiners each year the ability to successfully integrate them into the organisation is critical. The introduction of a "Livret de Parrainage" is an example of the straightforward approach taken to problem solving. Each new joiner has a personalised booklet explaining who his/her mentor is, what their role is and some personal information about the mentor. It is the style and tone of the booklet which communicate the purpose as much as the actual contents.

A Sense of belonging

Club Med cultivate and maintain the sense of belonging which GOs have to the Club Med family. This is done through communications such as the monthly "letter to GOs" from Gilbert Trigano which outline the important events which have occurred and the key issues facing the group in the future. There are also special editions such as the one in April 1992 entitled "metier GO", outlining what the GO's job entails and specifically what makes it different, challenging and rewarding. This special edition is being supported by a package of 80 35mil slides used by the village managers to explain the history of the "Club", its values and principles and the role of the GO.

The sense of belonging is also self-sustaining as GOs meet colleagues they have worked with before in different parts of the globe on taking up new positions. The head office in Paris plays an important formal role in maintaining this sense of belonging for example through training and inter-season meetings. It also has an important informal role as the centre of a network where GOs call in casually if they are in Paris. During the research project visits to head office, we invariably witnessed GOs "popping in to see someone and meeting with several other acquaintances".

This essentially human aspect of Club Med is central to its service philosophy. As Michel Perchet puts it "the client does not want to feel that he/she is the output of a standardised procedure. They want to feel special." Because of this, standards can only ever take us so far – what makes the real difference is the Club's values and the passion with which people live them.

Leadership

Leadership in a village is effected by example. As Francis di Landro, a village manager, says:

> *If the GOs see me talking to GMs, they will talk to GMs; if they see me checking the standards, they will check them; if I am approachable, they will be approachable.*

It is about village managers being "on the ground", being available to talk to customers and to staff. So much of Club Med's success is due to this contact and communication that the example from the top is crucial. Every opportunity to exchange a few words with a GM is taken. The village manager may run a business which has (at any point in time) up to 1,000 guests and 400 staff, with all the budgeting, planning and organisation that requires. He or she would still spend 6–7 hours a day "on the ground" with guests and staff.

It is also about clarity of purpose for all employees. What are the objectives? Why are we doing this particular task? How does it make the GMs happier? How do I contribute to its success?

It is about feedback: frequent and direct feedback. A word of praise for something well done. An explanation demanded if something goes wrong. Nothing is left to chance and nothing is ignored.

It is helped by the standards both as a control mechanism, a quality guarantee for the GMs and as an educational vehicle.

The role of village manager is critical in Club Med's success. He or she is similar to the captain of a ship being responsible for the wellbeing of GMs and GOs, often in far flung regions of the world. He or she has a high level of autonomy to implement the Club's philosophy, the guidance is the values by which Club Med lives.

Les gentil membres are the most important people of all

The GM really is considered to be someone very special and the feedback shows that they appreciate this. At the village in Opio, near Nice, a number of specific incidents provide an insight into how this is achieved. There is a rule which says not understanding a GM's request (because it is made in a language you do not speak) is no reason for not responding positively and appropriately to the request: you simply find a way of communicating. In one staff briefing it was announced that there were to be 400 Japanese people in the camp the following week. A GO asked the village manager in jest "How are we going to chat with this lot?" The next day two sides of A4 paper were given to each GO with the most common Japanese phrases in phonetic writing.

Another example is that GOs do not just say hello to everyone; they look them straight in the eye, when they have made contact they smile (with the eyes as well as the mouth) and then say hello, and if possible talk some more as well. Contrast this with a GM's experience at Nice airport where the airline staff member avoided eye contact as long possible then informed the GM that he was ten minutes too early to check his luggage in. In the words of the GM, the airport and Club Med Opio are only a few kilometres apart but they feel like different planets.

A third was explained by Valerie Frebot, in charge of administration at Opio.

> *We will always seek to avoid saying no to a GM. This may involve us spending a disproportionate amount of time and effort on a small number of guests. 99 per cent are happy with things as they are but we aim for 100 per cent GM satisfaction. If that requires spending 10 per cent of the time on 1 per cent of the GMs, then we do it.*

The GO's role in managing the atmosphere and climate in the village is put to the test here. The GOs spend more than 12 hours a day, seven days a week, in close proximity to the GMs. It would be difficult to maintain an "act" under those circumstances. The GOs genuinely enjoy meeting and living with a stream of new GMs and the unique relationship of service but not servility is rewarding for both parties.

This is exemplified by a GO working at reception who said:

It's only to be expected that guests arriving will be in a bad mood. After all they are stressed and tired by the outside world. We have been here for months and can help them unwind. They will be much nicer with us after a couple of days.

Little people

Club Med recognised before most of its competitors that family holidays did not necessarily mean all the family being together all the time. Its approach is to make the organisation of children's activities so good that the children want to be there. The mini-clubs and baby clubs are run to provide distraction and learning for children in complete security. This allows parents to participate for part of the day in sports and social activities where the presence of children would be inappropriate.

The increasing number of villages providing full child care facilities is significant. It shows how Club Med is enhancing its offerings to meet the changing needs of its existing customers as they become families rather than couples.

CLOSEST TO THE CUSTOMER

Club Med's ability to obtain, interpret and react to customer feedback is astounding. The subtle but significant changes which have taken place in its product over the last decade demonstrate this. The success with which the Club continues to manage "changing and staying the same" will be a key determinant of future success.

GM questionnaire

L'Oscar is the name given to the postage paid questionnaire which every GM receives following a Club Med holiday. Approximately 250,000 are returned every year, which Club Med feels reflects two things: a sense of satisfaction with the holiday and, more importantly, a sense of giving information to a club to which you belong rather than providing feedback to a supplier.

The questionnaire, which is waiting for holiday makers at their home on their return, first collects some marketing data: With whom did you make your reservation? Had you already been on a Club Med holiday? Which factors influenced you the most in your choice of holiday (word of mouth recommendation, advertising etc.)? Family situation and job type.

It then goes on to ask: "If you could improve one aspect of your Club Med holiday, what would it be?"

The next section asks the GM to "score" 16 aspects of the holiday on a scale from extraordinary to very bad. The example in the box is from a skiing holiday.

1. Avez-vous fait votre réservation par:
☐ Le Club Med ☐ Une agence de voyage ☐ Autres
2. Etiez-vous déjà parti avec le Club Med auparavant?
☐ Oui ☐ Non   Si *oui*, combien de fois?
3. Etiez-vous déjà parti en vacances en utilisant un organisme de voyage autre que le Club Med?
☐ Oui ☐ Non   Si *oui*, lequel?
4. Dans cette décision de partir avec le Club Med, qu'est-ce qui a *le plus* influence votre choix? (cochez *une* case)
☐ Un précédent séjour? ☐ Votre agent de voyages? ☐ Un article de presse? ☐ Un parent ou un ami?
☐ La publicité? ☐ La brochure?
5. Votre situation familiale:
☐ Célibataire ☐ Couple ☐ Célibataire avec enfant(s) ☐ Couple avec enfant(s)
6. Votre catégorie professionelle:
☐ Dirigeant, cadre supérieur ☐ Cadre, commercant ou employé ☐ Etudiant ☐ Profession liberale
☐ Retraité ☐ Autres
7. Si vous pouviez améliorer *un aspect*, ou une des caractéristiques de vos vacances au Club Med, ce serait: (cochez *une* case)
☐ Information à la vente ☐ L'équipe GO ☐ L'école de ski ☐ L'animation ☐ La table ☐ Le confort
☐ L'organisation pour les enfants (babyclub, petit-club, mini-club) ☐ Autres
8. Repartiriez-vous en vacances au Club Med?
☐ Oui ☐ Non

	L'impression d'ensemble	L'organisation	L'accueil des Bureaux du Village	L'équipe des GO	La table	Le bar	L'école de ski	Le choix des distractions	Le calme	Le mini-club	Le baby club/le p'tit club	La station	Le confort	Le voyage club	La propreté	Renseignements fournis à l'inscription
EXTRAORDINAIRE	6	6	6	6	6	6	6	6	6	6	6	6	6	6	6	6
TRÈS BIEN	5	5	5	5	5	5	5	5	5	5	5	5	5	5	5	5
BIEN	4	4	4	4	4	4	4	4	4	4	4	4	4	4	4	4
PASSABLE	3	3	3	3	3	3	3	3	3	3	3	3	3	3	3	3
MÉDIOCRE	2	2	2	2	2	2	2	2	2	2	2	2	2	2	2	2
TRÈS MAUVAIS	1	1	1	1	1	1	1	1	1	1	1	1	1	1	1	1

Pour nous transmettre tout autre commentaire, merci d'adresser un courrier au service Relations Adhérents – Club Med, 25 rue Vivienne, 75088, Paris Cedex 02.

It explores:

- Overall impression.
- Organisation.
- "Welcome" in the village offices.
- Team of GOs.
- Restaurant.
- Bar.

- Ski school.
- Choice of amusements.
- Peace and quiet.
- Mini-club (children).
- Baby club.
- Resort overall.
- Comfort.
- The journey to the resort.
- Cleanliness.
- Information given when booking holiday.

This information is used in a number of different ways. Immediate feedback is provided from head office (where the forms are received) to individual village managers if a GM has specifically highlighted a feature which left them dissatisfied. Given that the questionnaires are normally returned within 15 days of the end of a holiday this provides the village manager with the opportunity to identify the cause of the problem and take corrective action within 30 days.

Trends are tracked both in terms of customer type and profile and in perceptions of quality of different aspects of the Club Med experience. Correlations can be drawn between perceptions of quality and a range of different factors such as client type, nationality, location of holiday, mix of GMs, time of year, and so on.

Figure 2.1 below shows how the cumulative scores for each village for a season are presented graphically showing the rating for each key area. The qualitative comments highlight important aspects and also refer to the key points of the more detailed analysis on each village (by week, by customer type, etc.) which are not shown on this summary.

Figure 2.1 Key holiday areas ratings

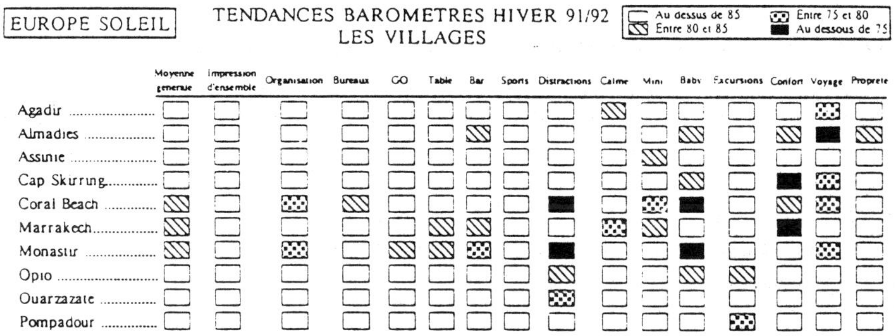

AGADIR	Toujours tres bon. La table redescend légerement
ALMADIES	Toujours tres bon. Table et distractions au-dessus de 90. Voyage en progression
ASSINIE	Toujours tres bon. Legere baisse en GO et a la Table.
CAP SKIRRING	Toujours tres bon. Hausse importante en GO 97,7 - Bar en baisse
CORAL BEACH	Les rubriques continuent de monter. Progression partout - Table a 92
MARRAKECH	Bon dans l'ensemble - Le confort en baisse - Les distractions remontent 85,1
MONASTIR	Peu de reponses. Legere baisse
OPIO	Excellent partout, tendances au-dessus de 90/95. Baisse en distractions
OUARZAZATE	Tres bon mais en legere baisse depuis mars.
POMPADOUR	Tres bon - Ensemble a 97,4 - Baisse en GO passant de 94,2 à 88,1.

Source: Club Med

Over time this wealth of information is used in various ways.

- Tackling specific, recurring problems. For example, with the buffets in the US villages a task force was set up to explore the problem and recommend solutions to be shared across the villages.
- Product and service development.
- Evaluation of village managers and of teams of GOs; marketing
- Human resources strategy.

La table ronde

To obtain feedback during a holiday rather than relying purely on the post-holiday questionnaires, Club Med instituted round table discussions in the villages. These involve the village manager or one of the departmental heads inviting a cross-section (5–8 people) to join him or her for a discussion about their holiday. This usually takes place after the GMs have been in the village for three days. It may happen over a meal.

Naive listening

GOs at Club Med are much closer to the GMs than are staff in a typical service environment. This means that the quantity and quality of listening is very high. This informal feedback process is crucial to the continuous fine tuning of each village to ensure GM satisfaction.

Telephone interviews

Another way in which Club Med broadens its ongoing customer research is by telephoning a random sample of GMs to discuss their holiday in more depth than is covered by the questionnaire.

ONGOING IMPROVEMENT

The latest developments in Club Med's drive to improve service quality include the following.

Focusing head office employees on customer service. Although many of the people working at head office are ex-village employees, not all are. Club Med is no exception to the apparently inexorable truth that those people removed or insulated from the external customer are less service oriented. This is being tackled by doing value analysis of functions and working on the concept of internal customers.

Retour au source. Managers in head office go back to work in villages during the peak summer months. This has made the gap between the operations and head office even smaller, improved communications and kept managers directly in touch with the GMs.

Coaching for quality. All middle managers are being developed to act as coaches. This process focuses on mentoring and development skills with very little emphasis on quality techniques. Club Med experimented with, but rejected most of, the formal techniques early in their initiative in 1986.

Reducing the number of core service standards. Customer feedback has shown that 15–20 core standards per service are the critical ones. The objective is to simplify the standards to make them easier to use and control. These new standards have adopted a slightly different format from the original ones. They are less detailed, containing information on what the GM expects and how the GO should meet this expectation (see Figure 2.2).

Figure 2.2   Simplified standards

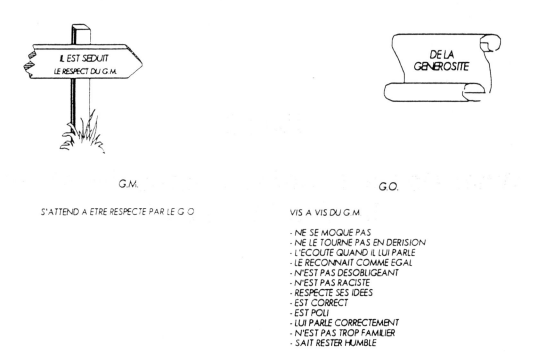

Source: Club Med

Revising the "Oscar" feedback form. Starting in the summer season of 1992 the GM feedback form has been modified to capture more detailed information about the GM's experience. It asks questions about aspects of each of the key elements in the holiday experience.

Part 2

What Do the Leading Companies Mean by Total Quality?

3 The Total Quality Principles

> *We are going to win and the industrial West is going to lose out. There's not much you can do about it because the reasons for your failure are within yourselves.*
>
> *Your firms are built on the Taylor Model. Even worse, so are your heads. With your bosses doing the thinking while the workers wield the screwdrivers, you're convinced deep down that this is the right way to run a business. For you the essence of management is getting the ideas out of the heads of the bosses and into the hands of labour.*
>
> *We are beyond the Taylor Model. Business, we know, is now so complex and difficult, the survival of firms so hazardous in an environment increasingly unpredictable, competitive and fraught with danger, that their continued existence depends on the day to day mobilisation of every ounce of intelligence.*
>
> Konosuke Matsushita, founder of the world's largest consumer electronics company

Total Quality has changed. Once associated just with process improvement and problem solving techniques, it now deals with quality in the broadest sense: how to achieve continuous improvement in the performance of an organisation. The companies interviewed during the research all agreed that this is what they are aiming at with TQ. The definitions of TQ set out in the European and the US Baldrige Quality Awards (see Chapter 6) confirm the point.

Customers define quality; it is their perception which matters. And the stakes have been raised. No longer is it enough to satisfy the customer's stated requirements. In an increasingly competitive world, it is customer delight which is sought: anticipating or exceeding customer expectations in order to build customer loyalty and make customers into the most fervent (and effective) advocates of your company's goods and services.

To achieve this an organisation must be continuously improving. Yesterday's marvellous new product or service is today's standard and tomorrow's reject. So the focus shifts from product or service quality to a process of continuous improvement in all aspects of the organisation. This in turn requires organisations to do three things – to focus on customers, improve processes and unlock people potential – and to do them together. TQ is now a holistic approach. A balanced diet of all three elements is required.

IBM's definition of quality

- Quality is the customer's judgement, not ours.
- Quality concerns both the product and associated services.
- Quality is not an absolute, but relative to competitors.
- Quality does not in fact include price; quality and service are remembered when price is long forgotten.

CUSTOMER FOCUS

The first and overriding principle is to focus everyone in the organisation on serving customers. Such customer focus has often been advocated before, so what does Total Quality add? There are three elements.

- TQ companies go to extraordinary lengths to find out exactly what their customers (actual and potential) want. They are not prepared to rely on received wisdom or secondhand information. Their recipe for understanding customers is "Go and ask them."
- The information on customer needs and wants must be customer driven; it must be based on the perceptions of customers and tackle the questions they, not the company, think are important.
- Direct personal contact with customers is important. Companies should have an informal and intuitive understanding of customers, gained by getting to know them and how they actually work, particularly when it comes to anticipating needs which the customer has not articulated.

THE TOTAL QUALITY PRINCIPLES

In order to improve continuously and delight customers, organisations need to:

- **Focus on Customers**
  Listen carefully to customers;
  Measure the things that are important to them;
  Maintain personal contact with them.
- **Improve Processes**
  See businesses as sets of processes, not hierarchies:
  – Consider systems as a whole, not blame individuals;
  – Break down barriers between functions;
  – Think of departments to whom goods/services are supplied as internal customers;
  – Set up long term partnerships with suppliers.

  Establish fact-based management:
  – Open people's eyes to the opportunity for improvement;
  – Prevent errors and reworking;
  – Speak with data;
  – Seek out root causes of problems;
  – Set standards.
- **Unlock People Potential**
  Foster continuous learning;
  Manage by values, not controls;
  Encourage team working;
  Continuously develop the self-confidence and sense of responsibility of staff.

Encouraging customer feedback

For every company there is an enormous reservoir of potential improvement among the customers who are dissatisfied but do not complain (see box). Companies need to encourage customers to complain; indeed to feed back as much as possible.

Companies need to encourage customers to complain

- For every customer who complains, 26 others remain silent.
- 91 per cent of unhappy customers will never purchase goods or services from you again.
- The average "wronged" customer will tell 8–16 people.
- It costs about five times as much to attract new customers as it costs to keep old ones.
- Remedy customer complaints and 82–95 per cent will continue to make purchases.

Source: TARP, Washington, DC.

Hewlett Packard stresses the range of sources of information it needs to capture fully the "customer voice" (see box).

Hewlett Packard collects customer information in many different ways

NEEDS/TRENDS/PERFORMANCE
(Company driven)

Market research
- Intelligence
- Product/service focused
- Red flag

Surveys
- Population/sample
- Broad/focused
- Selected objectives

Focus groups
- Focused issues
- One shot
- Dynamic

Face to face visits
- Sales interactions
- Account reviews
- Service visits
- User groups

CUSTOMER VOICE

External surveys
- Benchmarks
- Competitive products
- Markets

External process feedback
- Receivables
- Returns
- Delivery
- ATB
- Escalation

Product feedback
- Warranty
- DOA
- Repairs

Customer complaints
- Product performance
- Soft product issues

(Customer driven)
DEFECT REPORTING

Source: Hewlett Packard

Another example is Milliken, the US modular carpet company with operations throughout western Europe, which has been a leader in Total Quality implementation. Instead of "complaints" which customers often do not want to raise and staff see as criticism, Milliken has sought to change the attitude of mind by talking about "opportunities for improvement" (OFIs). The company has made extraordinary efforts to persuade customers to give them OFIs.

- Rapid response to complaints. The company measures the number of days each complaint takes to resolve. This has been reduced to 1–2 days on average. Customers receive letters confirming what action has been taken to deal with the issue raised.
- Thanking "difficult" customers. At dealer conferences, the company picks out for praise those customers who have complained the most.
- High levels of customer feedback. The company has a number of mechanisms to ensure the customer view is heard. For example, customers are telephoned after an installation to ask their views. Staff are trained to listen for things "we could learn from". Order confirmations include reply paid cards to ensure all details of the order are correct: 75 per cent are returned and close to 100 per cent show completely accurate order information.

Customer driven information

The challenge, particularly in large organisations, is how to obtain a customer's eye view of the world; and how to do so in a way that aids the company's own decision making. Customer surveys are now commonplace; they tend to produce masses of data but little understanding. Often the surveys do not ask the questions that really matter to particular customers; or they give weight to factors that are of little or no importance to customers; or they frame the questions in such a way that customers cannot really set out their opinions.

Libby Raper, formerly Total Quality coordinator for IDV, says quality managers should always keep in mind "the power of listening to customers". Her experience in a consumer products company is that careful listening forces managers to think afresh, "to think outside their own boundaries". With this objective, parts of IDV have regular meetings to which they invite groups of customers to discuss the quality and service they are receiving from IDV. The customers set the agendas for these meetings, raising the issues that they want to discuss.

For Ciba-Geigy Dyestuffs and Chemicals, as for many firms, a survey of customers by a third party was necessary to give an authentic view of customers' requirements. Dr Fadel Ibrahim, head of international marketing, comments:

> In a company such as ours there are lots of technical experts who are sure they know what customers want. We even had competing company "popes" leading different schools of thought on the real needs of customers. On the whole, though, we believed dyestuff customers were only interested in getting the lowest possible prices because that is what they always talked to us about. An anonymous survey by an outside consultant showed this was quite wrong. What customers want above all is consistency of quality. A small variation in product characteristics causes them huge problems. The message was clear: don't cut process corners. Even if it costs a bit more maintain absolute product consistency. It was a real eye opener.

Personal contact with customers

One of the strongest lessons to emerge from the companies we studied is the need, in addition to formal surveys and quantitative reports, to maintain strong personal contacts with customers. Mechanistic surveys and questionnaires may miss the understanding which direct personal contacts can provide. In particular, when it comes to trying to anticipate needs which customers have not yet articulated, it is necessary to get close to them, understand their real concerns and priorities and how they work and use your product or service.

ICL Product Distribution supplies and installs systems for very demanding supermarket and other retail customers, usually having to set up the systems out of shopping hours, overnight or at weekends. In the last five years the company has used factory staff to do the work and despite the unsocial hours the assignments are popular and there is no question of leaving the job till the installation is complete. One operator comments: "We're really lucky to meet the customers. It makes the whole job worthwhile." And knowing the customers personally has an effect on quality: "In four years we have hardly missed one installation date and no one would knowingly send out kit with something missing."

In Boise, Idaho, Hewlett Packard has a centre offering a free problem solving telephone service to its computer printer customers across the USA. The HP staff at the centre, many of whom formerly picked potatoes, provide advice to 700,000 people a year and in so doing collect invaluable information on what customers really want. Special HP teams track the calls and also assemble priceless data on competitors' products. John Golding, managing director of HP UK, says: "The centre may seem expensive but in fact it enables us to develop new products a vital six months ahead of the competition."

Milliken's view of the customer

- Customers are not dependent on us, we are dependent on them.
- Customers are not interruptions to our work, they are the purpose of it. We are not doing them a favour by serving them, they are doing us a favour by giving us the opportunity to do so.
- Customers are not outsiders to our business, they are an integral and most important part of it.
- Customers are not cold statistics, they are flesh and blood human beings with feelings, problems and emotions like our own. We must treat them as we would expect to be treated.
- Customers are not people to argue with; no one ever won an argument with a customer even though they may have thought they did.
- Customers are people who rely on us. If we have sufficient imagination and ability, we will serve in a manner profitable to the customer and to ourselves.
- Customers are not always right but they always deserve our understanding, patience and respect.
- Customers are the boss.

PROCESS IMPROVEMENT

Process view of business

TQ brings with it a profound change in thinking about businesses: seeing them as processes, not as hierarchies or bureaucracies (see Figure 3.1). Every customer order, every new product development, every purchase, every task in an organisation is dealt with by a chain of people all of whom are dependent on each other. Increasing value and reducing cost can only be done effectively by considering these processes (see box) as a whole.

Figure 3.1   TQ entails seeing business as processes, not hierarchies

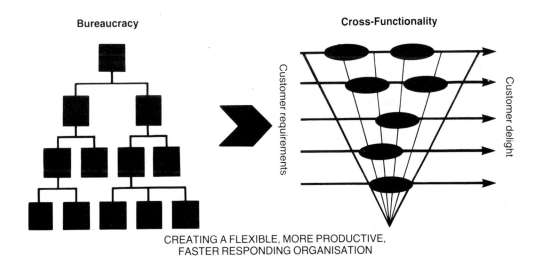

CREATING A FLEXIBLE, MORE PRODUCTIVE,
FASTER RESPONDING ORGANISATION

Source: Rank Xerox

Examples of critical business processes

Product creation	**Customer service**
Market research	Inquiry processing
Competitive analysis	Sales
Concept formulation	Order taking
Detailed design	Order fulfilment
Process development	Shipping
	Invoicing

Supply chain management	**Management of finances**
Purchasing	Capital budgeting
Inbound logistics	Expense budgeting
Inventory	Cash forecasting
Management	Tax planning
Outbound statistics	Revenue budgeting
Distribution	

Source: Arthur D. Little

Each process is a system with its own characteristics and its own inherent variability. Improvement demands that systems are considered as a whole and that individuals are not blamed for things which are not their responsibility but a function of the system they work in. Companies need to consider both the effectiveness and the efficiency of their processes: are they producing things which really add value to customers and are they doing them at lowest cost? Improving systems means bringing them under control by eliminating the one-off causes of error and then systematically reducing the variation of the different elements of the system. Careful factual analysis will show that most processes in most companies are capable of vast improvement. As Jonathan Smilansky, formerly a general manager of VISA International, puts it: "Most processes in life are a mess; the trick is to stand back and see the opportunity for improvement."

This in turn requires a fundamental and difficult shift in the way people look at their jobs and their careers. The barriers between the "functional silos", the departments and functions within a company, must be broken down. People must look at issues with a company-wide perspective and seek to serve the interests of the organisation as a whole, and not just their own part of it. They should be measured on their contribution to the organisation as a whole and see their career opportunities as linked to the success of the whole company, not just their own function.

Internal customers

Total Quality has made the phrase "internal customer" familiar. Each department or team is asked to regard the next process through which items pass as their own, internal customer. Service areas like finance or planning or personnel also have internal customers. Only if they provide a quality service to their customers will the users be able to provide quality to the external customer.

A common first step is for companies to map their key processes and then get to work to improve them. In Mercury Communications 33 top level processes were identified and teams put together to work on those of most strategic importance.

In Hewlett Packard there is a "war room" with a map of all key processes which are kept up to date as they are improved. The map is confidential because it is seen as part of the company's competitive advantage.

Supplier partnerships   *long term* —

The process thinking is also applied to the supply chains across industries. Total Quality draws attention to the importance of suppliers (often worth more than the value added within a company) and offers a complete change in the way they are managed. Single sourcing (or at least very few suppliers), long-term supplier partnerships, purchase decisions on the basis of long-term quality, service and cost (not short-term price), sharing of sensitive information, joint planning and scheduling, support for supplier improvement efforts, have all had an immense impact.

The Nissan Motors UK case study describes how that company has made a reality of this changed approach to suppliers.

Fact based management

Total Quality brings a scientific approach to the resolution of business problems. The need to pose challenging questions and frame hypotheses, the importance of measurement, simple tools for analysing data and getting to the root of problems, the necessity of experimentation, the value of recording carefully best practice so that it can become the norm are all are set out. Scientific methods which are commonplace in technical areas are now applied to the improvement of the business as a whole.

The challenge is to persuade people to stand back from what they are doing, look at it objectively and see the scope for improvement. Space must be made, amid all the day to day operational pressures of running a business, for planning and reviewing the way things are done.

The approach is most often summarised as the Deming or Shewhart PDCA (Plan, Do, Check, Act) cycle (see Figure 3.2): an iterative process of review and improvement.

Figure 3.2   The PDCA cycle

THE PDCA CYCLE

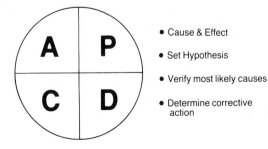

7. MAKE FUTURE PLANS
   - CONTINUE ON SAME ISSUE
   - SELECT NEW ISSUE

6. TAKE APPROPRIATE ACTION
   - CONTROL, STANDARDIZE & DOCUMENT PROCESS
   - TRAIN EMPLOYEES

1. SELECT THE THEME/PROJECT, PLAN THE SCHEDULE OF ACTIVITIES

2. GRASP THE PRESENT STATUS AND SET THE TARGET

3. ANALYZE THE CAUSE AND DETERMINE CORRECTIVE ACTION
   - Cause & Effect
   - Set Hypothesis
   - Verify most likely causes
   - Determine corrective action

5. EVALUATE & COMPARE THE RESULTS

4. IMPLEMENT CORRECTIVE ACTION, TRAIN WHERE NECESSARY

Source: Hewlett-Packard

At Hewlett Packard and Ciba-Geigy Dyestuffs, for example, the first half of the monthly management meeting is devoted to the quality initiative and only afterwards are conventional operational issues discussed. Continuous improvement is central to the strategies of both companies and is seen to have the attention of top management.

Opportunity for improvement

The greatest challenge is to open people's eyes to the scope for improvement. Ask the right questions and you are already most of the way to finding a solution.

The most famous device for doing this has been Phil Crosby's "Zero Defects" and "Price of Non-Conformance" approach. Instead of accepting certain levels of defect customers should ask why items cannot be produced defect free in the first place.

Estimates of wasted activity vary widely from company to company. Many companies participating in this research quoted 25–33 per cent of all activities as being wasted. John Golding, managing director of Hewlett Packard UK, says it may be higher. "Companies which really take a critical look at what they do realise that there is 30–100 per cent waste in everything they do."

The identification of wasted activities applies at least as much to service as to manufacturing businesses.

Benchmarking is being widely used to spur improvement; this is discussed further in Chapter 6.

Prevention

One of the main sources of waste is reworking things which should have been done correctly in the first place; repair or rework areas are often where companies start TQ work. More broadly TQ says that quality needs to be designed in; intense attention is directed at the "upstream" areas, seeking to develop products and services that can be produced reliably and will not have defects when used by the customer.

An example is Nissan Motors UK. From the first the company refused to set aside the large facilities for reworking faulty cars at the end of the production line which have been common in European car plants. Instead efforts were concentrated on ensuring that cars were made without any defects.

Speak with data

TQ managers are known for their passion for measurement, or as the Kaizen Institute describes it, the need to "speak with data". There can be few managers who have not experienced the frustration of meetings where participants exchange anecdotes and prejudices because no one has taken the time and care to collect good information on the problem being discussed.

How often does the problem occur? When does it happen? What are the main types of problem? About how much does it cost? In what circumstances does the problem occur?

Measurement involves leaving the managers' offices and looking carefully at what happens on the shopfloor or office where the work is processed. Do not talk about what you think happens or is supposed to take place; find out what actually happens.

An example is the passion for the facts demonstrated by the management team at ICL Product Distribution, described in the case study.

Seeking out root causes

TQ directs attention to the underlying causes of problems, not their symptoms. To get to root causes, people in Nissan are trained to use the "5 whys" technique; in other words to keep asking "why", to keep probing and not accept at face value the apparent cause of a problem. People also need some simple problem solving tools, such as 80/20 (Pareto) analysis and cause and effect diagrams, but the TQ companies emphasise that it is simple analysis which is needed, not sophisticated statistical techniques.

Set standards

Standard is a difficult word in the West. It is often seen as a threat to creativity and innovation.

TQ says exactly the opposite. Standards and procedures are seen as the way of holding gains in working practices and a base for further improvement. For each key operation or process there must be a best way of doing it. Is it not then obvious that everybody should be asked to do it in that best way? The writing of the standard provides the mechanism for those most involved to agree best practice and, provided they have participated, the commitment for them to stick to it.

The challenge is to develop standards which give specific practical guidance to front line operators and to involve the people who have to implement the standard in preparing and continuing to improve them.

The Club Med case study describes how that company has used standards very effectively to improve quality.

UNLOCK PEOPLE POTENTIAL

"I will listen. I will not shoot the messenger. I recognise that management is the problem," says Roger Milliken, president of Milliken.

It is a cliche among the Total Quality companies to say that "we hired hands and we discovered that we got people's brains for free". Unlocking the potential of employees has moved to the centre of the TQ stage. It is no use seeking to focus on customers and improve processes unless you use more of the energy and ability of employees.

The objective is an organisation in which staff feel they have the authority and the responsibility to initiate improvement and help the customer; to enable them to apply at work the energy, ability and creativity which they have in the rest of their lives.

Michel Perchet, Club Med's human resources director, says the staff (the GOs) "invent the Club every day". They are empowered to innovate wherever they can for the benefit of the holiday maker. Gary Roth, Federal Express's European director of marketing and customer services, says: "If a parcel is going to be late because of a mistake by Federal Express, our front line people can charter a helicopter if necessary to get it there on time."

The changes needed to achieve this are described under four headings: learning, values, teamwork and self-esteem.

Milliken says:

> The real skill of management is less in securing the talents of extraordinary people than in establishing structures which enable ordinary people to be successful.

Learning

Continuous improvement means continuous learning. Companies seeking to apply TQ need to become learning organisations.

What does this mean in practical terms? First it means changing the responsibilities of managers. From seeing their main job as control, they must shift to supporting staff and developing them for the future (see Figure 3.3).

Figure 3.3   Managers need to shift from controlling to enabling and developing their staff

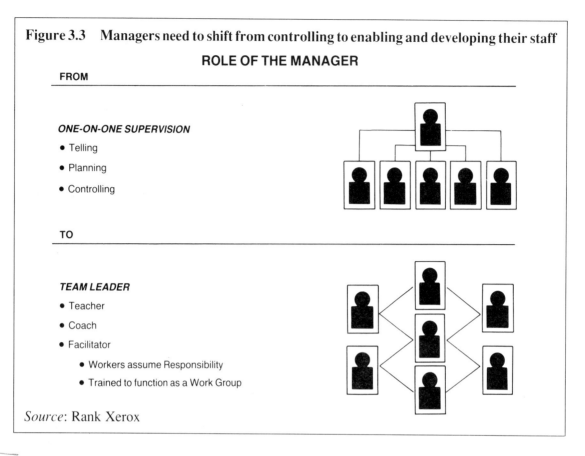

Source: Rank Xerox

It means that management must demonstrate that they too are prepared to learn; that they are listening to employees and responding to their needs and wishes; that they are prepared to admit to and learn from mistakes. There has to be an end to the "blame culture", in which when something goes wrong people are concerned to find a scapegoat, not to find the underlying cause and to correct it.

Review of experience must become the norm with feedback sought and welcomed from peers, bosses and subordinates as soon as possible after action (it is immediate, specific and constructive feedback that contributes most to improvement). Learning must be encouraged in all areas; it cannot be compartmentalised.

The case study describes the progress which Grundfos has made towards becoming a learning organisation. Front line employees say that "if you want to learn something, the company will help you". The accepted pattern of behaviour aids learning: people are open and managers are supportive when mistakes are made. "We discuss what the problem is, not the people. We go for the ball, not the player."

Each manager in Federal Express is evaluated by the team of people working for them and performance related pay depends in part on the evaluation. Staff complete an anonymous questionnaire and then discuss with the manager any points which need clarification. Managers must then produce a plan outlining how they will manage more effectively in future.

Values

Giving people room to experiment, to review and to learn means avoiding some controls; employees must be trusted to act in the best interests of the company and of the customer. But as older management controls become less important so the unifying effect of values becomes more significant. If "empowerment" and "learning organisation" suggest some soft option, of simply encouraging staff and letting them get on with it, think again.

TQ aims at a tough, performance driven environment. Talent and energy are to be unblocked in order to improve processes and serve customers. Shared values and peer pressure are, if anything, tougher on individuals than the old management controls. The difference is that people volunteer for these pressures; they opt to join organisations with values they share.

Thus both Club Med and NMUK appoint only a small percentage (3–5 per cent) of those who apply for jobs. Both select explicitly on attitude and values. Club Med people must be able to learn, to innovate and to help others to learn. NMUK staff must be flexible teamworkers and want to take pride in their work.

Teamwork

Teamwork, not surprisingly, is a requirement of TQ. Key objectives must be shared; management must set out a vision for the company, which embraces quality and which is credible and attractive to staff. Teamworking skills must be fostered and team loyalties nourished. Sensitive information must be shared with all staff; people need to feel that they are trusted. Managers need to be accessible and approachable, not hidden in far away offices but present where the work is done and visibly aware of what is happening. Line managers must recognise the contributions of everyone.

Club Med consciously cultivates the sense of teamwork among staff members. They meet regularly at training sessions; they change location every six months; the head office in Paris has an informal role as a networking centre where staff call in casually; everyone receives a monthly staff letter from Gilbert Trigano, the chairman, dealing with key events and issues.

Self-esteem

The great prize is to set in motion a self-reinforcing cycle of rising self-esteem leading to initiative taking and the seeking out of opportunities to learn and to develop; leading in turn to an increased sense of self-worth.

The Nissan case study describes the remarkable impact that many of its people say working in the company has had, both on their personal and work lives.

How Milliken does it

Milliken has achieved spectacular levels of employee involvement in its businesses in Europe by responding quickly and effectively to suggestions and by recognising the contribution of all staff.

Suggestions to deal with problems are called "opportunities for improvement" (OFIs). In 1984 each employee submitted an average of 1.4 OFIs per year; by 1990 this had risen to 39. Ninety per cent of all employees put in OFIs in that year and 70 per cent worked on some improvement team.

How is it done? The company commits itself to giving a response within 24 hours to the originators of the OFIs; and drawing up within 72 hours plans for the implementation of agreed OFIs.

The company stresses the need for managers to thank staff for suggestions, and mean it. Recognition comes through the award of "Associates of the Period", nominated by their peers: their photographs can be seen dotted around the Milliken plants. Cash is rarely given but there are reserved parking spaces for the winners. One associate had no car but was so pleased by the award that he parked his bicycle in the space.

WHAT'S IN A NAME?

The description given here of Total Quality is drawn from discussion with leading companies. This is what they say are aiming at in the 1990s. The great majority of the ideas are common to all the companies.

Often the companies do not describe what they are doing as Total Quality. Indeed it is argued in Chapter 6 that a company is well advised not to label its approach Total Quality but to find the name for change that best expresses its own goals and approach. Nevertheless they recognise these as being the TQ principles.

Presented together the TQ principles are formidable. In most cases they represent aspirations, not a description of current practice. One respected multinational which has used the US Baldrige for self-assessment said that it was disappointed to find its businesses scoring only about 300 points (out of a maximum 1,000 and with award winners needing at least 850).

It would be foolish to pretend that companies can apply all the principles. As described in Chapter 6, companies need to choose which principles they can and want to apply. In seeking change they must be selective and set clear priorities.

Nevertheless the core principles – of continuous improvement to delight customers, of customer focus, process improvement and unlocking people potential – are a whole. Companies must implement these together or they lose the value of TQ.

Hewlett-Packard's ten points for Total Quality

1. Focus on customers, their needs and expectations.
2. Regularly check how satisfied they are; establish the dissatisfiers.
3. The next person in the process is your customer.
4. Strive to remove the basic causes of customer defects; search continually for problems, deviations.
5. Have constancy of purpose: continuous innovation and improvement of products and processes in all activities.
6. Never fail to standardise to hold gains.
7. Build quality in upstream.
8. Break down barriers between departments.
9. Drive out fear throughout the organisation.
10. Continuously educate, train and retrain to realise our full potential.

SUMMARY

1. Customers define quality and their expectations keep rising. To be competitive an organisation must now delight its customers; that is, provide a little bit more than they anticipate.
2. The Total Quality principles are concerned with the continuous improvement in performance necessary to delight customers.
3. In order to continuously improve, an organisation needs to focus on customers and improve its processes and unlock the potential of its people.
4. A focus on customers means going to extraordinary lengths to understand their perspective, taking every opportunity to obtain feedback and getting alongside them to anticipate their needs.
5. Improving processes requires a radical shift to thinking about businesses as systems and an understanding of how to improve systems. It means fact based management in which there is a continuous cycle of planning, doing and reviewing.
6. Unlocking the potential of employees means creating an environment in which people can readily learn, teamwork can flourish and individuals grow in self-confidence and self-esteem.
7. Total Quality aims to develop tough, performance driven organisations where people fulfil more of their potential by serving customers.

Part 3

How Do You Start to Implement TQ?

4 The Challenge to Conventional Thinking

> *It has to be possible to dream and speak the unthinkable, for the only thing we do know is that we shall not know what tomorrow's world will be like. It will have changed more than even the most outrageous thinking is likely to encompass.*
>
> Sir John Harvey-Jones

The Total Quality principles are deceptive. When all the hype and jargon are stripped away the messages look simple, even obvious. Improving processes and involving people in order to delight customers. That is just applied common sense, so what is all the fuss about? Why is it so difficult to implement?

The first reason why the principles are hard to apply is that there is a problem of understanding. The changes demanded by TQ are not, as some literature would suggest, just a matter of applying common sense. Underlying some apparently banal thinking is a set of ideas which challenges conventional beliefs about management and organisations, indeed shifts the balance of power in organisations.

Managers think they understand when in fact they do not. To make progress they need to rethink important assumptions about how to manage. Such rethinking threatens the basis of competence of many middle and senior managers; it changes the rules they have been used to working by. Managers will not embark seriously on so difficult a shift unless there are compelling business pressures.

This difficult rethinking can be divided into five parts:

- Higher quality and lower costs.
- Improvement from effort not investment.
- The company as people not assets.
- Managing processes as well as results.
- Shifting power from shareholders to customers, employees and suppliers.

HIGHER QUALITY, LOWER COSTS

The old notion that companies had to choose between aiming at being the low cost producer or seeking to provide high quality, high value goods and services has been under increasing challenge in the last two decades. A succession of Japanese companies have demonstrated that low cost is the ally, not the enemy, of high quality.

Increasing yields, reducing defect rates, cutting out waste, meeting customer expectations 100 per cent of the time: all these have the double benefit of increasing quality and reducing cost. It is poor quality that increases costs, not working to satisfy customers. Quality companies can build a virtuous circle in which lower costs enable greater investment in the activities that add value to customers and increased focus on customers helps the efforts to reduce costs.

Many European managers know the words but have not accepted the message. As they come under pressure in the recession they believe they have no alternative but to apply traditional cost cutting. Cost reduction is imposed at speed from above and quality is sacrificed. Value adding activities are cut at the same time as waste in the scramble to reduce costs. As one manager put it:

> The people in head office are happy to go along with all this quality stuff until it conflicts with business as usual. Then it goes out the window. The finance brains take over and impose arbitrary cuts. What they don't think about is that their cuts don't stick. Soon the costs start creeping back.

The practical point is the choice of the focus of change. Is the overriding objective to cut costs, in which case you risk reducing the value you provide to customers and demotivating staff? Or is it to provide better goods and services, with cost reduction as one arm of an effort focused on customers?

IMPROVEMENT FROM EFFORT, NOT INVESTMENT

A second key assumption, which must be challenged if TQ is to succeed, is to equate improvement with investment. The research for this report revealed that many managers' unstated assumption is that major improvement requires large-scale investment. Of course they would like to improve, to reduce costs or increase the value delivered to customers, but it simply is not possible without new technology, new equipment and new facilities. Improvement, they feel, will only come when processes can be automated and people replaced or when the newest and most advanced technology is made available. If there were things that could be done without expensive investment, would they not have done them a long time ago?

TQ challenges these assumptions head on. It says that every individual and team has the potential to improve now, and that it need not cost a penny. It says understand what you are doing in real depth, map the processes where there are problems, look at the facts, look at the data. Examine, for example, rework; see what patterns there are in what is going wrong. Pursue the root causes, not the symptoms, and potential solutions will soon become apparent. No improvement, however small, should be scorned. It is more important to make some gains and give people confidence that they do have the ability to improve.

The availability of finance for large-scale investment may not just be unnecessary; it may actually impede improvement. It often allows managers to claim they are striving for improvement when they have not understood how work gets done at the moment and what the real problems are. It may lead in practice to a failure to collect data on what really happens in the workplace and to listen to the people who do the work.

Kaizen, the Japanese approach to continuous improvement, illustrates the change in thinking most vividly. The characteristic of *Kaizen* is that no improvement is too mundane or too small to be included. Everyone can contribute, every detail helps in the never ending march towards perfection.

In ICL's Logistics Division delivery reliability to customers has been raised in the last two years to 99 per cent. The improvement has only happened since the company stopped relying on a large automated warehouse for most of its deliveries. Instead it has adopted a process of unglamorous step by step improvements involving very little expenditure.

Milliken has redefined the levels of service customers in its business (modular carpeting) can expect from suppliers. Never before had seven day deliveries been considered possible. Now nearly 100 per cent of the promises to customers against these standards are kept. And the performance has been achieved by unrelenting efforts through people, not major investment.

In his book *Managing On The Edge*, Richard Pascale contrasts the approaches of General Motors and Ford in seeking renewal in the 1980s. General Motors invested $60 bn (enough to purchase Nissan and Honda outright) in new plant and equipment in the belief that the latest technology and automation would enable it to beat the Japanese.

The lesson Ford managers took away from visits to Japan in the early 1980s was that what they had to do was mainly concerned with organisation and people, and these have been the themes of its wide ranging change initiatives.

At the beginning of the 1990s GM is again in crisis and is losing heavily on its US car operations. Ford meanwhile has moved to number one among US automobile manufacturers in quality and profitability.

THE COMPANY AS PEOPLE, NOT ASSETS

TQ implies a new commitment by the company to its employees, and by staff to the company. If employees are to participate fully in continuous improvement they must identify with, and take pride in, the company they work for. This in turn requires that the company makes a long-term commitment, going beyond its contractual obligations to them. People cease to be tradeable assets, interchangeable with factors of production like equipment or finance. They become the company.

Such an approach is demonstrated by a new level of respect for the work and contribution of every employee. No longer is it only the skill and effort of managers which is recognised as really of value. The changed approach is also shown by sharing sensitive information; by being seen to listen; by opting to develop insiders rather than go outside for key appointments; and by making extraordinary efforts to look after people when redundancies are unavoidable.

Paul Watson, quality manager of ICL Product Distribution, comments:

> Quality is another name for pride in your work. Managers must show respect for their staff as individuals if employees are to be motivated to achieve high levels of service.

Federal Express has made particular efforts to help its employees find alternative jobs since it decided to reduce its European operations. Among other support, it placed a half page advertisement in the national press encouraging employers to recruit the redundant employees because of their training and quality.

The Grundfos case study describes the commitments in education and development, facilities and job security which the company has made to its employees and which provide the basis for strong sense of pride in, and identification with, the company.

MANAGE PROCESSES AS WELL AS RESULTS

The most subtle of the shifts in thinking required by TQ is the move to managing processes as well as contents or results.

The conventional model is of management by objectives. Good managers delegate; they become skilled in setting subordinates appropriate targets and trusting them to get on with it. If targets are met, subordinates are rewarded; if there is a shortfall there is some penalty, most likely rigorous examination of the problem area and, if necessary, reduction in salary and promotion rewards. Results are everything. The good manager seeks not to interfere but to give the subordinate maximum freedom as to how to reach the objective. The subordinate is then fully responsible for his or her success or failure in attaining the target.

TQ takes the process orientation of Japanese management and seeks to ally it with the Western concern for results. But what is meant by "process orientation"? The Kaizen Institute's Masaaki Imai provides an example.

In reviewing the performance of employees, Japanese management tend to emphasise attitudinal factors. When the sales manager evaluates a salesperson's performance, that evaluation must include such process oriented criteria as the amount of the salesperson's time spent calling on new customers, time spent on outside calls versus time devoted to clerical work at the office and the percentage of new inquiries successfully closed. By paying attention to these indices, the sales manager hopes to encourage the salesperson to produce improved results sooner or later. In other words the process is considered just as important as the intended result: sales.

Process oriented thinking seeks to tackle the dilemma that judging people purely by results often seems arbitrary and unfair. People can be prevented from reaching targets by factors beyond their control. Indeed the relationship between their efforts and the objectives may make the achievement of results seem (and be in fact) a lottery.

Process oriented management seeks to get behind the game playing that occurs in a strict results oriented environment. It aims at an open and honest atmosphere in which problems can be brought forward and resolved based on an objective review of the facts. It includes the following.

- An end to the "blame culture"; the emphasis is on digging hard to find out why the problem has occurred, not who can be blamed for it.
- Treating problems as "treasures", opportunities for the organisation to learn and improve, not things to hide away for fear of retribution.
- Managers seeing their role as support to their subordinates; staff become their customers and their job is to make available the resources, facilities and skills to enable them to do their jobs to the highest standards.
- A passion for the practical and the here and now; the manager must set the example of reaching for improvement now in everything, however mundane.

For Western managers there is a sting in the tail of process oriented management. It requires a thorough understanding of how the work actually gets done. It is not enough to "know the numbers", to understand the results and how to control them. They also need to understand the outline of the work processes, what happens in practice (or at least how to find out how the work actually gets done) if they are to coach and support. The skills and knowledge of financially oriented managers and of those parachuted in from other businesses are not enough.

But surely process oriented management cannot work in the West? In the end it is results that matter, however unfair. In the real world there are no prizes for trying hard. TQ says no. A combination of process and results management is needed. Results only and you fail to understand your processes, demotivate your people and get bogged down in internal politics. Process only and you will lose sight of the wood for the trees: immersed in detail without an appreciation of what it is all for. A synthesis of the two approaches is required.

Sumo wrestling

Japan's national sport is sumo. At each sumo tournament, there are three awards besides the tournament championship: an outstanding performance award, a skill award and a fighting spirit award. The fighting spirit award is given to the wrestler who has fought exceptionally hard throughout the 15 day tournament ... none of these awards is based on how many bouts the wrestler wins.

SHIFT OF POWER FROM SHAREHOLDERS TO CUSTOMERS, EMPLOYEES AND SUPPLIERS

Perhaps most challenging of all, Total Quality requires a shift in power. The focus moves from maximising returns to shareholders to providing outstanding quality and service to customers, to taking responsibility for the long-term interests of employees and suppliers.

It may well be (we believe it is the case) that putting customers first will improve long-term returns to shareholders; it may indeed be the only path to survival. Nevertheless it is important not to fudge the issue that customer, employee and supplier interests are given greater weight in a company applying TQ than in one which does not.

The paradigm shift

The rethinking of management and of organisations required by Total Quality is a "paradigm shift". Paradigms are the shared but hidden assumptions that shape the way we interpret everything around us. They are important because they enable us to make sense of what is going on around us, to see the patterns in all the chaos. They provide the code that allows us quickly to understand what is happening.

But they have a price. They prevent us from seeing the things that do not fit the patterns we are used to. It is not a question of individual cussedness or stupidity. The paradigm makes a whole community blind to the things that do not conform to its mental model.

Examples from science are legion: the refusal of Church leaders in the 17th century to consider evidence that the earth moved around the sun; the persistence of the practice of leaching patients in 18th century medicine; the reluctance in the 20th century to accept quantum mechanics and other ideas that overturned Newton's view of the universe.

The assumptions that make up a paradigm are unconscious, so much taken for granted that we are unaware of them. They are desperately difficult to change because we cling to them as our way of making sense of the world. And when change does come, it comes in a rush and is an emotional experience. For managers to give up their hidden assumptions about management and organisations is a painful process. It upsets the "recipes" by which they have been used to managing. It challenges the basis of their professional skill and self-respect. It is not something they will undertake lightly.

An end to either/or thinking

The rethinking being attempted by the TQ companies is difficult. It requires managers to change assumptions of which they are not even aware. It is not something that happens as a result of reading a book or listening to a presentation. It only happens by dint of experience and of achieving results, after some time, probably years, of seeking to implement the TQ principles. There comes a moment when managers challenge long held assumptions and start to believe in a new set of rules.

The rethinking is best summarised by Richard Pascale in two books: *The Art of Japanese Management* and *Managing On The Edge*. The key is an end to either/or thinking:

- no longer content or process management but both;
- not long-term perspective or action this day but both;
- not quality or lower costs but both;
- not incremental improvement or innovation but both;
- not concern for people or passion for results but both;
- not meticulous planning or improvisation but both;
- not procedures or individual initiative but both;

- not systems or culture change but both;
- not profit or broader objectives but both;
- not tackling today's problems or building long-term capability but both.

Does this seem impossible? The Japanese experience and the TQ companies say no. The trick is to see the characteristics not as opposites but elements in dynamic tension. The job of managers is not to balance the elements but find the right combination where ability on one side of the equation strengthens ability on the other.

Thus the right approach to process management helps you to deliver results and a proper concern for results focuses the process management. Because you have thought through your long-term objectives you are better able to act decisively today, and constant activity and experimentation helps sharpen your long-term perspective. Incremental improvement provides the time and resources for major innovation; innovation keeps you competitive; and so on.

IBM breaks the mould

Barry Morgans of IBM describes a game he uses on management workshops to illustrate the quantum leap in thinking and performance now being demanded in many industries. He gives managers a scrabble set and forms them into teams. In the first round he asks them to come up with ten words of four letters each; in the second with 50 words; and in the third with 25,000 words. There is a way: managers have to turn their thinking upside down to see it.

BEYOND TOTAL QUALITY

The rethinking espoused by the TQ companies represents a radical challenge to conventional Western management. But there are some, notably Dr Deming, who would go further. Indeed the implications of the TQ thinking go well beyond the paradigm shift described here. Four examples are given below.

An end to performance appraisal

Dr Deming argues in the 11th and 12th of his famous 14 points that companies should "Eliminate numerical goals for people in management" and "Remove barriers that rob people of pride of workmanship." For Dr Deming "internal goals set in the management of a company, without a method, are a burlesque". They show that managers have no understanding of variation.

> If you have a stable system, then there is no use in specifying a goal. You will get whatever the system will deliver. A goal beyond the capability of the system will not be reached.

If you have not got a stable system, then again there is no point in setting a goal. There is no way to know what the system will produce: it has no capability. Thus management by numerical goal is an attempt to manage without knowledge of what to do, and is in fact usually management by fear.

Performance appraisal "nourishes short-term performance, annihilates long-term planning, builds fear, demolishes teamwork, nourishes rivalry and politics".

The TQ companies participating in this research all disagree. They seek to ally results management and performance appraisal with process orientation in the way described above.

Managers in Federal Express have three sets of goals – dealing with profit, people and service quality – and are carefully monitored on them, receiving feedback from subordinates as well as superiors.

Long-term employment

Another issue which causes much concern among TQ managers is "job hopping". If a long-term view is essential, a real identification with the company and a thorough understanding of how work actually gets done, what chance is there of the necessary leadership from managers whose horizon is the next move in 2–3 years' time?

Again and again TQ people commented to the researchers on the damage done to TQ efforts by short-term perspectives and changes in teams which have just begun to understand and commit themselves to the TQ process.

Is it time for the MBAs and finance people to move over? Or could attitudes and measurement be changed so that managers could make their mark in a way that contributed to long-term success?

A change in the purpose of companies

Many TQ managers question if Total Quality is compatible with an overriding concern to deliver increased earnings for shareholders or a belief that the underlying purpose of business is profit. They point to TQ initiatives which have foundered when top management cancelled training or put volume and quick fixes before quality in an effort to shore up short-term profits. At least until boards of directors explain their long-term objectives and strategy to investors and cease relying on short-term returns, they argue, TQ will not succeed.

An end to managers versus staff

TQ brings with it a challenge to conventional hierarchies. Front line people gain in status and confidence; networks and support relationships are seen as at least as important as the old organisation charts. Authority is derived from skill, knowledge and peer respect more than from position. The old quasi-class distinction between managers and staff, modelled on the officers versus troops division, is eroded.

Perhaps then the words need to change. Maybe it should not be managers and employees but just people. In Milliken everyone is an "associate".

SUMMARY

1. One of the reasons TQ is difficult to implement is that it requires people to rethink fundamental assumptions about organisations and management.
2. The change in thinking has these elements: higher quality *and* lower costs; improvement from effort not investment; the company as people not assets; the management of process as well as results. TQ also involves a shift in power from shareholders to customers, employees and suppliers.
3. The theme running through the change is an end to either/or thinking: combining and getting the best from elements that people in the West have thought of as opposites.
4. Such a paradigm shift is difficult to make. It is not that individuals are stupid or obstinate. The assumptions they have in their heads do not allow them to see the evidence that supports the TQ approach.
5. Consequently the shift is not made as a result of reading a book or attending a presentation. It happens as a result of experience and seeing results from implementing the TQ principles. It will occur only if there are compelling business and personal reasons for change.

5 What Goes Wrong?

One consultant says that:

The performance improvement efforts of many companies have as much impact on operational and financial results as a ceremonial rain dance has on the weather ... a "rain dance" that is the ardent pursuit of activities that sound good, look good, and allow managers to feel good, but in fact contributes little or nothing to bottom-line performance.[1]

IBM's CEO, John Akers, has said:

I am sick and tired of visiting plants to hear nothing but great things about quality and cycle time – and then to visit customers who tell me of problems.[2]

In a number of the organisations participating in this research there is massive cynicism about Total Quality. In a meeting with front line staff in one company the researchers were greeted with an audible hiss of disapproval when they mentioned the name of the company's two year old quality initiative. In many companies a wide gap has opened up between the quality specialists, who are convinced advocates of TQ, and both senior managers and ordinary staff, who are deeply sceptical. As one manager said: "We got the religion and then we lost it."

Concerns have been highlighted by the problems encountered by two quality award winning companies in the USA. In February 1992 the Wallace Company of Texas, which won the Baldrige Award in 1990, filed for Chapter 11 bankruptcy protection. In 1991 a new chief executive was appointed to Florida Power and Light, the only company outside Japan to gain the coveted Deming Prize. He decided that many of the formalities of its quality programme did not help the company's business success and scrapped them.

So what goes wrong and why the cynicism and the lack of results? Consultants Booz.Allen & Hamilton describe the "Seven Deadly Sins of TQM" (see box) while ODI stresses the absence of top management commitment (see Table 5.1).

Table 5.1 Quality barriers ranked in order of "very significant" replies %

Top management commitment	92
Too narrow an understanding of quality	38
Horizontal boundaries: functions & specialisms	31
Vested interests	29
Organisational politics	28
Cynicism	28
Organisational structure	27
Customer expectations	26
Speed of corporate action	24

Source: ODI.

BOOZ.ALLEN & HAMILTON'S SEVEN DEADLY SINS OF TQM

1. Flight to nowhere

Without a shared understanding of company vision and strategy as its foundation, TQM will be undertaken without real change taking place. Florida Power & Light, for example, originally installed a TQM programme before developing a vision of how the company's economics and those of its customers were likely to change. Imposed from the top, it failed to address the strategic question of how to compete or cooperate with independent power producers. Although TQM has contributed to employees' problem solving abilities, basic questions of corporate vision, market strategy and organisational structure remained. FP&L has now rethought its role in the power supply business and is gearing its management processes to provide better service at lower cost.

2. One size fits all

If a company's survival is at stake, a long-term programme of continuous improvement is hardly the right first strategic step. Rather, a rapid assessment of capabilities followed by restructuring may be necessary. When TQM is appropriate, one size does not fit all, even within one organisation. For some companies the enhancement of quality customer service may be achieved through employee sessions that train or raise awareness. Yet, for many companies the individual's attitude and desire is only part of the equation.

3. Substituting TQM for leadership

When management does not lead the enterprise, TQM cannot follow. Leading means taking responsibility to define, select and deploy the firm's capabilities, and to determine the right priorities (such as speed to market, cost to serve, product cycle time), albeit with input from the front lines. Leading also means imbuing the organisation with a focus on customers and ensuring the organisation is capable of delivering quality.

As frequently practised, TQM alone has failed to remedy parochialism and the dangers of internally focused measures. Managers need to jump start a market focus perspective by re-evaluating customer inputs and best practices from outside their organisations.

4. Inside-out indicators: the trivial many

Many companies base TQM performance indicators on internal operations rather than on the dimensions like order-to-delivery time, defect rate and response time that are really important to customers. The result is often a long list of intermediate measurements – typically focused on inputs rather than outputs. The key is to understand what performance factors help drive the success of the enterprise.

The research for this report identified three underlying causes of these problems.

- Managements do not understand TQ. They see it as an incremental process only and never get to grips with the rethinking described in Chapter 4.
- Many managements are not serious about quality. They fail to give it real priority in resources and time. They do not change the measurement systems to include quality and service. Quality is often one of a multitude of initiatives and staff come to feel that management is only paying it lip service.
- Even those teams which are serious about quality do not know how to set about the necessary process of change. Often they fall into the programme trap. They launch, with the best of intentions, programmes which are company-wide, training led add-ons to existing jobs. Unfortunately they do not work.

When Hertz learned of its business travellers' dissatisfaction with getting cars at the airport, it did not measure the speed of checking in at the desk. As a result of looking at the business processes from a customer's perspective, instead of speeding up service at the counter, it eliminated check-in altogether which helped make customers confident they would "make it" to their destinations.

5. Mandatory religion

One of the surest ways to derive little benefit from TQM is to pass down autocratic edicts from the top. Even if top executives are convinced of the value of TQM – or have set their sights on the Baldrige Award – they must act to make TQM real throughout the organisation.

In his letter to employees in May 1990, FP&L's new CEO said:

> The vast majority of the employees with whom I spoke feel the mechanics of the quality improvement process have been overemphasised ... [depriving employees] of time that could be better spent serving customers.

The challenge is to define roles and responsibilities for people at each level and make the TQM message real and customised for them. Six sigma, for example, is the right model for Motorola, but it is not right for all companies (see page 80).

6. Quality as a separate activity

Many companies start the long journey toward TQM by creating the staff position of chief quality officer. During the start-up phase, the quality unit grows into a large department to support the training and systems needs. Then something happens: members of the quality group become enforcers and bureaucrats rather than offering service and support.

In the most successful programmes, management limits the TQM staff to an expertise and information role and encourages them to find ways to help others solve tangible problems.

7. Teaching to the test

Finally, the pressure to achieve TQM success drives some organisations to "look the part" instead of living the part. The symptoms show up in many ways. Management inspired reward and recognition programmes, for example, may drive internal competition rather than encourage commitment to better service and improved performance. Or the scatter diagrams and process flow diagrams are viewed as an end in themselves by the creators.

The real challenge for management and TQM staff is to develop employees who understand and can act on TQM principles. Again, Wallace Company may serve as a visible example. Reuters reported that the top executives spent too much time leading tours and leaving town for the lecture circuit, rather than focusing on turning around the troubled company.

MANAGEMENT TEAMS NOT SERIOUS ABOUT QUALITY

The most common barrier to effective implementation is failure to take the subject seriously (see Figures 5.1 and 5.2). There are management teams which have a TQ initiative because they believe they are required by head office to have one. They feel they have to show they are doing something; but they see TQ as yet another management fad. They acquire a simple first level understanding of TQ but they see no reason to invest time and effort in going any further. The realities of business have not changed. It is merely necessary to humour the bosses until they grow tired of TQ and go on to the next thing.

Less cynical approaches also amount to not taking the subject seriously. Many teams fail to give their TQ work priority in time or resources. TQ is the item that is mentioned briefly towards the end of management meetings when the real business has been done. The necessary training and development investments are never made or they are jettisoned when the company feels it has to improve its short-term financial results. Quality is traded off against volume and profit pressures; word gets round quickly that, when the chips are down, management's apparent commitment to quality is only skin deep. The key people with the skill, experience and commitment to make quality happen are not released from other tasks. Quality is not included in business or individual performance appraisal.

There are a thousand ways in which managements pay lip service to quality. The only certainty is that staff and customers soon get the message: nothing has changed.

Figure 5.1   The need for service quality is well recognised

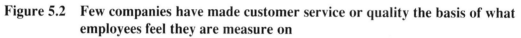

Source: Bain & Company

Figure 5.2   Few companies have made customer service or quality the basis of what employees feel they are measure on

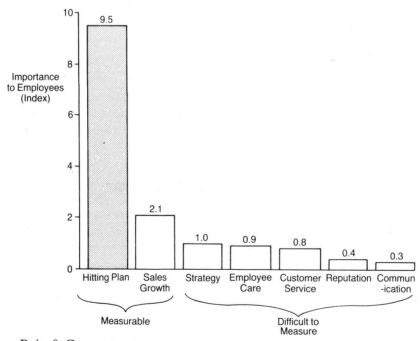

Source: Bain & Company

LACK OF UNDERSTANDING OF HOW TO IMPLEMENT QUALITY

Managers who are serious about quality often do not know how to implement it. Applying TQ means managing (or rather leading) change. There are some clear lessons about what to do and what not to do when leading a process of change.

Unfortunately many of the managers seeking to implement TQ have not applied these lessons. They frequently go for the "Big Bang" approach, throwing people, structures and systems up in the air and hoping that when they land things will be better. Usually they are not. Employees' sense of insecurity is increased and their willingness and ability to contribute to an improvement process is reduced.

Many of the processes adopted to implement TQ are themselves inconsistent with the TQ principles.

- They do not involve people; they are imposed from the top.
- They do not foster learning; they encourage people to go through the motions.
- They do not foster cooperation between departments but encourage competition.
- They do not push people to tackle root causes but allow symptoms only to be addressed.
- They do not look outwards towards customers but are preoccupied with internal issues.

Most often managers turn to programmes (see box). These fail for the following reasons.

- They are not clearly tied to business objectives.
- They are not "owned" by line managers.
- They fail to mobilise the commitment of individuals because they are imposed from the top and lack a compelling business justification.
- They do not significantly increase needed skills because most training is in the classroom and not rooted in application.
- They attempt to impose a uniform solution across different operating units and so lack relevance to the real and immediate business problems local managers are wrestling with.

The programme trap

Managers love programmes. They show that they are doing something; they can be easily measured; they allow copying from successful companies; they enable busy senior managers to delegate responsibility for improvement. The only problem is they do not work.

In their book *The Critical Path To Corporate Renewal*, Michael Beer and his colleagues from Harvard Business School analyse the limitations of programmes but also the reasons why they remain attractive to managers. "Programme" is defined as a discrete activity with definite start and end points, originating from a staff function and aimed at improving some internal processes, for example aspects of people management.

Total Quality, as espoused by the leading practitioners, is not a programme but a philosophy, a set of principles to guide a process of change.

Of the case study companies studied in this report, three – Nissan Motors UK, Club Med and Grundfos – have never had a TQ programme but have had striking success in applying the TQ principles. The three others – Ciba-Geigy, Federal Express and ICL Product Distribution – have had programmes but in each case they produced only superficial change. Real competitive improvement happened in these latter companies when the management overlaid the quality programmes with other initiatives, rooted in the business and their own objectives.

Programmes are not just ineffective; often they are counterproductive. In the words of Michael Beer they may "inoculate" organisations against change. Managers and staff can

PROGRAMMCO: HOW NOT TO IMPLEMENT CHANGE

Programmco is the division of a large (and fictitious!) international company. Three years ago a new group chief executive was appointed with a mandate for change. After years of complacent and conservative management, a corporate turnaround was needed; the corporation, once market leader in its field, had been losing share to a number of more aggressive rivals. While there was still considerable customer loyalty to the company, it was poorly placed in the most rapidly growing segments, its costs were out of line with those of competitors and the company lacked the cash for major investment or acquisition.

The approach to Total Quality

The CEO decided that in an industry where the products of different companies were increasingly similar, the company's main opportunity to differentiate itself was in terms of quality, in particular product reliability and durability and customer service. Within a few years the company must provide quality second to none.

To this end the CEO orders a Total Quality Programme to be set up. Because the corporation is only as effective as its weakest link, he decides that all divisions will participate. After researching the market, he appoints a reputable firm of consultants to guide the process in Programmco. On their advice, the quality programme commences with a massive training and awareness campaign. It is agreed that the objective is to change attitudes so that quality improvement becomes part of the job of everyone at Programmco. Everyone is to understand that they have customers – whether internal or external – and to learn basic techniques of process improvement and problem solving.

Starting with the board itself all managers go away for a week's training. To ensure the vital management commitment, each manager trains his or her own team in a cascade process. Over a full year every member of staff receives the same key messages, although by the time the training reaches the shopfloor it consists of one hour a week for eight weeks.

Messages are simplified and tailored to the different levels of audience. The training packages for shopfloor workers contain cartoons and the language is adjusted to that of the tabloid newspapers.

After a few months there is a "Quality Day" to celebrate the new initiative and give everyone the opportunity to show their commitment to quality. The day is a great success and everyone involved comments on what fun it was.

Following training, staff are immediately involved in teams examining processes and specific problems. Quality circles in each work area meet every week to consider how to improve quality and ad hoc teams are called together to solve problems across functions. An employee suggestions scheme is set up, with holidays and other prizes for those putting forward valuable improvements.

A team of quality facilitators works long hours organising training, assisting improvement teams, identifying priority quality problems and generally encouraging and motivating. They keep a count of all the improvement activities which is monitored at the monthly meetings of the board's quality steering group.

The results

After three years of hard work, the results are profoundly disappointing. Quality has improved but the relative standing of the company in the eyes of customers has actually fallen because of rising consumer expectations and rapid improvements by competitors. Market share is still falling and the poor profitability of the division is causing great concern. While divisional management continues to present a favourable view of the quality programme in its reports to head office (and does have some important one-off successes to talk about) its main attention is now focused on a top down productivity and cost reduction drive which has been started in an effort to restore profits.

Employee surveys reveal low employee morale and there has been a surprisingly high take-up for the voluntary redundancy recently offered by the company. Management is frustrated that despite all the quality efforts, employees still show little real awareness and regard for the needs and wishes of customers. The corporation's sales people, through whom the division must work, are regarded with suspicion and in many cases open contempt.

Front line workers are cynical; the behaviour they see from managers in no way matches the messages they hear from the TQ programme. They know that management is allowing the shipment of below standard products in an effort to meet volume and revenue targets. Shopfloor staff are resentful of what they see as the patronising presentation of the TQ training and contemptuous of middle management's failure to respond to improvement suggestions they have made and into which some people put a lot of time and effort. They say that the controlling and directing nature of management has not changed. As a result, they are reluctant to voice their real concerns and feel powerless to make improvements.

Some improvement teams still meet but they have lost energy and direction: operators describe them as "just talking shops". A number of incremental improvements within departments have been made but somehow the big issues – the cross-functional processes – have not been tackled.

How could it have been done better?

The managers of Programmco are not fools. They are capable managers with long experience of the industry. They fashioned in many ways a model programme. What else could they have done? Three lessons stand out.

- Local management in Programmco did not take ownership of the process of change and make it a clear priority. What they implemented was a process designed in head office. Local managers went along with it but they never really got behind it. They were doing many other things in the business, some of which were incompatible with quality.
- The quality initiative was not clearly grounded in a business imperative. There was no clear vision of why quality was important to the business. Staff generally still felt instinctively that Programmco was a powerful and successful company. They saw no compelling reason for change.
- The behaviour of managers did not change. Managers were asking staff to change but the example they set themselves was of business as usual. Occasional attempts by operators to change the pattern, for example by putting forward carefully worked out improvement ideas, met with no response from anxious middle managers who were themselves still treated with contempt by top management. The flickering light of employee initiative was therefore snuffed out.

emerge after 2–3 years of time consuming work, familiar with all the concepts and jargon of quality, yet without a real improvement in performance. People will then become cynical. Any later attempt to organise a true quality effort will be made more difficult.

In some large companies the use of programmes becomes the disease of programmitis: a mass of programmes and initiatives which are internally inconsistent, none of which bite deep into the culture of the organisation and which leave staff confused about top management's real priorities.

The key lesson is that TQ must be rooted in the business and implemented in a way that engages people's full commitment and increases their skills. The following chapters examine how an organisation should go about the process of implementation.

WHAT DOES NOT WORK

Jonathan Smilansky, formerly general manager of VISA International, describes some of the things he has learnt from his experience of implementing TQ. He says avoid the following.

- A quality day, at which everyone commits to quality. "Five minutes after people get back to the workplace and discover nothing has changed, they will be disillusioned."
- Training all staff. "If people don't have an opportunity to apply what they have learnt, they will soon forget it."
- Awards for good ideas. "This is the worst thing you can do. It is the triumph of marketing over substance."
- Using consultants to do everything. "It will result in people opting out of responsibility for change."

SUMMARY

1. Many Total Quality initiatives are coming under criticism for their failure to improve customer satisfaction and business results.
2. Some TQ initiatives have failed because managers have not fully understood the TQ principles, others because they have not been serious about implementing quality.
3. Even some efforts led by managers committed to quality have failed because they did not know how to set about the necessary process of change.
4. Many TQ initiatives are themselves inconsistent with the TQ principles.
5. Programmes – company-wide, training led add-ons to existing jobs – do not work.

References

[1] "Successful Change Programs Begin With Results", Robert H. Schaffer and Harvey A. Thomson, *Harvard Business Review*, January–February 1992.
[2] "When Quality Control Gets In The Way Of Quality", Graham Sharman, McKinsey & Co, *Wall Street Journal*, February 25, 1992.

6 Issues For The Board

> *We not have to outscale our competitors, we have to outthink them.*
>
> Steve Jobs, founder of Apple Computers

Total Quality can only contribute to real change if there is a shared understanding of how it fits into vision and strategy. Quality needs to be a board level issue and one for which top management takes collective responsibility; issues of continuous improvement and competitiveness are not ones that can be delegated to a quality director or function.

The objective of the board should be to develop a response to the TQ challenge which is home grown and distinctive. Unless it is home grown, it will not have the ownership necessary to push through change in the face of all the likely obstacles; unless it is distinctive, it will not in the long term contribute to improving the company's competitive position.

The evidence from the case study companies is that there are no predetermined stages to TQ work. The neat standard route maps to quality beloved of some management consultants are misleading and possibly dangerous. How to implement quality depends where you are coming from and where you want to go. Each company's path should be unique and never ending.

There are four issues which the board needs to consider when choosing this path.

- Where does our organisation stand now? What is an honest assessment of its strengths and weaknesses? How do we measure up against the TQ principles?
- Where do we want to be? What part can or should the TQ principles have in our vision and strategy? How will we integrate the principles to give us a distinctive strategy?
- What business objectives will we set, incorporating quality?
- Does TQ fit our values?

SELF-ASSESSMENT

The device which increasingly large numbers of companies are using, both to ensure their understanding of TQ principles and to measure their progress in applying them, is self-assessment against the criteria for one of the quality awards. The assessment is for internal purposes only and not to win an award; the objective is to learn.

Companies are finding use of the Baldrige or the European Quality Award (see below) criteria attractive for three reasons.

- The awards set demanding criteria, providing a template of genuine world class standards which can trigger action to develop continuous improvement. Numbers of companies comment on the rude shock an assessment can be to managers. Even some blue chip companies have found they have a long way to go to catch up with the best Japanese and Western companies. To win the Baldrige Award a score above 850 out of 1,000 is needed; one well known multinational was shocked to find that an honest assessment of its divisions produced an average score of just over 300.

MALCOLM BALDRIGE QUALITY AWARD: EXAMINATION CATEGORIES
(No. of points in brackets)

1. Leadership (100)

1.1 Senior executive leadership (40). Describe the senior executive's leadership, personal involvement and visibility in developing and maintaining an environment for quality excellence.

1.2 Quality values (15). Describe the company's quality values, how they are projected in a consistent manner, and how adoption of the values throughout the company is determined and reinforced.

1.3 Management for quality (25). Describe how the quality values are integrated into day to day leadership, management and supervision of all company units.

1.4 Public responsibility (20). Describe how the company extends its quality leadership to the external community and includes its responsibilities to the public for health, safety, environmental protection and ethical business practice in its quality policies and improvement activities.

2. Information and analysis (70)

2.1 Scope and management of quality data and information (20). Describe the company's base of data and information used for planning, day to day management and evaluation of quality, and how data and information reliability, timeliness and access are assured.

2.2 Competitive comparisons and benchmarks (30). Describe the company's approach to selecting quality related competitive comparisons and world class benchmarks to support quality planning, evaluation and improvement.

2.3 Analysis of quality data and information (20). Describe how data and information are analysed to support the company's overall quality objectives.

3. Strategic quality planning (60)

3.1 Strategic quality planning process (35). Describe the company's strategic quality planning process for short-term (1–2 years) and longer-term (3 years or more) quality leadership and customer satisfaction.

3.2 Quality goals and plans (25). Summarise the company's goals and strategies. Outline principal quality plans for the short term (1–2 years) and longer term (3 years or more).

4. Human resource utilisation (150)

4.1 Human resource management (20). Describe how the company's overall human resource management effort supports its quality objectives.

4.2 Employee involvement (40). Describe the means available for all employees to contribute effectively to meeting the company's quality objectives; summarise trends and current levels of involvement.

4.3 Quality education and training (40). Describe how the company decides what quality education and training is needed by employees and how it utilises the knowledge and skills acquired; summarise the types of quality education and training received by employees in all employee categories.

4.4 Employee recognition and performance measurement (25). Describe how the company's recognition and performance measurement processes support quality objectives; summarise trends in recognition.

4.5 Employee well being and morale (25). Describe how the company maintains a work environment conducive to the well being and growth of all employees; summarise trends and levels in key indicators of well being and morale.

5. Quality assurance of products and services (140)

5.1 Design and introduction of quality products and services (35). Describe how new and/or improved products and services are designed and introduced and how processes are designed to meet key product and service quality requirements.

5.2 Process quality control (20). Describe how the processes used to produce the company's products and services are controlled.

5.3 Continuous improvement of processes (20). Describe how processes used to produce products and services are continuously improved.

5.4 Quality assessment (15). Describe how the company assesses the quality of its systems, processes, practices, products and services.

5.5 Documentation (10). Describe documentation and other modes of knowledge preservation and knowledge transfer to support quality assurance, quality assessment and quality improvement.

5.6 Business process and support service quality (20). Summarise process quality, quality assessment and quality improvement activities for business processes and support services.

5.7 Supplier quality (20). Describe how the quality of materials, components and services furnished by other businesses is assured, assessed and improved.

6. Quality results (180)

6.1 Product and service quality results (90). Summarise trends in quality improvement and current quality levels for key product and service features; compare the company's current quality levels with those of competitors and world leaders.

6.2 Business process, operational and support service quality results (50). Summarise trends in quality improvement and current quality levels for business processes, operations and support services.

6.3 Supplier quality results (40). Summarise trends and levels in quality of suppliers and services furnished by other companies; compare the company's supplier quality with that of competitors and with key benchmarks.

7. Customer satisfaction (300)

7.1 Determining customer requirements and expectations (30). Describe how the company determines current and future customer requirements and expectations.

7.2 Customer relationship management (50). Describe how the company provides effective management of its relationships with its customers and uses information gained from customers to improve products and services as well as its customer relationship management practices.

7.3 Customer service standards (20). Describe the company's standards governing the direct contact between its employees and customers and how these standards are set and modified.

7.4 Commitment to customers (15). Describe the company's commitments to customers on its explicit and implicit promises underlying its products and services.

7.5 Complaint resolution for quality improvement (25). Describe how the company handles complaints, resolves them, and uses complaint information for quality improvement and for prevention of recurrence of problems.

7.6 Determining customer satisfaction (20). Describe the company's methods for determining customer satisfaction, how satisfaction information is used in quality improvement and how methods for determining customer satisfaction are improved.

7.7 Customer satisfaction results (70). Summarise trends in the company's customer satisfaction and in indicators of adverse customer response.

7.8 Customer satisfaction comparison (70). Compare the company's customer satisfaction results and recognition with those of competitors that provide similar products and services.

- Use of the criteria is not prescriptive: local managers decide for themselves what action they will take to deal with opportunities for improvement revealed by the assessment. Companies are more and more aware of the need to empower managers, that real change will not occur unless local managers are totally committed to proposed actions. Leaving managers the flexibility as to how they can best respond to the assessment is a good way to develop this commitment.
- The criteria provide a common yardstick to different divisions and businesses. Managers cannot escape by saying their business is different; the tests and implied standards apply to all.

The companies involved say they try hard to avoid the audit mentality: what Jim Havard of Rank Xerox calls "the desire to demonstrate excellence", that is, to show how wonderful things already are, rather than genuinely looking for opportunities for improvement. They are frank enough to admit that local managers can still be defensive but claim that as the examination process becomes more familiar, managers are seeing it as an opportunity to learn.

Companies differ on who they ask to make the assessment. Rank Xerox and Hewlett Packard select experienced and specially trained managers from other divisions to carry out the assessment. In Shell UK Oil and 3M managers participate in assessing their own businesses.

After the examination the results are reviewed with the local management and then passed back to corporate HQ. Hewlett Packard, exceptionally, does not release individual divisional scores to HQ but gives only regional and company averages in order to emphasise the point that the exercise is aimed at helping managers, not judging them.

There is criticism of some elements of the Baldrige assessment. The scoring system is felt by some to be difficult to use; they would rather have a qualitative assessment (from ++ to -- for each criterion) than a score which they believe is bound to lead to pretence, not a genuine effort to learn. Some managers are concerned that insufficient attention is paid to the views of customers and that quality is not linked to business results. Nevertheless use of the award criteria is an effective way of stimulating and measuring change.

The Baldrige Awards

The Baldrige Awards were set up by the US government in 1987. Named after President Reagan's secretary of commerce who died in 1986, they sought to stimulate US business to do more to take up the quality challenge by giving them an award to aim for and criteria that organisations could use to evaluate their quality improvement efforts. Awards are given to three types of businesses – manufacturing, service and small business – and the National Institute of Standards and Technology has developed, in cooperation with industry experts, the seven category, 1,000 point scoring system (see box). Companies submit applications of up to 75 pages describing their quality practices and performance in each of the seven areas and are then graded by teams of trained examiners. The Baldrige judges, who are all recognised quality experts from industry, academia and consulting firms, select a shortlist of high scoring applicants for several day site visits and then select the winners.

In terms of the awareness of quality issues, the setting up of the award has been an outstanding success. Presentation of the awards by the president gains national media attention. Since 1988 the National Institute has distributed 450,000 copies of the application guidelines throughout the world.

Yet the award has sparked off fierce debate. Dr Deming and his disciples say the award criteria are fatally flawed because they lack the foundation of a clear quality philosophy: they are "a list of things to do and to think about within the current system of management", not the new approach "that managers must understand ... if they are to improve the health of business".

From a different direction others have criticised the absence of financial measures of performance. They say it makes a nonsense of the award if the businesses of some winners fail. Other commentators criticise its emphasis on the process, rather than the results, of quality. Only 280 (categories 6.1, 6.2, 7.7, 7.8) out of the 1,000 points are tied to quality results.

The way in which awards are decided has been attacked. Companies (not customers) nominate themselves. Only six companies per year can become winners; it is suggested the

---

THE EUROPEAN QUALITY AWARD

The nine elements shown in the model correspond to the criteria which are used to assess a company's progress towards excellence. For convenience we use Results and Enablers to group criteria.

- The Results criteria are concerned with what the company has achieved and is achieving.
- The Enablers criteria are concerned with how results are being achieved.

For the purposes of meaningful assessment for the award a relative value must be ascribed to the nine criteria within the model.

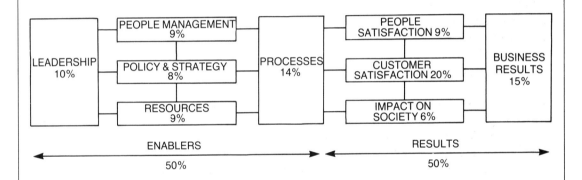

Enablers

1. Leadership (10%). How the executive team and all other managers inspire and drive total quality as the company's fundamental process for continuous improvement. Evidence is needed of:

1a – visible involvement in leading quality management;
1b – a consistent total quality culture;
1c – recognition and appreciation of the efforts and successes of individuals and teams;
1d – support of total quality by provision of appropriate resources and assistance;
1e – involvement with customers and suppliers;
1f – the active promotion of quality management outside the company.

2. Policy and strategy (8%). How the company incorporates the concept of total quality in the determination, communication, implementation, review and improvement of its policy and strategy. Evidence is needed of how policy and strategy are:

2a – based on the concept of total quality;
2b – formed on the basis of information that is relevant to total quality;
2c – the basis for business plans;
2d – communicated;
2c – regularly reviewed and improved.

award should be a "marathon", not a "horse race", going to everyone who reaches the qualifying standard.

European Quality Award

In 1992 the European Foundation for Quality Management is presenting its first quality award. The criteria (see box) are similar to those for Baldrige except in two respects: the award stresses business results and there is a category called "Impact On The Community".

---

3. People management (9%). How the company releases the full potential of its people to improve its business continuously. Evidence is needed of how:
3a – continuous improvement in people management is affected;
3b – the company preserves and develops core skills through the recruitment, training and career progression of its people;
3c – the company's performance targets are agreed and are reviewed continuously with staff;
3d – the company promotes the involvement of all its people in continuous improvement and empowers its people to take appropriate action.

4. Resources (9%). Evidence is needed of how the company improves its business continuously, based on the concept of total quality by optimisation of:
4a – financial resources;
4b – information resources;
4c – material resources;
4d – the application of technology.

5. Processes (14%). How key and support processes are identified, reviewed and if necessary revised to ensure continuous improvement of the company's business:
5a – how the key processes are identified;
5b – how the company systematically manages its key and support processes;
5c – how process performance parameters, along with all relevant feedback, are used to review key processes and to set targets for improvement;
5d – how the company stimulates innovation and creativity in process improvement;
5e – how the company implements process changes and evaluates the benefits.

Results

6. Customer satisfaction (20%). What the perception of your external customers, direct and indirect, is of the company and of its products and services. Evidence is needed of the company's success in satisfying the needs and expectations of customers.

7. People satisfaction (9%). What your people's feelings are about your company. Evidence is needed of the company's success in satisfying the needs and expectations of its people.

8. Impact on society (6%). What the perception of your company is among the community at large. This includes the views of the company's approach to quality of life, the environment and to the preservation of global resources. Evidence is needed of the company's success in satisfying the needs and expectations of the community at large.

9. Business results (15%). What the company is achieving in relation to its planned business performance. Evidence is needed of the company's continuing success in achieving its financial and other business targets and objectives, and in satisfying the needs and expectations of everyone with a financial interest in the company. You must be able to demonstrate that your company's business plan is sound.

Ashridge Assessment

For many businesses, particularly small ones, completion of the EFQM or Baldrige Awards is too time consuming and expensive a process. Simplified criteria (see box) are needed.

ASSESSING PROGRESS TOWARDS TOTAL QUALITY: ASHRIDGE CRITERIA FOR SELF-ASSESSMENT

Quality results

	strongly agree	agree	disagree	strongly disagree	don't know
1. Customers recommend the company to friends and colleagues.	☐	☐	☐	☐	☐
2. The company regularly exceeds customer expectations.	☐	☐	☐	☐	☐
3. The company delivers on its product/service promises very nearly 100% of the time.	☐	☐	☐	☐	☐
4. The company achieves higher customer satisfaction than its main competitors.	☐	☐	☐	☐	☐
5. The company's share of its markets is increasing.	☐	☐	☐	☐	☐

Customer focus

	strongly agree	agree	disagree	strongly disagree	don't know
6. The company actively encourages customers to feed back their views of the company and of its products and services.	☐	☐	☐	☐	☐
7. Complaints are systematically used to help prevent problems being repeated.	☐	☐	☐	☐	☐
8. Employees in most departments have personal contact with customers.	☐	☐	☐	☐	☐
9. The company uses customers' views to shape its products/services.	☐	☐	☐	☐	☐
10. The company uses the parameters which are most important to customers to define the information on customer needs and wants.	☐	☐	☐	☐	☐
11. The company is always trying to improve the quality of its goods and services.	☐	☐	☐	☐	☐

Process improvement

	strongly agree	agree	disagree	strongly disagree	don't know
12. Key processes are well defined.	☐	☐	☐	☐	☐
13. Key processes are continually reviewed to see if they can be improved.	☐	☐	☐	☐	☐
14. Staff take responsibility for checking the quality of their own work.	☐	☐	☐	☐	☐
15. All functions work in genuine partnership in the development of new products.	☐	☐	☐	☐	☐
16. When dealing with problems, staff are well informed of the facts.	☐	☐	☐	☐	☐

	strongly agree	agree	disagree	strongly disagree	don't know
17. Problem solving tools and techniques are used widely.	☐	☐	☐	☐	☐
18. Problem solving tools and techniques are used effectively.	☐	☐	☐	☐	☐
19. The company uses benchmarking widely to identify the need for change.	☐	☐	☐	☐	☐
20. Different functions in the company work well together.	☐	☐	☐	☐	☐
21. The company works in partnership with most of its suppliers.	☐	☐	☐	☐	☐

Unlocking people potential

	strongly agree	agree	disagree	strongly disagree	don't know
22. Top management has a clear vision which incorporates quality.	☐	☐	☐	☐	☐
23. This vision has been communicated to all employees.	☐	☐	☐	☐	☐
24. Top management consistently recognises the efforts of staff.	☐	☐	☐	☐	☐
25. Top management consistently provides the resources necessary for improvement work.	☐	☐	☐	☐	☐
26. Managers help staff improve the way they do their jobs.	☐	☐	☐	☐	☐
27. Managers see the development of their staff as one of their key responsibilities.	☐	☐	☐	☐	☐
28. Staff regularly give each other constructive feedback.	☐	☐	☐	☐	☐
29. Employees use their initiative to make improvements in the interests of customers.	☐	☐	☐	☐	☐
30. The company collects and uses the suggestions of employees.	☐	☐	☐	☐	☐
31. Employees are becoming more self-confident.	☐	☐	☐	☐	☐
32. Staff are becoming increasingly multi-skilled.	☐	☐	☐	☐	☐
33. The unions are partners in continuous improvement.	☐	☐	☐	☐	☐
34. Company values and beliefs are widely shared.	☐	☐	☐	☐	☐

Hewlett Packard's Quality Maturity Review

Hewlett Packard has devised its own process for measuring the progress of its divisions throughout the world in attaining quality. The company regards the use of the process to stimulate quality improvement as part of its competitive advantage.

The process is centred on a tough two and a half day review carried out by specially trained managers from other parts of the corporation. Drawing on the experience of inspection for the Deming Prize in Japan, the visiting managers measure the unit's progress along five dimensions (see Figure 6.1). They work with the local management team and can call for whatever additional information or documents they need in order to be able to satisfy themselves as to the unit's true position.

The group chief executive, John Young, has set every business in HP the objective of scoring at least 3.5 by 1994.

Figure 6.1   Hewlett Packard has developed its own TQ Assessment

No knowledge.	Some knowledge. Can talk but cannot demonstrate.	Doing and applying for the first time. Some struggle: exists in some areas.	Regular process in place. Exists in most areas. Some level of success.	Improved systems being developed. Exists in all areas: good level of success, shortcomings identified and better system planned.	Integral part of entire operation: exemplary, best known system.
0	1	2	3	4	5

Source: Hewlett Packard

3M

3M Europe is using the Baldrige criteria as the centrepiece of its efforts to galvanise managers to take action in support of Total Quality. All the European managing directors were sent on a three day course to learn how to become Baldrige assessors and then split up into seven teams, each assessing the European companies against one of the Baldrige categories.

Peter Pring, director of 3M UK, argues that the approach suits the 3M culture. "Effectively top management has set unit managers a challenge – tell me what you are going to do to live up to the Baldrige criteria." How they respond is up to the local managers. "They come up with their own action plans but they know they will be reviewed on their implementation of these."

Rank Xerox

Rank Xerox has adopted a process of self-inspection for "Certification For Excellence". Using a simplified list of six Baldrige categories (see Figure 6.2), first the national companies and then the units within these are examined.

Each year the company sets a minimum rating it believes every unit should attain ("the certification level"); it also identifies criteria which are of particular importance to the Rank Xerox business.

Coming out of the inspection is an overall rating of the unit involved and, more important, an assessment of the "vital few" projects which the unit will work on in the coming year. These "vital few" projects are integrated into the objectives set for units and cascaded down to individual managers.

Figure 6.2   Xerox uses a simplified version of the Baldrige criteria

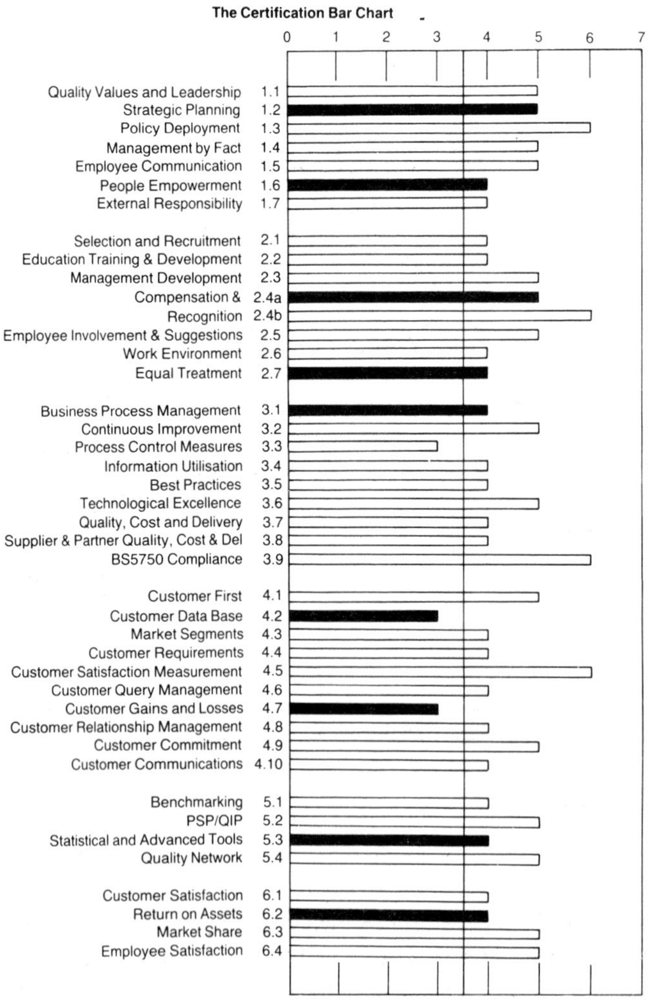

The Certification Bar Chart

Source: Rank Xerox

Jim Havard, director of Rank Xerox UK, comments:

> After we won the Baldrige Award in the USA, we needed a way to keep the heat up on quality. The Certification of Excellence did this for us. Senior managers like the approach very much: it's tough and demanding but gives local managers flexibility as to the actions they will take.

IBM Europe

IBM feels strongly that use of the Baldrige (it has slightly simplified the criteria) is a highly acceptable tool to stimulate action on quality. Barry Morgans comments:

> Marketing is a difficult area to get people to adopt the quality thinking but we have found that our marketing managers were really turned on by the Baldrige assessment. The trick now is to get genuine quality projects going in the aftermath of the assessment.

Shell UK Oil

Quality managers at Shell UK Oil are enthusiastic about the use of the Baldrige criteria. Jonson Cox, quality manager, says:

> The assessment does make managers think carefully. The criteria set out very useful and searching questions. Overall they provide a very effective way of grabbing managers' attention for continuous improvement.
>
> We have found that the criteria are reasonably easy to understand though there is a need for a facilitator to help managers be specific and avoid glib answers. The scoring system is difficult for managers to pick up.

Nevertheless what matters is the awareness and the action plans the events lead to, not the absolute scores. "Managers do need to understand the main quality concepts in order to apply the criteria effectively," Jonson Cox adds.

CRAFTING STRATEGY

Business strategies are, in the words of Henry Mintzberg, "crafted". They emerge as companies think and act, balance control and learning, and reconcile stability and change. They are developed most successfully by those with a passion for their businesses, those who love being intimately involved in doing. Organisations need the opportunity to review the past, to see what patterns are emerging so that they can manage the future. They should be involved in a continuous cycle of "plan, do, review".

So it should be with weaving quality into strategy. As described in Chapter 2, the most successful companies taking part in this study have grown TQ organically. When these companies have wanted to make a step change in some part of their approach, they have done so in a way that fitted their cultures and histories; they have built on their success in the past. The case studies examine how Club Med, Grundfos and Nissan Motors UK have developed strategies and philosophies in which quality is part of a wider whole.

In developing strategy the board needs make an objective but also realistic assessment of the company's quality strengths, weaknesses and potential. Essential inputs are benchmarking (see below) and listening carefully to customers and employees (see Chapter 3). These provide an antidote to complacency about a company's position.

Mapping of key business processes and assessment of key gaps and weaknesses is another tool often used by companies implementing TQ. It helps provide focus and objectivity.

However, it also important to avoid despondency. When looking at the quality award criteria or at results of benchmarking or listening to customers or employees, it is easy for some companies to conclude that they are too far behind; they will never catch up, much less leap ahead of, competitors. The best antidote is to stress distinctiveness, to avoid the "me too" strategies but consider realistically how the company can be different.

As Jonathan Smilansky describes it:

Everyone starts quality work by getting people to answer the phones faster. That's fine except that it may have nothing to do with the competitive advantage of your company. Go after the things that are really priorities for you.

Peter Scott-Morgan of consultants Arthur D. Little says:

The challenge for the board is to find a way to get hold of the big cross-functional issues. These are often where there is huge potential to increase value and reduce costs. Top management must focus attention on the big items and not let the value of process understanding and problem solving be wasted on a thousand small issues.

BENCHMARKING WORLD CLASS PERFORMANCE

Many companies interviewed for this report are now making use of benchmarking. Information is power and the best database of information is one that taps into the expertise of the world's leading companies. Benchmarking involves identifying the business practices in each functional area which are the best in the world, understanding why they are successful, comparing them with your own performance and then incorporating the relevant approaches in your organisation. Used correctly, benchmarking can jolt an organisation into much needed change – exposing large differences between the performance of best and of average companies – and it can foster a culture of continuous improvement. It can have enormous persuasive power, providing the hard data that show people what needs to change and why.

However, companies warn that benchmarking is difficult to do well and that much of the effort on it has been wasted. Effective benchmarking must have the following characteristics.

Target key processes. Organisations should home in on the processes that really matter to them and then look far and wide internationally for the comparisons that will help most, seeking the companies that are best in a particular activity. They will probably need to go to different companies to benchmark different processes and often the most powerful examples will be outside their own industry.

Focus on how, not just what. Managers should look beneath the surface to understand how superior performance is achieved (not just what it is) and use this understanding as a catalyst to change the processes in their own company. Too often managers see benchmarking as concerned only with measurement and target setting. The essence of the approach is learning how superior performance is achieved and thinking through how to apply, and improve on, those approaches in your own organisation.

Be rigorous. Good benchmarking is tough. It requires both careful analysis and selection of data – identifying the correct measures of performance and understanding what information collected means – and the use of imagination and lateral thinking to see the value of benchmarks in businesses apparently unrelated to your own and the ways to apply lessons from environments very different from your own. The thinking of those involved needs to be challenged all the time, for example by use of an outside facilitator.

Involve key line staff. Line managers and staff need to be involved in the benchmarking process and in visits to other companies so that they see for themselves that the benchmark performance is relevant and attainable. A well conducted benchmark exercise automatically generates enthusiasm among staff to come back and apply the new approaches seen in the benchmark companies.

Aim at continuous improvement. Benchmarking should not be concerned just with one-off efforts to catch up with best practice. Instead it needs to be seen as a continuous process which aids "breakthrough" thinking and encourages staff to continuously question and challenge existing ways of doing things and look for improvements.

How companies have used benchmarking

Notable among those TQ companies which have used benchmarking to generate leaps forward in competitive performance are Xerox and Motorola. They have both surmounted the block of thinking that "we are different": both are therefore able to learn from a broad range of companies in different industries. They include careful consideration of broader processes like how suppliers are managed and new products developed as well as reverse engineering products and making comparisons of overall business system economics.

Motorola tries to start every new product or programme with a search for "best of breed" in the world as a whole. A Motorola manager comments:

> The further away from our own industry we reach for comparisons, the happier we are. We are seeking competitive superiority, after all, not just competitive parity.

Xerox has gained a formidable reputation for benchmarking. A summary of the original assessment in 1980 which was the trigger for rapid change in the company is shown in the box below.

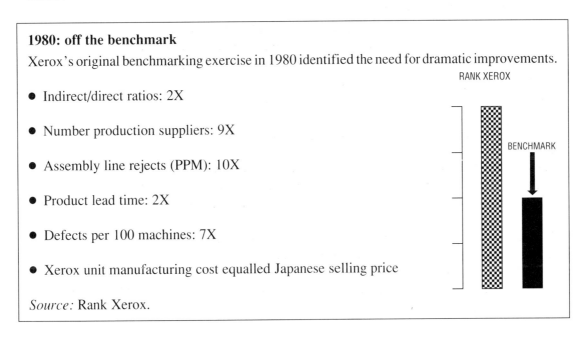

1980: off the benchmark

Xerox's original benchmarking exercise in 1980 identified the need for dramatic improvements.

- Indirect/direct ratios: 2X

- Number production suppliers: 9X

- Assembly line rejects (PPM): 10X

- Product lead time: 2X

- Defects per 100 machines: 7X

- Xerox unit manufacturing cost equalled Japanese selling price

Source: Rank Xerox.

The case studies examine examples of the use of benchmarking. For instance, Nissan Motors UK has continuously used the company's plants in Japan as a benchmark of best practice in the car industry. Staff at all levels have worked in the factories in Japan and seen for themselves how superior performance is attained. In addition experienced Japanese engineers are used in the UK plant as sources of information on all aspects of excellent practice.

ICL Product Distribution carefully benchmarked best practice in the supply and support of personal computers. The staff involved in the exercise came back with recommendations for a radical change in the service to be offered to customers which went beyond what management had previously contemplated. However, the people concerned had persuasive data from the benchmarking work to support their ideas. As a result management agreed to set up a new operation, providing 24 hour delivery service and selling customised software with the PCs, which was quickly successful with customers.

Information sources for benchmarking

When getting started on benchmarking, managers often wonder where to go for the necessary data. Some suggestions are as follows.

- Trade and professional associations may be helpful in suggesting contacts and information on specific topics.
- Consultants and academics may have done research in particular areas and be able to suggest people to talk to.
- Business magazines and newsletters can help you to tap into their expertise and sources.
- Computer databases in a good business library will enable you to read up published information about a potential benchmarking partner.
- Investment analysts have financial data and can identify who industry leaders are.
- Customers and suppliers can be very valuable because of their active involvement with potential benchmarking partners and their interest in stimulating improvement.
- Executive networks: there are often strong informal links between those in the same function and industry.

Ten steps to effective benchmarking

1. Select the process or function to benchmark. Consider the processes that are of real importance and where substantial potential for improvement seems to exist.
2. Identify the best company in that process. Look far and wide, at home or abroad, for the best performer.
3. Choose the key performance measures and collect data. Agree with the benchmark company the type of information to be collected.
4. Analyse and compare the data. Get to grips with how superior performance is achieved, not just what it is.
5. Project future performance levels of the benchmarked company. Be sure to look ahead and think about what will be excellent performance in three or five years' time.
6. Establish goals for own performance. Decide how to translate the lessons learnt into change in your own organisation.
7. Communicate benchmark findings among staff to develop support for change.
8. Develop action plans to support the agreed objectives.
9. Implement changes and monitor progress.
10. Recalibrate benchmarks. From time to time review the benchmarks to ensure they still reflect best practice.

SETTING OBJECTIVES

From the start the quality efforts need to be integrated into clear business objectives. This is often not the case when managers start on TQ work; yet, if they do not take the time to start clarifying objectives and agreeing them as a team, they have little chance of successful implementation.

The companies studied provide good examples of clear objectives.

- ICL Product Distribution has relentlessly concentrated on delivery reliability to customers. In his early days as general manager, David Palk was prepared to go through customer orders one by one finding out exactly where each stood and what needed to be done to keep promises to customers. Over four years service reliability has been improved from less than 50 per cent in some cases to more than 99 per cent.
- In its main factory in Denmark, Grundfos has targeted the reduction of the costs of scrap. Over five years this has been cut from 6 to 0.6 per cent of the value of raw materials.
- Nissan Motors UK has focused the attention of everyone in the organisation on the objective of achieving quality (meaning absence of defects) and productivity levels on a par with those in the company's Japanese factories.
- The worldwide Federal Express system of eight service quality indicators allows everyone to understand both the priority given to customer service and exactly what they need to do to meet the company's objectives.

In multi-divisional companies corporate centres can choose between two approaches to the setting of objectives: setting company-wide stretch goals or encouraging divisions to do something about TQ without prescribing what.

Setting company-wide stretch goals

A number of Western companies have adopted the Japanese practice of setting targets which are deliberately stretching: objectives which cannot be reached by doing more of the same, but require staff to rethink the way they do things. The goals are set in terms which can be applied to all units within large groups, whatever the particular business they are in. Typically the objectives are a response to intense competitive pressures; management has become aware that an order of magnitude improvement in performance is needed in order to survive.

Top managers focus on a few powerful goals. The selection of the goals is all important. Top managers need to understand their own business thoroughly – its customers and their needs and wants, its own processes, how the work actually gets done – and the nature of the competitive pressures to set the right objectives. They also have to be prepared to take risks and to look foolish. By definition the stretch goals will look unattainable when they are first launched. Top managers must have the self-belief to push on regardless.

In a number of cases the use of stretch goals has been spectacularly successful in triggering dramatic improvements in performance.

Hewlett Packard. In 1981 John Young, chief executive of Hewlett Packard worldwide, kicked off the quality movement in HP by asking all divisions to improve product quality ten times in ten years. A measure was devised which applied to all HP companies across the world and was then used as the acid test of quality. The defect rate for each company in 1981 was defined as 1; by 1991 the company's average defect rate was to be reduced to 0.1. Over the ten years the company did exactly that.

John Golding, managing director of Hewlett Packard UK, comments: "That one decision ten years ago has contributed more than anything to the success of HP and our recent increases in earnings."

HP related defect rates to $ of sales. In product performance terms HP's quality has improved by much more than ten times because of the rapid fall in the price of products.

Milliken & Co. Roger Milliken, president and CEO, set all units in his company the challenge of 10/4 goals: increasing performance on a number of key customer and cost variables by ten times between 1989 and 1993. The goals he decided had to be stretching objectives if the company was to get ahead of competitors. Goals have been established using common measures for all Milliken units around the world and included:

- reducing the price of non-conformance to one tenth of its previous figure;
- a tenfold reduction in defects;
- reducing the non-value added time in processes to one tenth of what it was.

The company says that some of the goals have already been achieved; others have not.

Motorola. Worldwide the company has adopted the challenge of reaching by 1994 the famous Six Sigma level of performance in everything it does. This means that for every million parts or steps there will be no more than 3.4 defects (Figure 6.3).

Figure 6.3 Benchmarking quality in some everyday tasks

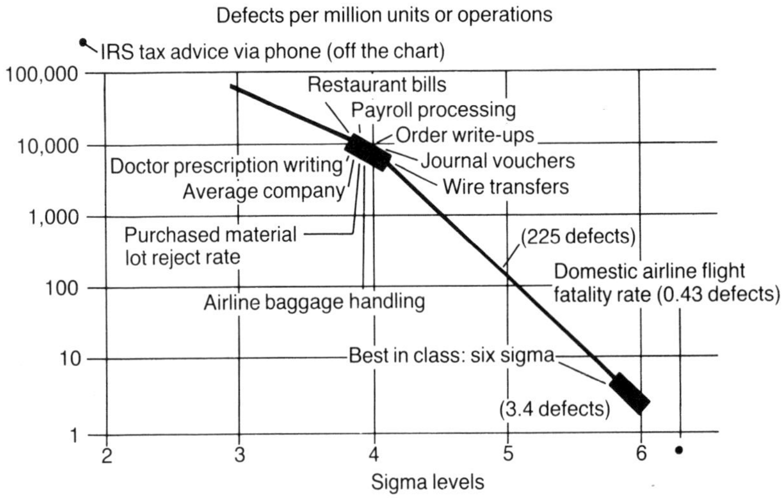

Defects per million units or operations

Source: Motorola

IBM Europe. The company is moving to focus its managers' attention on two key numbers. The first is the satisfaction rating given by customers; the second is the score achieved by units when measured against the Baldrige Award criteria. The ultimate objective is a rating of "85/875" meaning delighted customers and world class quality processes.

Enabling role of centre

The second approach is for corporate centres to adopt an enabling role. They ask divisions to consider the TQ challenge and to do something to respond but leave it to local discretion to decide exactly what. They have small central teams which help to get unit managers thinking about the TQ challenge; they encourage those who take effective action and celebrate their successes; but they do not dictate to their divisions.

3M, Xerox, and Shell UK Oil are using the Baldrige Award or similar criteria as a mechanism for stimulating change.

Other companies have found different ways of encouraging divisions to change.

- Brian McMurray, general manager of Daintyfit, a clothing company in Northern Ireland and subsidiary of Courtaulds Textiles, describes how his group CEO, Martin Taylor, and chairman, Sir Christopher Hogg, encouraged him to start continuous improvement without specifying how he should do it.

- IDV has given the maximum freedom to subsidiaries to choose the form of TQ that suits them but insisted they do something.
- Ciba-Geigy has a small corporate team encouraging group companies to start TQ work but is careful to leave ownership with them.

DECIDING VALUES

Before embarking on TQ work, management needs to consider whether TQ fits their values. Work with the case study companies shows that two values are preconditions to effective TQ work.

A passion about quality. This is akin to people's pride in their craft; the delight in striving for perfection, fulfilling themselves in creating something that is useful for others. It means cherishing the past and those who have mastered the business before them but also a desire to go on experimenting and improving the product or service. It means a gut commitment to delivering quality every time.

Belief in people and their potential. This is the belief that people do not need to be controlled, managed, manipulated or motivated to do useful work. It is the belief that people want to take pride in their work, want to learn and to develop. The job of top management is seen as one of liberating individuals to fulfil more of their natural potential.

Barry Morgans of IBM says:

> The pride is naturally there; the job of managers is to release it. Often our systems of measurement and our short time horizons get in the way. We have to find a way of clearing them out of the way.

Why these values are preconditions for TQ

Repeatedly in talking to companies the researchers heard that quality starts with a frame of mind, an emotional commitment, a passion. Logic alone is not enough. If every decision relating to quality is subject to careful analysis, some poor quality will slip through: there will always be some marginal decisions where it appears cheaper in the short term to compromise on quality than to ensure 100 per cent performance. As Professor Charles Handy of London Business School puts it: "Quality is like truth: one slip and your reputation can be tarnished for ever."

Peter Wickens, director at NMUK, explains:

> Everything you hear about the Japanese attitude to quality is true. Commitment to a zero defect product is absolute throughout the company. Assembly workers take a pride in building the perfect product, and they insist that the components they receive are of the same high standard.

Paul Watson, quality manager of ICL Product Distribution, adds: "Quality is about pride in your work."

The commitment to learning also has immediate practical implications. Amid all the hustle and bustle of day to day operations, companies need to find time for reviewing and learning from what they have done. They need to work hard to foster an environment in which people admit to errors and genuinely see them as opportunities to improve. What chance is there of that space and that openness unless there is an ethic of learning?

Grundfos encourages staff at all levels to learn. It has lavishly equipped and heavily used workshops where employees can learn anything from pottery to car mechanics, languages to communication skills. It reasons that people who are skilled at learning in their private lives will also be good learners in their work lives. "If you want to learn the company will help you" is their motto.

The belief in people is essential if management is to make the shift demanded by TQ from controlling and directing to leading and releasing potential. Top managers in the TQ process need to "let go", to give up the detailed controls on which they have relied for their sense of comfort in the past. They should delegate much more and take risks in assigning people to responsibilities so that people can develop. They need to invest heavily in training and development and to protect those investments against short-term pressures.

Finally the TQ values are important because of their energising effect on those who believe them. The TQ teams studied are prepared to work long hours and to give maximum commitment to their companies because they share a passionate belief in the ideas they are seeking to implement.

GETTING STARTED ON QUALITY

Do

- Start at the top if humanly possible.
- Assess honestly where your organisation is, where it wants to be, what needs to change and what needs to stay the same. Very careful listening to customers and to employees and selective benchmarking are essential to this process.
- Begin experimenting soon. Lots of study is fine but the real learning comes from "having a go", seeking to apply the quality principles and reviewing what works and what does not.
- Start small. Do not take on the big issues straight away; try instead for projects that are potential "easy wins" that will help you to learn and to convince the sceptics. If possible projects that everyone will agree are of real value to the business.
- Have a look at organisations that are years on in applying TQ; seeing and feeling what implementation is like is better than any number of presentations and books.
- Support and encourage the champions of change to start working on quality projects; accept that there will be many sceptics at first and work with the willing few to achieve actions and results that will begin to convince others.
- Avoid the ready-made answers offered by some consultants; the path to quality must be home made or it will not have sufficient commitment to push it through.
- If senior management cannot be interested, start where you are with other willing participants. Let your successes begin to convince top management to give quality the necessary priority.
- Set up cross-functional and multi-level teams to work on the quality projects. People need to experience the value of working across the old organisational boundaries.

Do not

- Think of it as "doing quality"; the reason you are taking action is to address your strategic objectives. Understanding and applying the TQ principles will help you reach those objectives.
- If you have a choice start with ISO 9000 (BS 5750). (See Chapter 7.)
- Start with training; provide this only as and when it is needed to progress the quality projects (see Chapter 11).

SUMMARY

1. Senior management as a whole must take responsibility for quality.

2. Make use of the European or Baldrige Award criteria (or a simplified version) to clarify your understanding of the TQ principles and how you measure up against them.

3. Decide how to integrate the TQ principles into your strategy in a way that is distinctive and suits the culture and history of your organisation.

4. Set clear objectives incorporating quality.

5. Before embarking on TQ work, review whether you do have a passion for quality and believe in people; if you do not you are better off not starting.

CASE STUDY

FEDERAL EXPRESS: QUALITY IS NOT ENOUGH

Federal Express, the worldwide parcels transportation company, has an enviable history. Started in 1974, FedEx grew rapidly to become the first US company to reach an annual turnover of $1 bn in under ten years without benefiting from mergers or acquisitions. Its business performance is largely based on, and supported by, a total and rigorous commitment to customer focused quality initiatives in every aspect of its operations.

However, Federal Express admits that its success in the USA has not been easy to duplicate in other parts of the world. Most notably, in March 1992 Federal Express announced that it was withdrawing from its UK domestic and intra-European operations.

Although adopting Total Quality principles may improve many businesses beyond recognition, even save them from failure, the FedEx case illustrates that quality is not enough. It can help a company deliver a well thought out strategy, but is no substitute for asking some timely questions about the intrinsic viability of its business.

Summary of FedEx case

What it got right.

- The personnel and management policies and procedures brought from the USA supported a Total Quality approach.
- It had clear support from all senior managers in Federal Express, nationally and from the USA.
- The rationalisation of 1991 handled change sensitively but implemented, in one go, some tough decisions which completely changed the nature of the company.
- Throughout resources were made available for training and supporting employees and quality action teams.
- The effective use of technology and sophisticated measurement techniques backed up the initiative.

What it got wrong.

- Understanding and solving the difficulties of customs and VAT operations across Europe, and the extremely complex logistical operation required to guarantee intra-continental and intercontinental deliveries through a single system. This meant that the anticipated synergies and economies of scale between the domestic, intra-continental and intercontinental businesses never occurred.
- Overestimating the demand for a premium priced 24 hour delivery service in Europe.
- Starting the initiative too late.

There are three main streams of activity in the Federal Express story in the UK.

- The gradual introduction, from 1987 onwards, of successful management and personnel policies used in the US company.
- The development of a specific UK quality initiative from 1989 onwards.
- The strategic and operational review of 1990 which resulted in a major reorganisation of UK operations from April 1991.

Federal Express entered the UK parcels distribution market in 1986 by buying an existing distribution business, Lex Wilkinson. Deregulation was in full swing and the market appeared to be expanding with rich pickings to be had as the monopoly of the Post Office was challenged. However, the acquisition presented FedEx with a very different challenge from the business which had been developed organically in the USA. In the first couple of years, fearful of alienating the workforce, few changes were made. Eventually, however, a TQM approach was introduced in 1989 as the US company was already qualifying for the Malcolm Baldrige Award in the USA.

Results of TQ initiative

The TQ initiative was not unsuccessful, based as it was on the proven US formula of people, customers, communication, style, problem solving and technology (see box), with a particular focus on the problem solving. However, it was not all plain sailing; for example, the "survey, feedback, action" process caused surprise and disbelief in the UK workforce. As one seasoned British manager said of the staff feedback sessions:

I thought they (the staff) would really go for me, and they did. But we worked our way through that first time and now (two years later) it works really well.

The British workforce also reacted positively to FedEx's policy of empowerment, although it took time and a gradual shift in management style before employees felt confident to use this freedom to real effect.

Similarly, the focus on customers generated real results. For example, in the fiscal year 1991/92, the cumulative SQI (service quality indicators, see page 87) figure was 98.9 per cent. This was achieved from a starting position of around 80 per cent in 1986. And there was a 92 per cent reduction in the number of problems with "overages and shortages": either parcels which arrive without documentation or documentation which arrives without parcels.

An interesting and specific example of how the quality improvement process happened in practice was at the call centre. Abandoned telephone calls went from some 1,400 per day down to 90 per day.

Nearly all the incoming calls to Federal Express in the UK were handled at the national call centre in Coventry, an average of 6,000 per day. All incoming calls at the centre are monitored constantly; for example, how many "holding", how many answered within 20 seconds, how many hang up without getting answered. This information supplies a performance rating. It demonstrates the need for improvement and shows when real improvement has taken place.

The manager of the centre, Tom Aahl, who had previously managed a 16,000 call per day centre in Memphis, decided to implement a quality improvement feedback process (QIF). This ensured that the problems being reported to the centre by customers phoning in got dealt with back where the problem had been created, such as in a depot or at the "hub" (the central sorting operation).

QIF involves customer service agents logging every problem reported to them by a customer, by type and by location, tracing back to where the problem originated (such as where in the transportation process it got lost or delayed) and informing the employee concerned and the employee's manager. This provides the employee and the manager with the opportunity to find out why the situation arose and how to avoid it happening again.

Although this created some discomfort, it did strengthen the relationships between the call centre and the individual employees at the stations. It also produced 600 opportunities for improvement, 106 in the call centre itself and 494 in other parts of the company.

Managers additionally started to spend two hours per month with customer service agents, listening in to their conversations in order to get a first hand view of how calls were being handled. Again this caused some concern initially but it was seen to have benefits as managers and staff could have much more informed conversations about what was happening.

THE FEDEX TOTAL QUALITY PRINCIPLES

A lot of Federal Express's success is explained by its "people, service and profit" philosophy. These three concepts are at the heart of its worldwide approach to business. A staggering amount of effort is put into translating these concepts into reality "on the ground".

People

Federal Express believes in its own people and their right to be treated with respect. This is not a sentimental wish, it is a business reality lived in all aspects of their work. Performance is discussed openly and objectively. It is measured visibly. Commitment and success are recognised, positive behaviour is reinforced. Training is provided and valued. Anyone can progress if they have the ability and the commitment. People are empowered, within specific guidelines, to help the customer.

A key procedure is "survey, feedback, action", where employees' opinions of their managers and the company are solicited (survey) and discussed (feedback), and change is implemented to improve leadership and the organisation (action). It is designed to ensure that open and honest feedback between managers and their reports is given, received and used. It provides an accurate ongoing indicator of employee relations within the company.

Additionally, each year employees complete an anonymous questionnaire providing feedback on specific aspects of how they are managed. The questionnaire is split into three main parts: how employees are managed by their immediate superiors; how they are managed by their superiors' superiors; and questions about the company in general. The questions take the form of statements which the individuals respond to on a five point scale from strongly agree to strongly disagree.

The information from a group of employees is processed centrally and produces a score or rating for that group's manager. This rating is one of the key elements in the manager's performance assessment and is critical in determining whether he or she receives a bonus. (The other two components for management bonus are service quality standard scores and profit.)

Continuous poor scores are a significant problem for a manager. He or she is provided with help and support to develop an appropriate management style, but repeated low scores indicate that the manager is not living the people, service, profit philosophy in the way it is intended and can lead to dismissal. This concept of employees assessing managers' performance is refreshingly new, but it is the next step in the process which creates the real impact.

Having received his or her rating the manager reflects on it and organises a meeting with the people who completed the questionnaires to explore their concerns and understand the causes of any problems. (If the manager has scored poorly, a personnel professional is called in to help facilitate the discussion group.) The output from this meeting takes a number of forms.

- The group produces an action plan outlining what actions will be taken in order to improve the way in which people feel they are managed in the highlighted problem areas. (One of the questions in the survey asks if the individual employee feels that last year's agreed action plan was properly implemented.)
- The manager has a fuller picture of how he or she is perceived by the people he or she manages.
- There has been an opening up, a sense of being listened to.

To managers used to cultures in which such open feedback is not encouraged this may appear to be "the tail wagging the dog". In reality it is not. It is a rigorous and demanding process for managers which enables them to be more effective leaders.

The employee calendar is another technique designed to encourage honest communications between managers and employees. A simple sheet of paper showing each day of the year provides an ongoing record of an individual's performance at a detailed level. For example, compliments or congratulations for good work are noted as are criticisms for poor work. This document allows the manager and the employee to have regular, informed discussions about training needs, promotion opportunities or recurring problems from a basis of fact rather than from vague souvenirs.

Although initially given a cool reception, the calendar became accepted by most employees because it was seen to be fair. Like many aspects of work at Federal Express it is not "easy" (there is no hiding from facts), but it is fair, it is open, it shows respect for the individual and each person knows what is expected and how they are doing.

It is a policy of Federal Express that every individual should be guaranteed fair treatment. This policy is put into practice through employees knowing what is expected of them, what is in it for them and where to go with a problem. This means that employees can question a manager about anything and expect a reasonable answer. If they feel they are not getting one they can go to that manager's manager. Indeed if an employee has a query about a Federal Express policy he or she can expect a written reply from the owner of the policy within 14 days.

Integration around the customer

"Excellence for the customer" is the message in everything. The business focus is simple: "absolutely, positively on time". Everyone in Federal Express knows that their job is to get the parcel to its destination on time. The key quality indicators all reflect this focus, the systems are designed to achieve it and Federal Express people exude it.

A key technique to enable this to happen is empowerment. This is more of a policy than a procedure. It requires belief on the part of individual employees that initiatives taken and decisions made will be rewarded not punished. Staff know that they will have the support of management if they have considered the best interests of the customer first. The story of the front line employee who hired a helicopter (without seeking approval) to fix communication lines during a snowstorm is part of Federal Express folklore and shows employees the scope of their empowerment.

One of the features of the company is the clarity of the framework within which people are empowered. In some ways Federal Express is a very rigid organisation with procedures and policies to cover every eventuality, yet, at the same time this is what empowers people because the limits are so clear. People seizing initiative are rewarded, indeed celebrated, if the result is customer satisfaction.

An example of this happened in March 1992 when the articulated lorry bringing parcels from Scotland to the central distribution "hub" in Nuneaton broke down. In order to get the parcels to Nuneaton before the 2.00 am deadline for sorting and redistribution to other depots three drivers unloaded the lorry (1,974 parcels) into three smaller vans and drove in convoy down to Nuneaton. The drivers in question saw 1,974 potentially unhappy customers the following morning and did not need to seek anyone's authority before taking the necessary action. They were thanked, given a token financial reward, given a terrific amount of public recognition in the form of an award and articles in the company press and they received a note from company president Fred Smith personally thanking them for their efforts.

Federal Express measures service quality using eight criteria critical to the customer's perception of quality. These are:

- delivery service failure;
- missing or late PODs (proof of delivery);
- overages and shortages;
- abandoned calls;
- traces;
- complaints reopened;
- lost packages;
- damaged packages.

These standard measurements are used by Federal Express everywhere in the world. Each of these "top level" measures is supported by more detailed local or issue specific measures. A system of points and weightings translates raw data on a multitude of specific dimensions into the eight SQIs and one overall quality rating. Measurement is a crucial part of quality management and improvement in Federal Express.

The scores reflect the customer's view of quality. For example, if a parcel was to be delivered to a Mr X and on arrival at the delivery address the courier discovered that the house had burnt down, forcing Mr X to go to stay with relatives, the parcel would be classified as a delivery failure because it did not get to Mr X on time.

The simplicity of the measures allows for easy trend analysis and comparisons between one unit, area or region and another. They also provide vital feedback on the overall effectiveness of the various quality improvement efforts.

Communication

Regular communication from the centre (both globally and nationally) helps keep people informed and reinforces a sense of belonging. Clarity around specific policies and procedures ensures clear expectations of staff. One to one feedback is formalised and effective; good and bad news is communicated.

External customer communications are managed and monitored constantly for effectiveness. For example, each customer service agent receives two weeks' classroom training before handling any calls. They then spend two weeks with an experienced agent before being left on their own. Subsequently they receive two hours' training per month.

Style

The organisational style is classless and open. It has an American, success oriented feel to it that cuts through British taboos and reservations. The award schemes play an important part in this, much more through their public recognition than any monetary value they represent.

The badges, stickers, medals and plaques appear to be widely appreciated, and the potential to win one provides a "bit of spice", an incentive to try harder.

One story which epitomises the reward style is that of the courier who saw a child in difficulties in a river. He parked his van and got the child out of the water. It was only when he arrived back at the station in normal clothes (since his uniform was wet) that the incident came to light. The following week during his round the driver was stopped by the area manager who asked him to get into his car. Together they drove to Heathrow airport where the driver's wife was waiting. They were put on to a Federal Express plane and flown to Memphis, Tennessee, to have lunch with company president, Fred Smith, and spend a few days on holiday at the company's expense.

This type of incident is part of Federal Express life. Such events are always widely communicated inside the organisation.

Problem solving

Within Federal Express people take a practical approach to problems. Everyone has a common base and language for tackling problems and they do so with vigour. The aim is always first to do the necessary to satisfy a customer quickly, then to trace back to the root causes of a problem in order to eliminate the source thus avoiding repetition of the problem.

The focus of the quality initiative in the UK was problem solving, and although the approach taken was very similar to that used in the USA, great care was taken to ensure that the training materials used in the USA were appropriate for the UK.

The first step was check that senior managers knew and had experienced the concepts, tools and techniques which the staff were going to learn. The managers therefore all attended quality workshops run by in-house trainers in 1989. Following these workshops the managers set up quality action teams (QATs) to work on real problems affecting their part of the business.

The next step was to develop a network of quality facilitators across the network of stations (depots). Each of the facilitators received 22 days' training and could act as a resource to help any QAT.

After this QATs made up of employees from different functions and different levels were set up in regions and stations. Members were trained in the philosophy of TQM and specifically in the tools and techniques of problem solving. A number of QATs have achieved significant results. The criteria used to evaluate a project are: will it improve service, will it reduce costs or will it do both?

For example, a team of Federal Express employees at the Birmingham station (working jointly with HM Customs and Excise staff) produced an improvement in the way parcels were cleared through customs at Birmingham airport which resulted in the number of parcels "held" by customs being reduced from an average of 625 per day to under 50 per day. This has reduced the amount of time being spent handling customer complaints from 54 hours per day to 5 hours per day and saved the company over $1 mn a year in refund costs.

To support and expand on the energy being created by the QATs a number of award schemes were introduced to recognise individual and team contributions to quality. Some of these like the Bravo Zulu awards were already in existence in the USA; others such as the Legendary Service awards were created for the UK operation.

Customer/supplier alignments

Customer/supplier alignments were formally introduced in Federal Express in the UK in 1990. They marked a recognition that the quality efforts needed to emphasise more specifically the customer's requirements. Federal Express defines quality as "doing the right things right". The quality initiative had got people thinking and working on quality improvement (doing things right) but not necessarily on matters that were critical to the customer (doing the right things).

The customer/supplier alignments apply to both internal and external customer relationships. They clearly identify who is the customer and who is the supplier in any situation, but recognise that it is a "two way street" and that in order to receive the required service from a supplier the customer has to recognise and agree certain conditions.

An example of this working internally is the relationship between marketing and sales. The sales department is clearly the customer since marketing provides it with promotional materials, customer leads and the types of products to sell. The starting point for the alignment is for the marketing director to ask the sales director how what is being supplied meets his or her needs. This might lead to an agreement on some modification of materials and time frame guarantees. The marketing department, however, needs regular feedback from sales on which promotions are running well, and so on, and this would also be built into the alignment.

An external customer alignment involves someone from Federal Express, usually a sales person, sitting down with a customer and exploring in some depth the type of service that customer requires and working with the customer to create a solution which is right for them. This could involve, for example, a special pricing arrangement, or some of Federal Express's technology being installed at the customer's premises, or particular pick-up or delivery arrangements. What was agreed would be thought through in terms of the implications for each of the parties and guarantees put in place. Sometimes a solution to a particular problem is not obvious, in which case Federal Express and the customer might form a joint QAT to develop options for a way forward.

Technology

Federal Express uses technology throughout its operation to improve speed and reliability, to eliminate errors and to reduce costs. Computer technology is in the hands of all employees not just management.

The 1990 performance review

It became apparent during 1990 that a dramatic change was necessary to make the UK operation competitive given the difficult market conditions in which it was operating. The result was a major rationalisation in operations. Federal Express withdrew from the heavyweight part of the market (which involved a three day delivery cycle) to concentrate on its core business of delivering express parcels, overnight or within 48 hours. This rationalisation involved opening a number of new stations (depots) and redesigning all the routes and schedules.

At the same time, hand held computer terminals (known as supertrackers) were introduced into the vans so that as soon as couriers accepted parcels from clients, they were entered into a worldwide tracking system (Cosmos) which enables Federal Express to know at any point in time where a given parcel is in the system.

These physical changes in operations were accompanied by some significant changes in personnel and management policy. A flatter management structure was introduced. Greater flexibility and reductions in overtime among the workforce were achieved through negotiation with the trade union.

The introduction of these changes was orchestrated with the precision and thoroughness of a military operation. The plans were finalised and announced to managers in a document entitled "Partnership for Change" in February 1990. There then followed a three month period during which managers finalised the implementation details for their particular location and counselled staff on the options open to them. Retraining, particularly in using the technology and in customer care, was provided for those who chose to stay, and redundancy packages made available to those who did not want to or who the company did not wish to retain.

A cathartic experience

On April 8, 1991, the new operation was launched. In the words of a station manager "it felt like a new organisation, Federal Express had finally arrived". These sentiments were echoed by many people the researchers spoke to. The time leading up to the big change was difficult for everyone, with some tough decisions being made. Once this was done, however, things felt different; the climate of openness and cooperation aspired to became a reality. People had the tools to do the job and felt that the organisation was fit to meet the challenges it was facing.

This major change helped the quality initiative to grow into being part of life within Federal Express in the UK. Assessed by those critical criteria of customer perceptions of quality Federal Express UK was a success story. Why then was the company finally unsuccessful in its bid to enter the UK domestic and intra-European markets?

Gary Roth, managing director of marketing, communications and customer service (north west Europe), explains that Federal Express's primary interest in international business has always been intercontinental transportation. Entry into the European domestic and internal markets was seen as a way to develop and reinforce the intercontinental work.

However, when Federal Express entered the European arena there were already a number of well established competitors whose market share allowed them to better cover the fixed costs which are inevitable in providing a country-wide distribution service. For example, in the UK domestic market Parcelforce and Securicor were strong while in the intra-European market DHL and TNT had several years' experience and a reasonable market share. These and similar companies were better placed than Federal Express (with a 5 per cent UK market share) to survive the recession driven cost and price cutting activities of the late 1980s and early 1990s. As Federal Express says "no one was making any money at that time but some were losing less than we were".

Downturn of UK economy

Expansion was predicted in the UK market following deregulation but this did not occur, with resulting overcapacity in the transportation business. This was compounded by the low barriers to entry in the domestic delivery business encouraging many, often tiny, firms to set up. Although usually shortlived these firms helped to exacerbate the severe price competition the market was experiencing.

Too little, too late

When it entered the UK market through acquisition in 1986 Federal Express was aware of a number of changes it needed to introduce into the operating practices of the acquired company. It was also aware of the potential danger of introducing wholesale changes too quickly. It did not want to "Americanise" the UK operation for fear of rejection from the employees and/or the customers.

With hindsight it was perhaps oversensitive to this. Two of the managers who were long-term employees of Lex Wilkinson expressed surprise at the low impact Federal Express had when it took over in 1986. One said, jokingly: "We thought, here we go, it's going to be like the GIs – 'over paid, over fed and over here' – but in reality we carried on as before."

In fact this delay had a significant, if perhaps unplanned benefit. The old Lex Wilkinson operational managers were initially relieved that there was no radical upheaval. After a while, however, they began to feel frustrated that although working for a (arguably the) world leader in their business, things were not improving. They were becoming aware of the US operation and wanted to emulate it. This created a "pull" for change and for US management methods which meant that they were readily accepted when they were introduced. It did, however, take (possibly vital) time.

Insufficient customer awareness

Gary Roth's comment "if people don't know you are there, and what you can do, they are not going to buy from you" rings true. Federal Express put a tremendous amount of energy into getting the operational business sorted out. It is possible that the company was too late in undertaking major awareness raising activities within the UK, given the tough market conditions and the high levels of public awareness of longstanding competitors.

A new ball game

It could be argued that since all Federal Express's experience in the USA was in growing an organisation organically, perhaps it lacked the knowhow, the ability to make an acquisition work. It seems that the company was working hard at disproving this (successfully in our view); however, other factors caused it to run out of time.

Ultimately, however, the quality improvement activities did not tackle the fundamental strategic issues of the business in the UK. Improving customers' perception of product and service quality is a necessary but not sufficient condition in overall business success. TQM applied in this way cannot be a panacea for all business difficulties.

CASE STUDY

CIBA-GEIGY ITALY: THE LONG ROAD TO QUALITY

Ciba-Geigy Italy is responsible for the sales, marketing and distribution of products from all six divisions of Ciba-Geigy. It handles:

- dyestuffs and chemicals;
- pharmaceuticals;
- agrochemicals;
- polymers;
- additives;
- pigments.

Its 1990 turnover was £500 mn (6–7 per cent of worldwide sales) and it employed 3,200 people, 1,100 of whom were based at the Italian head office in Origgio. Apart from intercompany trading, Ciba-Geigy Italy primarily sells into the Italian market, with most products supplied from the group's manufacturing centres in Switzerland.

Why Total Quality?

The Total Quality initiative was introduced to Ciba-Geigy in 1985 by Heinz Lippuner, then CEO of the group's worldwide dyestuffs division and now group chief executive. Faced with a need to reduce costs drastically in order to remain internationally competitive, yet unwilling to do this through redundancies, TQ appeared to represent a way of making cost cuts that would stick, and to do so in a way that saved jobs and motivated staff.

Lippuner's decision to adopt a Total Quality approach was helped by a visit to Milliken Industrial, a maker of contract carpeting and one of the dyestuff division's principal customers in the USA. Initially sceptical, Lippuner was convinced by what he saw.

Asked to introduce TQ only in his own dyestuff division, Sergio Giuliani, head of Ciba-Geigy Italy, saw much greater opportunities. Although the company had a strong reputation with customers and was financially sound, he felt that product excellence alone would not be enough to maintain his group's leading position in Italy in years ahead. The company had to become more market driven, providing new products to meet the needs of customers rather than those of the R&D division. It also had to cut costs on a continuing basis.

Did it work?

His optimism about TQ was not unfounded; seven years later Ciba-Geigy Italy has cut costs significantly, and achieved many incremental improvements in quality and service. Its people have a common understanding of quality principles and techniques which will enable them to maintain the quality momentum. In 1991 the company was presented with the "Beacon of Quality" award by Crosby Associates.

However, senior managers are realistic. They admit that they were overconfident of the speed with which Total Quality would deliver benefits, and there is still a lot to do to realise the real benefits of TQ.

An important aspect of the Ciba-Geigy story is the time and care that the local management took to "own" and shape the quality initiative. Before Crosby Associates were involved, the management team spent two years clarifying their objectives and pushing through priority improvement projects. Forthright leadership was given by a close-knit management team who have worked together for years and know their business intimately. A clear sense of passion, involvement and enthusiasm comes through when talking to them. And, after a period of Crosby style work, the focus is now again on integrating quality into the running of the business (see box).

The Italian team stress that they started the TQ work at a time of comparative business success. "TQM must start when a company is successful. It takes time. You have to give people time to change," says Sergio Giuliani.

CIBA-GEIGY QUALITY CONCEPT

Ciba-Geigy's vision

By striking a balance between our economic, social and environmental responsibilities we want to ensure the prosperity of our enterprise beyond the year 2000.

Quality at Ciba-Geigy

Our commitment to quality is a key guiding principle of our vision and provides the basis for action in the Ciba-Geigy Group.

Quality to us means that we continually meet mutually agreed requirements within the company, between Ciba-Geigy employees, as well as in all our dealings with business partners and society in general.

Quality management

Quality management is a company-wide, management led, continuous improvement process to ensure that the attitudes and behaviour of every employee are focused on:

- identifying, understanding and reviewing the requirements of external and internal customers (users/partners);
- satisfying these requirements efficiently and effectively;
- continually monitoring the fulfilment of these requirements and carrying out corrective measures whenever necessary.

All activities following these steps must result in providing value to Ciba-Geigy and our customers.

Responsibility for implementation

The responsibility to implement quality management lies with the heads of the divisions, the business sectors, the central service units, the corporate units and the corporate staff units in Basle and the heads of group companies worldwide.

H. Lippuner, chairman of the group executive committee

FORTHRIGHT LEADERSHIP

The top team at Ciba-Geigy Italy have known each other for many years. They have worked closely together and come across to the observer as a strong and coherent team. This undoubtedly has helped when struggling with the emotional difficulties of changing the organisation, starting with themselves.

The first stage in the process was to define what quality meant to Ciba-Geigy Italy. With the assistance of a consultant facilitator, they agreed that it had four elements:

- customer orientation;
- widespread innovation;
- controlling costs;
- improvement through people.

It was then necessary to involve the rest of the management team and gain their commitment. This was done through a series of three day seminars at which managers reviewed the four principles, the obstacles to change and the suggestions for quality related projects.

Ciba's Italian term for TQ is MPQ (*Miglioramento della produttività e qualità* – continuously improving productivity and quality):

MPQ in Ciba-Geigy means improving our capability to respond to the expectations of our customers with products and services at declining costs. We will reach our goal through consistent, widespread, constant improvements realised with the involvement and participation of all the employees, introducing new values in our way of thinking and behaviour.

TQ projects

In April 1987 senior managers initiated four cross-divisional and multi-disciplinary quality projects:

- staff involvement;
- reward/recognition systems;
- increasing awareness;
- monitoring systems.

These were undertaken on a part-time basis and the results presented in July 1987.

Employee communication programme

As projects got under way in the operating units, a comprehensive communications campaign was launched. Posters, brochures and notice boards all emphasised the need for quality improvement. This was supported by senior management holding a series of meetings in an effort to develop awareness of, and commitment to, quality.

A taskforce of 17 worked on the advertising and communications campaign and started to prepare a training programme. The message sent to all levels of staff was that they should "challenge managements' commitment and will to change". Quality was to be achieved "through people".

Suggestion scheme. A suggestion scheme was set up by the taskforce to encourage people to innovate. In an effort to improve communication and understanding between departments, suggestions had to be outside the person's own area of work. The implementing department had to evaluate the success of the idea. If the idea was rejected, the rejection had to be justified to the proposer.

Successful ideas were rewarded by the award of a number of gold coins (each worth about £70) to a value approximately 5 per cent of the benefit obtained from implementing the idea. If someone won 12 gold coins they were presented with a Ciba-Geigy share (approximate value £1,500) by the president of the company. The person also had to present his or her idea at a seminar.

After some initial enthusiasm the number of ideas put forward to the suggestions scheme declined. Nevertheless the company argues the approach did have value because it provoked people to suggest improvements, raised awareness of costs and helped reduce barriers between departments.

BRINGING IN THE CONSULTANTS

It was only at this stage that the company commissioned Crosby Associates to support its quality work. The consultants helped in three areas: training; introducing the "price of non-conformance concept" (PONC); and setting up quality teams.

Training. All senior managers attended the Crosby College. A number of managers and staff were selected to be trained as course instructors for internal training. Quality awareness programmes were organised for blue collar workers and training modules were prepared for new staff. A total of 52,000 hours over two years were dedicated to quality training.

Putting every employee through the same TQM training has given people in the company – across all divisions – a common language of quality and a shared way of thinking about business problems. Before the TQM initiative there were often misunderstandings of what external and internal customers wanted. Now that the TQM concepts are generally understood and used, communication is much easier. A common understanding of TQM concepts enables both suppliers and customers to participate in a process of determining requirements.

The price of non-conformance (PONC). The well known Crosby concept was adapted to the company's own use. For all activities Ciba defined the acceptable levels of cost or resource required. Everything above these levels was considered to be non-conformance and reviewed to see how it could be reduced.

Ciba-Geigy managers stress that their use of PONC is a relative measure rather than an absolute one. The target is a larger decrease in PONC year by year. The figure for total PONC in the company has increased as people have become more aware of the opportunities for improvement.

Recent figures for PONC reduction are L3 bn in 1989, L5 bn in 1990 and L13 bn in 1991 (the latter includes a reduction of 100 corporate staff). Typical PONC savings in 1991 included reductions in credit notes, stockouts, unnecessary sales calls and telephone calls not returned on time.

In 1990–91 the company used TQ tools and techniques to help implement the SOAP project (Structures Organisation Activities Processes): a systematic redefinition of the relationship between the divisions and central functions aimed at reducing costs and giving more responsibility to operating units. Apart from finance, accounts and information systems, business units were given the freedom to decide whether to source services internally or from outside the corporation. The result in Italy was a reduction of 100 corporate staff, the value of which was included in the PONC reductions for 1991 (see above).

Quality teams. The company set up two types of group to look at quality improvement. Gruppo Reale bring together people who work in the same place or who do the same job and are aimed at improving the efficiency or effectiveness of work in that area. The groups typically meet for 3–4 hours a month and anyone in the group can propose a topic for the group to work on. They have had the effect of ensuring that problems are brought to the surface to be resolved and that they are dealt with in a fact based and constructive way. Increasingly they are taking over from the suggestion scheme as the source of incremental improvements.

A typical example is a project to reorganise the input of work to the laboratory. Internal customers of the laboratory were dissatisfied with the service they were receiving and this was traced back to poor systems for scheduling and allocating the work. There is now a big wall chart updated by the people who work in the laboratory which provides the focus for scheduling work.

In addition to the Gruppo Reale, cross-functional corrective action teams (CATs) were put together to work on specific problems. People may spend significant amounts of time on a CAT, with projects lasting up to two years.

The Gruppo Reale and CATs have caused significant local improvements. An example is the supply of information on the status of goods coming from Basle.

The logistics department received frequent requests for information from people in marketing but did not know the answers and had to keep chasing the warehouse staff in Basle. The solution agreed was that every day at a fixed time the warehouse in Basle would provide logistics in Italy with an update of certain information. Marketing knows what time this is and when it will get the latest information. It saves a lot of time chasing information and has simplified and streamlined the whole process of information supply.

Top managers reckon that after the Gruppo Reale were set up it took about a year and a half to begin to get real value from them and overcome the fear of employees that measurements would be used to assess people's performance, and to make clear that improvement comes from looking at processes not blaming individuals.

Persuading people to alter their behaviour and breaking down barriers between departments remains difficult. For instance, there is a continuing problem with supplying the samples sales staff need.

The sales staff should get samples from the warehouse, but the laboratories also hold small quantities so sales staff often obtain their samples direct from these because it is quicker. This disrupts operations in the laboratory. Agreement was reached that sales staff would go to the warehouse and in return the warehouse would supply orders within one day. However, a year later sales staff were still getting samples from the laboratory. A CAT was set up to resolve the situation but the team decided it was not something it could sort out. Instead the issue was referred back to the head of textiles as a people issue – unwillingness of the sales staff to change – rather than a problem the quality team could solve.

Unions kept at arms' length. The company had an unhappy history of confrontation, strikes and unrest in the late 1970s and early 1980s, and the TQM project was started without union involvement. When the union later asked to be included in the corporate TQM project this was refused. The company wished to re-establish a direct line of control and communication to the shopfloor rather than through the union. By providing stronger direct links between management and staff the TQ initiative has helped reduce the union's conflicts with the company.

Plateauing of TQ initiative

After two years the enthusiasm of participants for the TQ work faded. Top management had to re-energise the initiative. Comments Sergio Giuliani:

> *Every programme needs a midway crisis to spur it on to the next stage. Ours was after two years and 52,000 hours of training when we realised very little was happening. People understood the concepts – TQM had been absorbed in their brains but not in their hearts or guts. Since TQM is not new any more, people are not sure if TQM is still important to top management. We then saw it was all about motivating people.*

One reason for the plateauing of the TQ initiative may have been the impact of Italian culture. While Italians seem able to cope with the very high levels of communication in the workplace and the climate of continuous change that TQ requires, they are perhaps less good at the steady, consistent application of improvement concepts and techniques. The quickest solution may not be the best.

In the opinion of senior managers at Ciba-Geigy Italian workers are more prone to become discouraged if results do not come easily. In this respect they feel somewhat at a disadvantage compared with, for example, their Swiss colleagues.

RE-ENERGISING THE TQ INITIATIVE

Pay and compensation. One important way that enthusiasm for the TQ process was rekindled was rethinking the reward system to include quality objectives. Everyone, including shopfloor workers, is partly paid according to results. For managers only 80 per cent of salaries is regarded as basic pay. The remaining 20 per cent, plus a further 20 per cent on merit, is paid according to company results, department performance/special projects and personal improvements.

Greater involvement. Another change was drawing the TQM coordinator from line areas as well as management, and rotating the job every 2–3 years. This not only brings fresh ideas to the TQ work and but also reinforces the idea of TQ as the responsibility of every person throughout the organisation, not just the management team.

Leadership review and assessment. Communication, trust and getting to the bottom of ingrained attitudes and beliefs is vital to TQ. Ciba-Geigy introduced a system of subordinates reviewing the leadership style of their managers. This is cascaded down from the top. Every manager has done a self-assessment and compared this with an anonymous review by their subordinates. The results have been discussed and managers have undertaken to change aspects of their behaviour. Groups of more junior staff are currently repeating the approach.

TQ IN 1992

The objective now, five years after starting the TQ initiative, is unchanged. Quality concepts must be built into the running of the business and become part of the normal way of working. In 1992 the company plans to do a self-assessment using the Baldrige Award criteria. The objective is not to apply for the award but to use the assessment to identify further opportunities for improvement.

External focus. While the reputation of the company with customers is good, there is further scope for linking systems more closely with external customers. The company also recognises that it needs to get closer to its suppliers within the group in Switzerland. One manager comments: "You need the whole supply chain to apply TQM or else you won't achieve quality for the customer."

Corporate culture. The company now sees quality as a much bigger task than before. Broad organisational change is needed to make a reality of quality. Looking back Mr Giuliani believes that top management advertised TQM too positively.

There was no recognition of the extent of the necessary culture change: from bureaucracy to everyone believing that "quality is my responsibility". There was insufficient understanding among managers that their own style would have to change: from being autocratic to empowering people to do things for themselves; that communication would have to become genuinely two way; that people must have the opportunity to experiment and make mistakes.

7   ISO 9000

ISO 9000 is like passing your driving test: it means you know the rules of the road but it doesn't mean you drive well everywhere, all the time – which is what TQ is about.

A manager taking part in the research

The International Standards Organisation 9000 series of quality assurance standards (originally based on BS 5750) is currently the biggest development in quality in Europe. Thousands of manufacturing and many service organisations, first in the UK but increasingly throughout Europe (and to some extent North America), have sought certification to ISO 9000. Many have done it from choice, in the belief that certification helps win customers. For many others customers have made it a qualifying criterion: if they do not meet the standard, customers will not even consider them as potential suppliers.

Yet when ISO 9000 is examined closely what it says about a company's quality, and what it does not say, makes it a strange place for most organisations to start the implementation of quality. ISO 9000 has an important supporting role to play in quality, provided it is handled correctly. It is not, in our view, for most companies the place to begin.

WHAT ISO 9000 IS AND IS NOT

The ISO 9000 standards deal with quality assurance: the setting up and maintenance of effective quality systems. If implemented correctly it ensures that an organisation has:

- a quality policy;
- standardisation of processes;
- monitoring of defects and a system for corrective action;
- management reviews of the system.

This can support implementation of Total Quality but it is only one part of a much larger picture. The European Quality Award allows only 14 per cent of its marks for the management of processes, of which quality assurance is a part; the US Baldrige Award gives 14 per cent for quality systems (see Chapter 6). ISO 9000 does not deal with leadership, people involvement, customer delight, continuous improvement and business results.

However, the difference between Total Quality and ISO 9000 is more than this. If implemented outside the context of TQ, ISO 9000 can lead in a different direction. The thinking which underlies the standard is very different (see box). It stems from the different definition of quality. ISO 9000 sees this as conformance to requirements; Total Quality, as explained in Chapter 3, now looks outwards to the customer and thinks of quality as that which delights customers. Compared with TQ the quality assurance definition is too limited. Specifications may be wrong and not what the customer wants; competitors may come up with better products that mean yours are no longer acceptable to customers; service and image may be important parts of what the customer expects (even in manufacturing businesses) but not included in the explicit requirement.

Viewing quality from an internal perspective – does the product conform to predetermined specifications? – misses the point that is at the centre of Total Quality.

ISO 9000 confirms that a company has an effective quality management system. It does not guarantee that the goods and services the company produces are of quality; that depends on whether the systems serve the interests of customers and are supported by a quality culture. A number of managers commented on companies which in their view supplied poor quality but which nevertheless had been certified for ISO 9000.

The other danger with ISO 9000 is that people may believe it represents Total Quality. They then ignore all the other things there are to do. When they see the quality manuals needed for ISO 9000, they may decide quality is just bureaucracy and become disillusioned with the whole subject.

Total Quality and ISO 9000 compared

	ISO 9000	**TQ**
Focus	Conformity to requirements Product or service centred	Customer delight All activities
Objective	Standardise practice	Continuous improvement
Responsible	Quality manager or director	Top management
Involvement of staff	None required	Essential
Development focus	Training	Education and development
Functions involved	Marketing and finance not mentioned	All
Attitude to defects	Inspect and test Corrective action	Design them out Eliminate root causes
Thinking about statistics	Techniques	Understanding
Approach to quality systems	Audit to ensure compliance	Weave into fabric of organisation

SUPPORTING ROLE OF ISO 9000

Implemented within the context of the TQ principles, ISO 9000 can play a valuable role: ensuring that, as described in Chapter 3, best practice is standardised and used as a base for further improvement (see Figure 7.1).

Figure 7.1   The endless improvement cycle

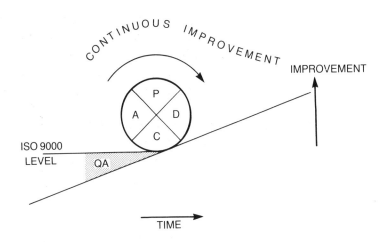

Source: Kaizen Institute of Europe

Many quality managers taking part in this research – and most are implementing ISO 9000 in at least part of their organisation – view the standards pragmatically. They recognise the limitations of ISO 9000 but see it as a way to place quality on the management agenda in their companies. They are delighted that preparation of certification forces managers to stand back and look at their processes. They seek to gain a foothold from which to move on to improvement. They see certification as a useful contributor to a long-term quality initiative, provided it is handled with care.

Jonson Cox, quality manager of Shell UK Oil, comments:

ISO 9000 helped us focus on getting the basic processes right after a period of rapid reductions in employee numbers and it identified improvement opportunities.

Maxine Slade, TQ manager of CMB Packaging Technology, adds:

The work on ISO 9000 has shifted attention from blaming individuals to examining the underlying problem.

Barry Morgans, director of market driven quality at IBM UK, says:

We have ISO 9000 in our UK business and we aim to get it for all our European operations. It's a vital foundation stone for quality work.

Companies stress that to get value from the work on ISO 9000 you must decide yourself what procedures and systems need to be recorded in the interests of customers, and at what level of detail. If the task is delegated to junior managers or consultants, a costly paperchase will result which will have little impact on the way people actually do their jobs.

It is also vital to consider how to build in challenge to traditional ways of doing things; otherwise you end up confirming processes which could be both inefficient and not serve the interests of customers.

The attitude to the auditing of systems is important. Is this seen as a policing operation, with the objective simply to obtain a clear report? Or is it considered an opportunity to learn?

NOT THE PLACE TO START QUALITY

As is stressed in Chapter 6, every company must decide its own route to quality, in the light of its own history and culture and its own objectives. It is impossible therefore to prescribe what role ISO 9000 should play for a particular company. Nevertheless for most, given a free choice, we believe it is the wrong place to start.

The evidence from the case study companies is mixed. ICL Product Distribution wholly and Grundfos in large part are certified to ISO 9000. Ciba-Geigy is planning to seek certification. Nissan Motors UK, Club Med and Federal Express – for all of whom selected operating standards are an important feature of their quality efforts – see no reason at present to be certified. It is not essential for companies in their industries and they prefer to be able to choose freely what procedures and systems they adopt.

Their views are seconded by some of the quality managers who see ISO 9000 as something to acquire because of pressures from customers but still a diversion from their main thrust towards quality improvement. One manager in a US multinational summed it up:

> If the Japanese have a quality problem they go and fix it: if the British have a quality problem they go and write a procedure.

Writing procedures is an essential part of quality but it's the writing of them that is valuable for those involved, much more than the manuals that result. ISO 9000 has made the production of paper an end in itself and people have lost sight of what it is all for.

The important thing is that the Japanese are already way beyond ISO 9000. It's only your ticket to play the game; it doesn't say you will win.

There is indeed a telling indifference among leading Japanese companies operating in Europe to ISO 9000. "It's like asking a post-graduate student to go back and get an A Level in his own subject. Yes he could do it, but why bother?" says another US manager.

Jonathan Smilansky adds:

> Starting with ISO 9000 is like beginning by preparing for exams. It's good for some but I wouldn't recommend it for most. Better decide first what you want to learn and why.

SUMMARY

1. ISO 9000 deals with quality management systems which are only one part of Total Quality.
2. Many companies are obliged to seek ISO 9000 certification because of pressures from customers and competitors. They need to ensure they go about implementation in a way consistent with the TQ principles.
3. For most of the other companies which are free to choose, ISO 9000 is not the best place to start quality efforts. They should begin further "upstream" with the issues of how quality fits their philosophy and strategy, which was examined in Chapter 6.
4. ISO 9000 can play a valuable role in TQ implementation by focusing management attention on the need to consider processes and develop clear standards.

Part 4

What Guidelines Should a Company Follow in Implementation?

8 Forthright, Listening Leadership

> *Management must mean what it says. As soon as a senior manager allows a car to go through which is not at the right quality level "because I have to meet the schedule", the battle is lost.*
>
> Peter Wickens, Nissan Motors UK

Not surprisingly the research for this report shows that strong leadership has been present in the companies that have an effective process of change. What is more interesting is that the leadership is of a particular type: forthright and listening, willing to take personal risks and go out on a limb for key objectives and standards but confident enough to listen and involve others in deciding how to reach the objectives. It is also operationally credible leadership; overwhelmingly engineers in manufacturing companies and in service companies people who have worked their way up through the ranks and who know how the work actually gets done.

In what circumstances do you find this leadership? There are three conditions, each of which must be present.

- Need: a strong sense that the status quo is unacceptable, a personalised need to change.
- Want: a vision of where the organisation needs to get to, a passionate wanting to change.
- Personal confidence: individuals must have the personal confidence to lead at the same time as listening and responding to others about how to achieve the vision.

Leaders must have a powerful reason for change. Without it they will not see their companies through the inevitable difficulties and frustrations that lie ahead.

Finally, in order to initiate the process of change leaders should pick a theme, a focus for change, and stick to it.

FORTHRIGHT LEADERSHIP

A characteristic of the leadership observed in the successful case study companies is that it is at times "out on a limb" leadership, involving significant personal risk for the leaders. Each of them has made clear that there are quality and service objectives or ways of doing things which they insist on. These objectives or standards are non-negotiable: if people want to work for the company this is the way it will be done.

In Grundfos Finn Moller, the quality director, first insisted on a systematic approach to quality in the factory. Informal deviations from drawings and specifications were no longer acceptable. Operators would agree specifications and procedures that were realistic and up to date and then people would stick to them. Initially people did not see why the new approach was necessary; there was resistance. Finn insisted and saw the process through.

Later he pushed through the self-management of quality. The same pattern was repeated: a leader with a clear vision of what he wanted to achieve forcing change through despite the sceptics and cynics; someone willing to face the initial loss of volume and sales because he was convinced this was the right way to operate.

In ICL Product Distribution the general manager, David Palk, inherited an operation that was in a mess. As a 28 year old he only got the job because older "wiser" managers thought the post too risky. David flouted corporate policies when it was necessary to get things done for customers. He provoked protests from the corporate quality and financial staff by hauling people out of quality meetings and dispensing with some reports in order to get things done now for the customer. He harried and pushed on the detail of what had happened on each individual shipment until people got the message that serving customers was the one thing that mattered.

In Nissan Motors UK the start-up team made clear that quality standards would be exactly the same as those applying in Japan. No concessions would be made because of difficulties with suppliers or the need to train and develop a new approach among UK workers and managers. If quality meant that volumes were low and costs higher at the beginning, so be it. Costs and volumes would be worked on later once quality was consistently obtained.

Serge Trigano, chief executive of Club Med, made his commitment to the quality initiative of 1986 crystal clear by meeting with the team leading it every week for half a day. He and his financial team took on the spot decisions about capital expenditure to put in place changes necessary to improve customer service.

IBM's definition of vision

In today's changing environment to have a vision is of the utmost importance. A vision shows direction, it is the lighthouse on the horizon. A puzzle is an even better analogy. You may have all the pieces of the puzzle, but without the picture of how the puzzle is supposed to look, it is very difficult to do.

Action without vision is activity, vision without action is reverie, vision combined with action moves the world.

Source: IBM, *Manager's Handbook for Market Driven Quality*.

LISTENING, RESPONSIVE LEADERSHIP

Total Quality companies need to become learning organisations. Continuous improvement implies continual learning throughout the company. To enable this to take place, leaders have to give managers and workers room to work things out for themselves, to make mistakes, to review and to learn from what they have done.

The successful TQ leadership is not overbearing nor indeed charismatic. While insistent on objectives and standards it seeks to involve others in deciding how to reach objectives; it is modest, even self-effacing. It does not pretend to be the source of all wisdom. It admits to facing problems, not knowing the answers to them and looking for support from anyone around to solve them. It loses no opportunity to stress that real achievement flows from teamwork, not the inspiration of one or a few individuals. It does not aim to prescribe how the change should be carried through.

An example is the attitude of the Japanese managers who worked with the start-up team in Nissan Motors UK. Despite their vastly superior track record of running car businesses, they did not come to the UK to tell the British team how to do it. They questioned, they challenged, they drove the British managers wild at times with their examination of the accepted way of doing things and their attention to detail; but they made it plain from the start that the decisions and the responsibility for running a British plant with British workers rested with the British managers. They insisted on quality but they left the "how" to the UK team.

The style of the British top managers at Nissan bears this out: they are quietly spoken, questioning, listening, not status conscious, often referring to "we", much less often to "I".

Similarly in Grundfos the senior managers are credited with listening. Values and objectives they are insistent about. The group managing director, Jorgen Madsen, spends

30 days a year in management workshops, reinforcing the message about the core values of the company. But he is seen as being flexible about how those objectives and values can best be realised in current circumstances. The style of senior managers is quiet, rather reserved, interested in others, factual, logical: more like a sympathetic doctor than a business tycoon.

Leadership in both companies is not based on personality but on consistent, meaningful support. At Grundfos Finn Moller says: "The most important thing was that top management supported me even when they disagreed with what I was doing." Moral support, assistance with making available money or people's time, space to make progress without being obsessed with this month's operational results: this was what motivated people and enabled them to carry through the process of change when the going got rough.

Club Med seeks to foster innovation by supporting those who have unsuccessfully taken risks and tried to make improvements. This was exemplified by the chairman, Gilbert Trigano, in his speech to shareholders at the annual general meeting in April 1992. He admitted his own mistake in thinking that he could bring together two airline companies Club Med had been hoping to work with. He sought by his openness to encourage others to take risks, to innovate and to learn from their experience.

Managers at 3M describe the change in the approach of management as the single most important factor in the implementation of TQ. Cesare Bruschini, TQ manager for 3M Europe, says:

> Managers must grow into leaders if the full potential of the organisation is to be realised. We have recently had one general manager who has shifted his style to being much more supportive of subordinates as a result of visiting some of the Baldrige finalists in the USA and some internal coaching.

In his book *The Fifth Discipline – The Art And Practice Of The Learning Organisation* Peter Senge argues that a shared vision is a necessary part of a learning organisation and that this vision should not be imposed, as it often has been. Imposition leads at best to compliance, not commitment, and will discourage people from learning. Charismatic leadership by a very strong individual can therefore be counterproductive; a less dramatic and less personality based leadership is needed.

INVOLVING PEOPLE IN DECIDING HOW TO CHANGE

To own the process of change employees must be involved in designing it; they feel responsible because they have shaped the changes which are happening.

The most dramatic example of this was in Nissan Motors UK. Nissan Japan had decided, following its experience three years earlier of starting a plant in Tennessee, USA, that this time it would be a local team building a local organisation. Despite the lead of the Japanese car maker, it concluded that only a British team with full responsibility could get the best from the local conditions. The company questioned many things the British team took for granted; it challenged at length and in remorseless detail; but it did not dictate. Some things were non-negotiable, like the quality standards mentioned earlier, but the rest was for the British team to decide.

The result was a remarkably consistent and powerful sense of ownership among the British team in NMUK. They know the company created is their achievement.

When Club Med decided to focus on improving quality in 1985 it set up a team of six key managers, taken from line jobs, to develop the way forward. This core team was small enough to act quickly and was supplemented by each member involving a network of 15 other people in the process.

OPERATIONALLY CREDIBLE LEADERSHIP

The other characteristic of leadership observed was that it is technically credible, able to understand the detail of process, to question, to challenge and to support improvement in how the work is actually done.

In Grundfos the leaders described in the case study are all capable engineers in addition to their other qualities and experiences. Finn Moller, quality director, had 20 years' experience, before joining the company, of introducing quality in ITT, Denmark, and in Bang & Olufsen. The other directors had grown up with the company, working in it since at least their 20s.

The leading figures in Nissan Motors UK had all spent over 15 years working in the car industry. The managing director is a physics graduate with long experience, before coming to NMUK, of managing operations in Ford.

The general manager of ICL Product Distribution joined the company from school and, although he did an MBA in his twenties, had worked his way up from junior positions in the same division.

Club Med managers have all been promoted through the ranks. They feel it is impossible to run a village without having worked as a staff member (a *gentil organisateur*). Even head office staff are mainly ex-village employees. There is, however, little chance of stagnation as no one stays in the same function or service for more than five years.

Why is such operational and technical grounding important? There appear to be two reasons.

First, managers with this background have the self-confidence to press ahead with change in key operational areas and to challenge existing ways of doing things. They are not relying on the technical judgements of others. They can call on their own sense and intuition of what will work to support them through the critical early days of change when many around them are likely to be sceptical or outrightly hostile.

Second, such managers carry greater weight with the key operational managers and staff who must be convinced to change. The leaders are not peddling theories out of a textbook but understand their subject. Part logically, part intuitively, their subordinates trust them more than they would a manager without the same operational understanding.

POWERFUL REASONS FOR CHANGE

In what circumstances does this forthright but not aggressive leadership exist? In each of the case study companies there was a sense that the status quo was unacceptable combined with a strong vision of how things should be organised. These were personal views and feelings; the starting point for change was individuals personally committed to change.

For the start-up team at NMUK the individual motivation was nothing less than the desire to show that Britons could run a world class car company. Each had worked in the UK car industry in the 1960s and 1970s and had been sickened and frustrated by the poor quality, inadequate management and appalling labour relations of those days.

In the case of Grundfos the transformation required was less extensive. Nevertheless Finn Moller, the quality director, came to the company in 1980 with a strong sense that it could not maintain its quality reputation by its ad hoc approach in the factory and by using inspection. From his experience at ITT and Bang & Olufsen he had a clear vision of how it should be done.

In ICL Product Distribution the need for drastic change was all too apparent when David Palk became general manager of part of the unit in 1988. What had been missing up till then was someone with the courage to drive through the process of change and the clear sense of what the business could be like if customers were given priority. These Palk and his team provided.

A sense of crisis can be created or used by leaders to motivate change but it is not the only way to do so. The previous management in ICL Product Distribution had avoided coming to terms with the crisis that was all around them. On his arrival David Palk brought people hard up against the crisis they were facing. On the other hand, the change seen in NMUK and Grundfos built on previous success.

Where a sense of crisis is used to induce change it needs to be allied with the vision of how things could be better organised and a conviction that the alternative vision is attainable. The job of the leader is to point the way out of the crisis.

Andrew Campbell, author of *Sense Of Mission*, distinguishes between mission (which he defines as timeless and a function of a company's purpose, strategy, values and standards of behaviour) and vision (which he sees as the hoped for outcome of a particular process of change). The processes of change described here started with a vision of how things should be organised. A sense of mission takes longer to develop and emerges as the result of applying together the guidelines for change (forthright, listening leadership, involving people early, integrating quality and learning by doing) which are described in this report.

THE PERSONAL CONFIDENCE TO LEAD

A powerful reason for change was not all that was observed in the most successful case study companies. The other requirement for effective implementation of Total Quality is the personal confidence not to insist on getting your own way all the time; the ability to identify the objectives that are non-negotiable while allowing those who will have to implement them and who are closer to the work to define how the objectives will be reached. The ability to listen, to learn from others, to admit to ignorance and to error: this is the self-confidence that was seen in Grundfos, NMUK and Club Med.

PICK A THEME AND STICK TO IT

What is required first from the leaders of a change process is that they should pick a theme, a focus for change. What was seen most often in companies whose change processes were not leading to results was a lack of focus, a sense among staff that they were receiving mixed messages from management and did not know what was really expected of them.

The characteristics of an effective theme

The research identified five elements.

Business fit. Chapter 6 discusses the need to integrate quality into the objectives and strategy of the business.

Simple and easy to communicate. This is obvious, perhaps, but often forgotten. Some management teams love to overcomplicate things. The theme must be one that will be interpreted consistently at all levels in the organisation and not be muddled in the passing of the message from one person to another.

Strike a chord with staff. There is a tendency among companies to adopt "me too" visions and aims. The theme should not be one of these. It should be relevant and credible to the company and its staff, given the industry it is in and its history. It should be one that offers meaning to employees, that will help them take pride in their work and the company.

Easily translated into action. The theme should be one that staff can put into action, which they can readily see will make a difference to behaviour.

Lived by management. Finally, and most difficult, the theme must be lived by management. They must show by their behaviour that they are serious and they must be seen to be demonstrating the theme. They should consider what symbols are effective in their culture and use them shamelessly to communicate the message. They should demonstrate the theme in action by the decisions they take, not just talk about it.

A good example of such a theme is the work of the management team at ICL Product Distribution. Here the theme has never been summed up in a single slogan but it has been lived since David Palk and his team took control. The implicit theme of "Action now to serve the customer" is highly appropriate to a distribution operation; it is simple and generally understood; it makes sense to the people working in the division; and it leads straightaway to action.

Federal Express's advertising slogan "Absolutely, positively, overnight" communicates to all staff the primary purpose and success criterion of the business. Other punchy sayings such as "The sun does not set on an enquiry to Federal Express" reinforce the desire to provide customer service.

Find your own name for the change process: do not call it total quality

What about the use of Total Quality as the theme for change? Following the research we advise strongly against it. Total Quality is not a simple, easy to communicate message, it does not translate readily into action and it is unlikely to strike a chord with staff. The Total Quality principles are too broad to provide an effective focus; they need to be internalised, translated into themes specific to each organisation in the way suggested in Chapter 5.

Thus, paradoxically, the less a company uses the phrase "Total Quality", the more likely it is to be applying the TQ principles.

"Quality" alone may be an effective theme, provided managers define it carefully in terms relevant to their company.

- Milliken & Co calls its continuous improvement effort the "Pursuit of Excellence". Susan Cottrell, director, says: "We do not use the word 'quality' because we feel it would be confused with quality assurance."
- Xerox calls its initiative "Business Excellence".
- International Distillers Vintners, the division of Grand Metropolitan with leading drinks brands in Europe and North America, decided in 1989 to avoid the term "quality". Peter Cox, technical services director of IDV Europe, recalls:

  Even that word was interpreted differently by different managers. After much consideration we decided that "Closer To My Customer" was the phrase that in our organisation best expressed what we are trying to achieve.

- Kate McCormick of the Wellcome Foundation similarly advises against calling an initiative "Total Quality". Companies should instead "find the title that relates to the business purpose it will fulfil in your organisation".
- Barry Morgans of IBM says:

  It's important to get the language right if you are going to embed quality in the business. We now talk about "Market Driven Quality" because that is the key reason that we're doing it and those are the words that have worked with our managers.

Setting a quality example

Top managers need to be aware of the messages their actions and behaviour are sending to staff. Often the signal that is sent about what is regarded as important depends on their use of time.

Rarely in the companies observed is it a matter of heroic gestures; much more often it is consistent support and use of time which has impressed employees. Examples from the case study companies are as follows.

- David Palk, in his early days as general manager of ICL's literature and software operation, demonstrating his commitment to securing excellent service for customers by sitting down with his team every day at 4 pm to review action on each customer order.
- Jorgen Madsen, chief executive of Grundfos, showing his commitment to quality and to listening to, and learning from, staff by devoting 30 days a year to participating in management workshops reviewing the implementation of the company's philosophy.
- The top managers at Nissan Motors UK showing their belief in learning and approachability by sharing open plan offices and wearing the common blue uniforms.

PERSISTENCE AND CONSISTENCY

The leadership observed in the most successful TQ companies is a prosaic one. It does not depend on charisma or personality but derives its strength from persistently emphasising over an extended period the same key objectives and giving subordinates practical support to achieve them. In the case study companies the virtue staff most often praise is consistency; this is what convinces them that management is serious and motivates them to fight for quality.

SUMMARY

1. The leadership required for TQ is forthright and listening, willing to take risks and very assertive about standards and objectives, but responsive to the views of others on how change should occur.
2. TQ leaders need to be operationally credible.
3. They must have powerful personal reasons to force change and the personal confidence and insight to know what is non-negotiable and what is not.
4. Find a theme for change which fits the business strategy, is simple, strikes a chord with staff and can be readily translated into action. Total Quality is not the right name for change; find the label that suits your own organisation and objectives.
5. TQ leaders should be persistent and consistent.

CASE STUDY

GRUNDFOS: WORLD CLASS QUALITY

Grundfos is a remarkable company. Starting from a small town in rural Denmark in 1945, it has used a Japanese type of approach to win world leadership in a specific market: clean water pumps. It now sells half of all the domestic circulators sold in the world and has a leading position in commercial and industrial water pumps. It employs 7,500 people in 27 countries and is the acknowledged quality leader in its markets.

The company has the feel of an organisation where the motto is "if something is worth doing, it is worth doing well". From the outstanding leisure centre for employees to the large and comfortable guest house for customers and suppliers; from the light and spacious colour matched offices to the courtesy and efficiency of reception; from the remarkable educational provision for shopfloor workers to the strength of the relationship with suppliers; from the award of "Best Supplier" by Bosch in Germany to the winning of the title of "Best Employer" from Denmark's largest union for blue collar workers: this is a company which strives for quality in everything it does.

Grundfos products have a reputation for reliability and durability and for being consistently innovative. Grundfos pioneered the use of expensive but corrosion resistant stainless steel in pumps and the building of modular units to provide flexibility and quick delivery. Many customers pay a price premium for its products.

Costs are carefully controlled. In the main factory in Denmark the value of scrap has been reduced to an impressive 0.6 per cent of the cost of raw materials and labour.

Yet the company has never had a Total Quality Programme. It has little time for consultants and is wary of the quality gurus. There has been little emphasis on formal process improvement in areas other than production. The company has drawn consciously on the TQ principles and is in fact applying most of them but the process it uses to do so is entirely home grown.

So how has the company achieved success? What has enabled a small Danish company to turn itself into a world leader in quality? The answer is in three parts.

- The company has had a series of forthright leaders, people willing to go out on a limb for the things they believed in. Their style has not been macho or aggressive. They have listened but they have also made clear that there are objectives and principles they are not prepared to compromise.
- Quality, defined as superior products which meet and anticipate customer needs, has been part of the business strategy from the first. If the product is not more reliable, more innovative and more appropriate for the customer's needs than those of the competition, then it is not something Grundfos should put its name to.
- The company has gone a long way towards creating a learning organisation. There is a passionate belief in the appetite and ability of individuals to learn. Standards and approved behaviours reinforce this and training and development are widely available and taken up.

GRUNDFOS'S PURPOSE

From the earliest days the company's founder, Poul Due Jensen, decided to plough most of the profits back into investment, rather than take them out for use by him and his family. In 1975, shortly before he died, this situation was formalised. The Poul Due Jensen Foundation was set up and is now the only shareholder in Grundfos Holding AG.

The aim of the foundation is as follows:

To consolidate and expand the economic basis of the continued existence and development of the Grundfos Group. The capital and the profits of the foundation are to be used solely for the aim of the foundation, that is the profits are to be reinvested in the Grundfos companies.

World leadership in the chosen market is the driving objective and that implies continuous growth and improvement. Virtually all profits are reinvested in the business. Effectively there are no other shareholders to satisfy and so the purpose of the company is to realise the potential of all those working within it. Indeed in a sense the company is its employees.

GRUNDFOS PROFILE

With annual production of 7 mn pump units, Grundfos is one of the world's leading pump manufacturers. Circulators, submersible and deep well turbine and centrifugal pumps are made for domestic, commercial, industrial, land drainage, water supply and environmental applications.

Grundfos's production is vertically integrated. It manufactures the electric motors for its pumps (and sells many motors to other companies), makes and develops its own materials and produces electronic control systems. It develops its own process technology and makes its own advanced production equipment.

Trading results for the last five years are shown in Table 8.1.

Table 8.1 Grundfos: key figures, 1987/88–1991/92

(Dkr mn; approx 6.4 Dkr 1US$)	87/88	88/89	89/90	90/91	91/92
Turnover	2,665	3,182	3,380	3,995	4,537
Trading profit	259	355	404	504	634
% of turnover	9.7	11.2	12.0	12.6	14
Profit before tax	188	309	352	435	476
% of turnover	7.1	9.7	10.4	10.9	10.5
Consolidated equity capital	1,058	1,247	1,334	1,612	1,906
Return on equity capital (%)	11.5	13.5	17.5	19.6	16.9
Total assets	3,695	3,922	4,135	4,887	5,315
Employees (no.)	5,794	5,906	6,616	7,179	7,514

FORTHRIGHT, LISTENING LEADERSHIP

Grundfos has had a succession of strong leaders. Four are particularly relevant to the story of quality in Grundfos: Poul Due Jensen, the founder of the firm, and his son Niels, the current president; Jorgen Madsen, employed as an industrial engineer in 1963 and vice group president since 1986; and Finn Moller, appointed quality manager in 1980 and quality director since 1989.

Serving customers at the heart of the founder's mission

Poul Due Jensen was a combination of intensely practical engineer and business visionary. He was absorbed by the detail of how to design and produce a better pump. He determined to use stainless steel at a time when other companies thought it far too expensive a material. He designed unique equipment for manufacture of the pumps. Engineering excellence was for him an article of faith.

However, he also developed a highly distinctive and surprisingly comprehensive mission for the business. The approach is not unlike that of some famous Japanese companies. Grundfos aims at world leadership in a very specific market: clean water pumps. The implicit purpose of the company is nothing less than serving mankind by realising to the full its potential capability in pump knowhow and service. The objective is in the best sense self-serving: to strive for perfection and make the most of the skills and resources the company has.

The values which Poul Due Jensen built into the fabric of Grundfos support this purpose. They are simple but powerful – values which many companies talk about – but Grundfos has managed to make them real and thereby to provide a solid foundation for quality. People at all levels in Grundfos say: "Quality is lived, not just talked about, by the managers here."

Serving customers – interpreted as providing pumps which are the most reliable, state of the art, most appropriate for the customer's purpose – is a core value. Reinforcing this is a belief in engineering excellence, both of product and of process, and a desire to exploit the latest technology. Also central is the commitment to learning (see below).

The vice group president, Jorgen Madsen, stresses communication as a value of the company from its earliest days:

The key is to keep people as informed as possible. People want to do things right. It's up to management to give them the chance to do so.

Belief in teamwork is very visible. The words family and partners are often used. As one MD of a sales company comments: "You feel part of a family in Grundfos. Anyone who needs help gets it." Knud Madsen, the purchasing director, adds: "We have very few kings or departmental barons. If people don't like being part of the family, they leave."

In the words of another manager:

Grundfos is very special. We have to have rules but what is really important is the attitudes. We have created Grundfos attitudes throughout the organisation.

These attitudes are reinforced by the current leadership. Niels Due Jensen, president of the company, is seen by staff as being "a development engineer first" and someone with a "passion" for the contribution Grundfos pumps can make to the welfare of people around the world. Given the importance of supplies of clean water and the priority of environmental issues, such ethical concerns seem to resonate with employees and are an important motivator.

Fearless introduction of self-managed quality in production

Finn Moller, the quality director, has also displayed forthright leadership. An electrician and electrical engineer, Finn joined Grundfos in 1981 with experience of implementing quality in ITT, Denmark, and in Bang & Olufsen. He saw that Grundfos had the foundation for quality assurance but was not doing it. His appointment came at a time of rising management concern about whether Grundfos could hold on to its reputation for quality. Increasing complaints from the assembly and production plants abroad were frightening management, factory scrap at 7 per cent of raw material and labour costs was viewed as much too high and procedures in the factory were lacking or ignored. In the words of one manager: "We were just a big blacksmith," with different procedures and approaches, depending on who was doing the work. "The aim of producing quality was always there, but we didn't know how to achieve it."

Top management and Finn Moller set about a process of change which continues to this day and which at times involved him in high personal risk. First he raised awareness and understanding of quality throughout the company. He obtained agreement from managers that a quality policy was needed but refused to write it himself. An MD from one of the sales companies was responsible for compiling it and getting consensus among all the MDs of group companies, with Finn providing only two pages of handwritten suggestions. Finn visited all the production plants abroad and drew them into the discussion about quality. Back in Denmark he highlighted the scale of the problem by setting up an inspection team of 50 of the most experienced production workers who red tagged all the (many) raw materials and items of work in progress which did not meet the specifications. Sign-off systems were set up so that exceptions to specifications were made explicitly.

Next it was insisted that drawings of parts must be followed to the letter or changed. Project teams were established to review all drawings and specifications and ensure that they were up to date and correct. Teams also looked at the capability of processes to check that specifications were realistic.

Initially production and volumes fell as people adjusted from the informal to the systematic approach to quality. But management did not waver in its support for the changes. The quality department had the authority to stop sub-standard production and to refuse new products which were not ready for consistent quality production. People had to fall in line and began to see why the changes were needed.

With quality assurance in place, the evolution process could move to the next stage: the self-management of quality. The move was carefully prepared; every operator received two sessions of training, each two weeks long. Blue tables (blue is the Grundfos company colour) were set up around the factory solely for operators' use in measurement and quality control and much new measurement equipment was purchased. Then, operation by operation, the factory switched to workers controlling their own quality and external inspection was stopped (except for minimal tests at the end of the line). Again there were teething troubles and many worried faces. Finn recalls:

One MD in an assembly plant abroad protested to me about the end of inspection. I said no, we haven't stopped inspection; we've moved from 50 to 2,000 inspectors.

It was a nerve racking time. "The most important thing is that top management showed confidence in me," says Finn. With self-control of quality in place, the company realised that it had changed attitudes. There had been a powerful positive signal to employees. "We had shown our confidence in them," recalls Finn. Once the process began to work in some areas, others were convinced. "Your ears will doubt but your eyes will believe," says Finn, quoting an old Danish proverb.

Now quality managed by the employees themselves is second nature. Shopfloor staff demonstrate how they are responsible for setting up, producing and controlling their own areas of work. Procedures are drawn up, and so owned, by them. As one worker describes it: "It's very simple; you decide what you want to do, write it down and then do it." Another compared work at Grundfos with his previous job in a major German car company:

> Here every person really is responsible for quality. Operators are trained to read drawings, check components and use measuring equipment.

The plant in Denmark has been certified to the ISO 9000 series of standards with the work done by operators and not imposed by outsiders. "We built up the quality manual for each area and this gave everyone a lift."

The latest change has been in product development. This time there was a false start. The first attempt to make the process systematic failed because the quality engineer could not establish the necessary rapport with the development teams. Finn had to go back and try again. This time the procedures took root. Nine engineers now work with the development teams helping them to build in quality from the start of a new product.

Focus on people and results

Jorgen Madsen took over as managing director of Grundfos A/S in 1987. He has reinforced original values and beliefs – particularly the need for teamwork – and brought in a new emphasis on results and profits.

He is not shy about managing by values. He spends an average of 30 days a year sitting in seminars with all levels of managers, going through the philosophies of Grundfos including quality and discussing with them how far the company is living up to them. "It's what you believe in that matters; communicating what you care about," he says.

He has also introduced a tough new budgetary control system. Each year sales companies are expected to come up with higher sales and lower costs. Standstill is not accepted. If performance falls below objective during the year, quick remedial action must be taken. One manager recalls the effect during the Gulf crisis:

> As soon as it became apparent that the crisis would hit sales, we reduced costs. However, training and product development expenditure were not touched.

Profit is stressed (see Table 8.1) but as a means to continued growth, not as an end in itself. Throughout Madsen has quietly but consistently led on quality and backed Finn Moller whom he originally appointed. As Finn puts it: "I don't want management behind me: I want them out in front."

QUALITY INTEGRATED IN BUSINESS STRATEGY

For Grundfos quality is part of strategy; not a programme or initiative but central to its efforts to win a sustainable competitive edge.

Highly distinctive strategy

Grundfos competes not on cost but on quality, product innovation and fit with the customer's application. The company has expanded organically, avoiding the risk of acquisitions compromising quality and the company's philosophy.

The company has spurned diversification and concentrated on becoming better at serving its focused world market. As one manager describes it: "The objective is to become the IBM of the pumps business: the company you have to justify not going to."

The sales engineers play a key role. They must be able to win the trust of the customer and understand fully each application so that they can advise on the best Grundfos solution. The company sees customers as partners. "With the installers of our pumps, relationship is everything," says one company MD. "They're our friends, our business partners." Grundfos UK, for example, has since the 1970s run a "Better Business Club" which organises workshops for installers providing training information on the industry as well as on Grundfos products.

Production is vertically integrated (see above). Wherever the company identifies an opportunity to add value or increase the differentiation of its pumps by producing its own materials and components, it does so.

Since the 1960s the company has taken a world view. On average every year since then one and a half new overseas companies have been opened. Selling outside the small Danish market is handled by fully owned subsidiaries, managed by local nationals and with very close links to the local market. At the same time key product and process knowhow is kept within the plant in Denmark.

Innovation is an abiding objective. Teams in Denmark constantly scour the world for potential or competitive improvements; an important part of the role of sales company MDs is to feed in market intelligence on possible improvements.

If it is quality, invest in it

Whatever the pressures on company performance, time and expenditure devoted to quality are protected. Two examples (in addition to training and development, which are described below) are as follows.

Customer care. Management invests substantial time and money in listening and responding to customers. The work starts with top management. Every key customer is visited at least once a year by a member of the senior management group. 28,000 customers visit the Grundfos HQ in Denmark each year and 3,000 of these stay at the elegant company guest house.

The company operates a no quibble return policy for its customers; if customers are not happy with their pump they can return it and get a replacement without any questions asked. One MD comments:

> In our experience there's nothing wrong in fact with 50 per cent of the returned pumps. However, the guarantee is an important expression of our desire to get it right for the customer.

Quality control and measurement. The company has invested heavily in state of the art measuring equipment. The attitude of staff is: "We can get anything if it's for quality." Sophisticated statistical control techniques are not extensively used; it is simple tools and techniques that staff value.

Supplier partnerships supporting quality

The company sees partnerships with suppliers as an essential contributor to quality. It has a policy of very few (but not sole) suppliers of materials and components. With each supplier it draws up a "framework agreement" which sets out the main terms and number of units required for the coming year. The company also seeks personal relationships with suppliers and invests time and hospitality in an effort to develop the necessary closeness. As the purchasing director describes it: "The moral agreement with suppliers is more important than the legal one."

Detailed requirements for suppliers are spelt out and the top managers of supplier companies invited to regular seminars. "We do very little checking of incoming supplies," says the purchasing director. Instead the company seeks to work with the suppliers to improve their quality. The result is that rejections of supplier materials have fallen to 0.5 per cent.

A LEARNING ORGANISATION

At Grundfos there is a strong sense of the pride which employees at all levels take in the company. As one operator puts it: "The salaries are only average; everything else is fabulous." Another says:

> People are proud to be here. We're proud to tell our friends and neighbours that we work for Grundfos. We have high quality, well thought of products. It's a pleasure to go and sell them.

How has the company achieved such pride? Because it helps its people to learn, to develop and to grow as individuals.

Learning as a value

The standards and approved behaviour of Grundfos support learning. One manager says:

We're very open; we talk about everything. If you make a mistake, colleagues and management are supportive. We discuss what the problem is, not the people. We go for the ball, not the player.

A factory manager adds: "We tell people: if you have a good idea, go for it; if it goes wrong, there will be a hand of support and help." Comments quality director Finn Moller: "The first thing if you do make an error is to tell everyone so that it can be corrected. Honest and open mistakes are not penalised."

Complementing this is a passion for training and development. In Grundfos these are not subject to cost/benefit analysis. "If you want to learn something, the company will help you learn," is what staff say.

Commitment to training and development

Shopfloor workers receive most training, more than either managers or administrative staff. The training starts as soon as people join the company with an overview of quality lasting four days. Quality comes first. "When we employ new people, we train them to make one good product first and then we go for volume."

There are six levels of operator skill and the aim is to move individuals through all levels over six years. A training package goes with each grade involving about 30 days' training. Thus over six years an operator may have 150 days of training.

Education extends to subjects not directly linked to job skills. Operators study areas such as leadership and communication skills. "Nobody is forced to go on courses," comments one operator, "but only 50 out of 3,500 people here have not volunteered to attend." Learning outside work is encouraged. A superbly equipped centre allows individuals to learn a wide range of subjects from pottery and motor mechanics to woodwork and sports.

Feedback from training courses is carefully monitored to improve the quality of succeeding events.

Everyone has a personal development plan. The discussion between manager and individual is held six months before the time for salary review. Individuals propose their own objectives for the coming year. "They are often tougher than their managers would be," comments the group personnel manager. There is no rating; instead the output is a carefully designed plan for the individual which emphasises training and education. "I feel I can go for it in working for Grundfos", says one production worker. "When I got frustrated with my job, I was quickly offered another one." Or another: "I have learnt in a positive way that I am not as good as I thought I was and how to re-educate myself." "They try to make the workers grow and get involved."

For all employees an average of 4 per cent of working time is devoted to training.

A management style that encourages learning

Top management stress their objective of providing "open and visible management". People at all levels in the organisation confirm that it does exist.

One middle manager says: "Top managers do listen." He describes an incident when the system for notifying production dates to service personnel was not working well because different departments were using different definitions. The issue was raised with senior management and quickly resolved. A standardised approach across departments is now in place.

Shopfloor workers describe management as "very approachable". "Grundfos is good at giving and receiving feedback," says one operator. "Good ideas are easy to implement."

The ethos of good two way communication is supported by simple systems and procedures. Once a week teams come together formally to go through quality issues and the state of the business. Newsletters appear weekly and monthly and management brief staff on financial performance three times a year. The company is driving towards a flatter organisation structure. "Currently there are two levels between the factory manager and shopfloor workers", says Jorgen Madsen. "We are aiming to reduce that to one level."

Management has demonstrated that it will respond to criticisms from staff. A 1987 employee survey identified employee concerns about lack of challenge in the job and not enough influence on how the work was done; irrelevant training courses and too little job rotation; and tensions between management in different departments. By 1991 many of these points had been tackled. The overall satisfaction rating by employees increased from 84 to 95 per cent.

Respect for employees

Mention has been made already of the stylish recreation and educational centre which is heavily used by staff and their families. Since 1986/87 everyone who meets certain seniority and skill criteria has been able to move to monthly paid status and terms and conditions. The company promises job security. There are close and friendly company/union relations.

THE NEXT STAGE OF QUALITY

Grundfos recognises that much remains to be done on the never ending journey towards quality. Externally it sees faster product development, more emphasis on customers rather than products and still lower defect rates as priorities. Internally it wants to foster more teamwork between departments, reduce absenteeism (still 4.8 per cent), reduce the sense of hierarchy and encourage risk taking. In a sense, 47 years after the founder put quality at the centre of his philosophy and 11 years after the beginnings of Total Quality, the company is just starting.

However, its prospects of moving to the next stage of quality work are greatly strengthened by the values and attitudes foundation the company is building on. What is most impressive is the reserve of commitment, talent and knowhow at middle and junior levels that remains to be released.

What has Grundfos learnt after all these years of work on quality? Jorgen Madsen says he is often asked how to introduce Total Quality:

I can't give one simple answer. It's a process. Be involved, be there. You have to do the lot. You can't improve profits without improving relationships with people. If you want to be a leader, you must do the lot.

GRUNDFOS'S MANAGEMENT PHILOSOPHY

Management consists of a number of functions which can be learned if the people themselves are interested in learning and developing. The following basic management attitudes are targeted.

1. Employees are motivated by goal direction and less by detailed instruction.
2. The employee's commitment and feeling of responsibility is increased when given more responsibility and competence.
3. The employee has a need to see him or herself in relation to the totality and he has a right to know the relationship between overall goals and his own functions.
4. Employees are interested in learning and developing when confronted with tasks that make heavy demands and when they have feedback on the result.
5. Employees commit themselves actively as they have an influence on conditions and decisions which affect their own working conditions.
6. Employees are interested in new fields of activity.

CASE STUDY

ICL PRODUCT DISTRIBUTION: A TRANSFORMATION OF CUSTOMER SERVICE

ICL was formed in 1968 by merging the UK's leading indigenous computer suppliers, English Electric and ICT. Brought together by the government, it enjoyed protected markets in its early years. However, shielded from the full effects of international competition it acquired a reputation for low quality products and poor service, which put the company in a poor position to survive the combined effects of the 1981 recession and the Thatcher government's increasing moves towards privatisation and deregulation. One manager recalls a remark by a pharmaceuticals customer: "If our products were as unreliable as yours, half our customers would be dead by now."

The government acknowledged its responsibility to the company by providing an exceptional £200 mn rescue package in 1981, but the intense pressures to achieve market share in the fiercely competitive European computer market led to the company's acquisition in 1984 by STC, the UK electrical and electronics group.

In 1990 STC sold 80 per cent of ICL to Fujitsu of Japan, the world's second largest computer company, and in 1991 ICL merged with Nokia Data to create a company with 27,000 employees, operating in 70 countries. With manufacturing and development centres throughout Europe and the USA, ICL now specialises in the provision of integrated business solutions, such as retail information systems (of which it is the world's third largest supplier), and retains a dominant position in the UK government and local authority markets.

Although the frequent changes of ownership would appear to indicate a company continually on the brink of disaster, in fact ICL has provided one of the most striking examples of European turnround in the 1980s.

In 1990 ICL was the only one of Europe's four remaining full-line computer manufacturers to make a significant profit (see Figure 8.1). It has cut costs and moved towards open systems and computer services earlier than other manufacturers.

Figure 8.1   Europe's full-line computer makers

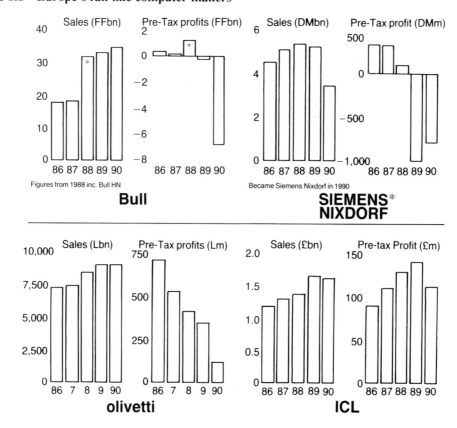

Fujitsu, although it owns 80 per cent of the shares, is more of a powerful partner than an autocratic owner. The *Financial Times* remarked in January 1992: "In contrast to earlier fears, Fujitsu's management style at ICL has proved light to the point of invisibility."

In fact the Japanese company has announced its intention of floating ICL's shares on the London Stock Exchange and says it wants to continue to manage ICL as an arm's length subsidiary.

A quality led recovery

Part of this remarkable business recovery has been ICL's conversion to the principles of Total Quality. Starting in 1985, the chief executive, Peter Bonfield, has personally spearheaded a company-wide drive which has drawn heavily on the approach of Crosby Associates but has also received praise from Dr Deming.

In order to discover exactly what this meant in practice, the researchers focused on a specific business unit: Product Distribution in Stevenage. This unit is responsible for the storage and distribution of hardware, software and literature around the world. Employing 310 people and handling over 2 mn items per year, the division has four sections.

- A literature and software operation (LSO).
- A retail logistics centre (RLC) which provides supply and installation of systems to major retail customers such as Sainsbury and Whitbread.
- An integrated supply unit (ISU) for accelerated supply of personal computers.
- A product distribution centre (PDC) distributing mainframe systems.

Subsidiary activities include purchasing, provisioning, new product management, customer services liaison and process development.

THE PROBLEM

In 1988 the literature and software operation (LSO) had a very poor service record, with a six month backlog of work. Says David Palk, general manager:

> *The unit was about to die. More experienced managers had turned down my job because they thought it was too big a risk. We either turned the unit round or it would close.*

The unit was in a muddle. Different departments didn't talk to each other. Systems were outdated. There was such a big backlog of material that a number of off-site warehouses were needed to store it. People didn't care; there was a happy country club atmosphere. There were lots of strategy plans but no action to sort things out for customers.

Palk's responsibilities were extended to include the main distribution unit (PDC) in 1990, and the retail operation (RLC) together with the newly established fast service unit for PCs (ISU) in 1991. In each case the problems were similar, although on a smaller scale than those of LSO. In PDC delivery reliability was poor and staff demoralised by the failure of an expensive new automated warehouse. In RLC service was inconsistent and costs far too high.

THE ACHIEVEMENTS

The achievements of Palk and his team can be summarised under the following headings.

- Improved service to customers.
- Reduced costs.
- Increased flexibility.

Improved customer service

Product Distribution measures its delivery performance against the complete orders delivered as requested on the dates promised to customers. It now regularly achieves 100 per cent or near 100 per cent performance. The change in LSO has been the greatest. From a 27 per cent delivery record in 1988, the unit now reports very nearly 100 per cent. The other units achieve between 97 and 99.7 per cent performance. A manager in LSO quotes an example of a recent distribution: "Out of 44,000 items, two were returned with an incorrect address."

The company keeps innovating in the interests of customer service. Customers are now telephoned before deliveries are made to check that delivery times and address details are exactly right. In the retail centre a system has been set up to ring a sample of customers the day after an installation to check that the customer is entirely happy. The unit is working hard to deal with the pressures of quarter and year ends when many customer deliveries are concentrated. As one manager comments:

> We take it for granted now that service to the customer comes first. The challenge is to keep the focus going and keep reinforcing the message.

It is not just the managers who care. There is now a passionate and generally held commitment to customer service. One worker in the retail unit says: "We would now never send something out with something missing." "We know the pressures to get material out of the door but getting it right comes first," comments another. A manager with the PC unit says:

> The customer is always right – even when it is the customer's fault that something has gone wrong and it costs us money to remedy the error.

Or an installer with the retail business:

> However late it is (they usually work out of shopping hours – weekends or overnight), you just don't leave the job until it's done.

A manager comments:

> We're used to working for the most demanding customers – Sainsbury's (the leading UK supermarket chain), for example. Working for them helps raise the standards for everyone else.

The accent is on action now to serve customers. Numbers of staff comment that if they have an improvement idea they do not take it to a process improvement team. They talk to their manager and, if the suggestion is a good one, something gets done right away. Within work teams there is a strong sense of energy and commitment. The researchers got the impression that individuals feel personally responsible for quality. People at all levels say that the "ICL culture is to underpromise and overdeliver".

Reduced costs

Everyone understands that competitor costs are falling rapidly and that ICL will not be able to provide them with jobs unless the company's costs come down at least as fast. Again the LSO example is most striking. Productivity there has risen three and a half times (£19 mn worth of items are now handled by 88 people compared with £12 mn worth of goods distributed by 193 people in 1988).

Overheads have been cut even more sharply than people costs; for example, operations which were handled on three sites are now concentrated on one. Small items are tackled alongside the big ones. One manager comments:

> There is a passion to tackle detailed costs. We recently took up an employee suggestion to send out some items in "Jiffy" bags rather than boxes. This protected the items better and cost less.

An order processing clerk says her section of two people now handle more orders than four people two years ago. They are more skilled and more flexible.

Increased flexibility

Examples abound of action orientation, of managers and employees "mucking in" to get things done for customers. Staff recognise (as they did not four years ago) that in a distribution business, timescales are short and the prizes go to those who act now, not those who think about the problems too much.

In the middle of the recent move of ISU, the 24 hour PC service, to the consolidated Product Distribution site, the printers ceased to work for a day. Equipment and staff were borrowed for the 24 hours until the normal printers were working again so that customer service was unaffected.

All stock data in LSO were lost once because of a system crash. Staff worked around the clock for 36 hours to recount all 100,000 items and restore the system. A later audit showed no errors in the new count.

A major brewery customer was very dissatisfied with the service it was receiving. A joint sales and marketing and installer team met the customer several times to understand his problems and act on them. The customer now feels very positive about the ICL service.

THE PROCESS

Getting it right in the Product Distribution division, as with all TQ initiatives, has taken hard work, trial and error and tenacity. The effort can, however, be grouped into three categories: leadership; creating supplier partnerships; and working with consultants.

Leadership

The key success factor in achieving these results is the quality of the management team. David Palk and his operational managers are all bright graduates, competitive and high achievers. Their average age is 30. They work long hours and their central objective is to improve the value of their service to customers.

David Palk made clear to everyone as soon as he arrived as general manager of LSO that there was just one thing that mattered to him: getting products to the customer on time. Every day at 4 pm he sat down with his team of 20 managers and supervisors and went through every single part number, asking if deliveries were on time and if not what was being done to remedy the position.

Because he had worked through more junior roles, including a post in LSO, he did not hesitate to challenge, to examine the detail, to seek to find root causes. He adopted a zero defects mentality; nothing less than 100 per cent performance was acceptable. Soon people got the message that they had better do their utmost to get things to customers or they would be embarrassed in front of their peers and superiors.

Everything is focused on the customer; it's as simple as that. We only do what the customer wants; the rest is a waste of time. I will happily get people out of quality meetings in order to get things done for the customer.

In their first year the new team had to overcome the personal problems resulting from LSO's move from Reading (west of London) to Stevenage (north of the capital). Out of 188 people only 30 transferred to the new site. Yet the performance was maintained. "People wanted to go out on a high," says Palk, "to show that they could do the job properly."

When he and his team were put in charge of the main distribution centre in Stevenage, he again had to take risks. A new and expensive automation system was not working properly and causing erratic service performance. Palk decided to scrap most of the system, "to go back to basics and allow operators to do their jobs" without being stymied by unreliable equipment.

Palk now manages the business through a weekly service review with the heads of his four units. He expects managers to compete to come in with the best service performance for the previous week. "It's amazing what a bit of competition can do. We're a participative autocracy."

The message has got through: "Managers are committed to quality," is what staff say. Individuals have a clear understanding of their work and objectives and how these serve the overall delivery performance targets. Managers are credited with listening to their own teams and responding quickly to suggestions. One office worker recalls an example:

There was an idea to move our section. We said we didn't want to move and explained how our current seating pattern enables us to answer customer calls more quickly. Our manager agreed and did as we wanted.

The results mentality is reinforced by a strong culture of control and measurement. As one manager puts it: "We're paranoic about measurement." The ones that matter, not surprisingly, are the ones that get carefully reviewed. David Palk and his team have no doubt which these are: service, quality and costs. Annual appraisals and quarterly reviews with every individual translate objectives into clear personal accountability and rewards for service achievement.

The company also benchmarks against a range of outside companies. For example, comparisons with best industry practice have led to important product and service developments: the setting up of the 24 hour PC delivery service and the selling of customised software with equipment. Study of distribution operations in other industries has helped achieve better use of automation in the plant.

Creating supplier partnerships

The new team have worked hard with suppliers outside the ICL group to improve their quality. All major suppliers have to be accredited. There is a weekly review of the quality and service of key vendors. The company has moved to single sourcing of key supplies as selected suppliers improve their quality and service to meet the demanding standards set.

In a number of cases suppliers have transformed the service they give in order to meet Product Distribution's requirements. One packaging supplier has completely changed its packaging design and presentation and invested in new plant in order to become the sole supplier of some types of packaging.

Working with consultants

The transformation in service and cost has been achieved even though the company's formal quality programmes have had limited impact. The weaknesses of the businesses the new management team inherited in 1988–91 are a comment on the inadequacies of the quality initiatives the company had experienced since 1985.

The initiatives did provide a common understanding and language of quality, but they did not change attitudes. They were not integrated into the running of the business and they did not lead to action that really helped customers. They did not take root in a way that enabled them to become a self-sustaining process of continuous improvement.

CROSBY BASED APPROACH TO QUALITY

Like so many companies ICL started with Crosby. At first this meant quality awareness and understanding training. Managers were educated, then the messages were passed down in a cascade process with each manager training his or her own team. By the time the process reach the shopfloor level training consisted of a one or two hour session each week for ten weeks.

The concepts and language of quality according to Phil Crosby became part of ICL. Quality was thought of as conformance to customer requirements. A lot of work was done on defining the requirements of both internal and external customers. The measure of progress in introducing quality was the price of non-conformance (PONC). The importance of measurement was repeatedly stressed. Quality was to be designed and managed by the people doing the work, not by inspectors.

Teams were set up to improve quality. In Product Distribution continuing process improvement teams in work areas (PITs) and corrective action teams (CATs) were brought together by management, as and when needed, to tackle specific problems. A procedure called error cause removal (ECR) was set up to deal with particular defects or errors. An employee suggestion scheme was established. "Excellence Awards" were given to recognise individual and team success and outstanding effort.

However, in David Palk's division the new management stopped meetings of some PITs and CATs. They wanted action now for the customer, not reflection on things that might get done in several months' time. With the support of senior management, desperate to sort out the mess in LSO, they concentrated on the substance of quality improvement, not the appearance.

The company won registration under BS 5750 (the UK equivalent of ISO 9001). Training was focused on quality and by 1991 each employee received an average of eight training days. Employee opinions were surveyed every year.

Posters and slogans were used in the effort to motivate staff and increase understanding of the role that everyone could play in improving quality. Measurement charts dealing with customer service levels, process improvement and personal and departmental performance were widely maintained and displayed.

The reaction to the original training was mixed. One manager says the messages were "Brilliant; I realised that quality applies to everything you do. I take it home. It drives the wife nuts." Another praises the Crosby emphasis on individual responsibility for quality: "It gave us hope that we could pick things up and solve them."

But another manager says the Crosby messages were "so obvious they were silly". An operator comments that the training she had was "childish, obvious; it didn't make a difference". Some were unhappy with the US style of the material; others were not bothered by this. The "poor quality" of the training and materials were criticised.

One manager says he saw two types of negative reaction to Crosby. "Some said they couldn't do it, it was too difficult. Others thought it didn't affect them, it was somebody else's problem."

FAILURE TO LINK TO BUSINESS PRIORITIES AND MANAGEMENT BEHAVIOUR

The more fundamental weakness of the quality work prior to 1988 was the failure to integrate it into the running of the business. Management failed to provide a focus, to link quality clearly to business priorities. As Palk puts it: "There was a danger that staff were discussing the price of coffee from the vending machines while the building was burning down."

Management behaviour did not change. "We didn't have much teamwork then," says one shopfloor worker. "If you want the shopfloor to believe the message, you must stick to your commitment," comments a manager; and the commitment of managers was only partial. They had made time and money available for the training but they had not changed the way they were running the company.

Slogans and posters had little impact on motivation. Measurement posters were not looked at. Skills training and procedures were inadequate. In an environment of constant structural and management changes, some teams which suggested improvements became demoralised because their ideas were overtaken by organisational changes.

Against this background the Crosby process failed to take root. The ECR procedure was dropped because it was thought to be bureaucratic and unhelpful. There is no formal suggestions scheme. Some improvement teams – PITs and CATs – soldier on but most have folded or become ineffective. As one operator describes it:

> We used to have meetings once a week, then once a fortnight, but then we dropped it. Meetings were pointless, just staring at each other with nothing to say.

Awards for quality seem to interest only a minority. The PONC is no longer widely used as a management tool.

WHERE NEXT?

Despite the transformation, quality in Product Distribution is, in a sense, just beginning. Seven years have passed since Total Quality was launched in ICL and four years since the step change began in the division. Yet, as local management recognises, there is still much to do. Relationships with other parts of ICL need to be strengthened so that the total service provided to the paying customer can be improved. More of the ideas and energy of middle management and manual workers need to be tapped. The results orientation needs to be balanced by more general support and concern for people. Direct employee contacts with, and understanding of, external customers need to be increased.

The division is now working through the new corporate-wide customer care initiative launched in September 1991. This aims to sharpen the focus on customers and to raise the sights: from meeting customer requirements to delighting customers. It seeks to achieve that simplest but hardest of all tasks: to enable staff to put themselves truly in the shoes of customers, to see ICL's service from their viewpoint. All employees will go through an innovative educational programme (including a video of customers giving their views of ICL) by the end of 1992; managers have been challenged to come up with action plans for the improvement of customer service appropriate to their businesses; and customer care measures have been included in systems for review and reward of managers.

9   Provoking But Not Imposing Change

> *Management of quality requires quality of management.*
>
> Dr Deming

There is a dilemma at the heart of efforts to implement Total Quality. Leaders impatient for change are likely to have difficulty "letting go": giving subordinates the space and time to take ownership of the process of change. Yet it is this transfer of ownership which is essential if a true process of continuous improvement in the interests of delighting customers is to start. TQ requires much more than the passive acceptance of employees. It demands their full blooded participation; and the release of their energy, skills and knowledge. Securing this transfer of ownership is the greatest challenge TQ leaders face.

The objective is to provoke but not to impose change. The acid test is: are people trying to change because they have been told to by management? Or are they changing because they want to?

This is particularly important for those in international companies, seeking to lead a process of change across differences in local and national cultures. Examples from the case studies emphasise the value of ensuring ownership of change is with the local management team who can choose to implement TQ in a way that fits the local culture.

One of the keys to transferring ownership is to involve managers and staff, particularly opinion formers, as early as possible. They should be drawn into understanding the challenge the organisation faces and deciding how to change.

A second theme is that leaders need to encourage the champions of quality but not impose a particular process of change. There is a trap here for many advocates of quality. They understand that TQ in time needs to be applied by everyone in an organisation and that each person must take responsibility for quality. They conclude from this that change must take place across a broad front. Everyone must march in pace together.

The evidence from the companies taking part in this study is that this view is wrong and bound to lead to frustration. It confuses ends with means, where you are trying to get to with how you get there. Change, particularly radical change, does not happen evenly across organisations. To be effective managers should work with the grain of organic, localised experimentation and development, giving support to areas where change is particularly urgent or where there is energy for change.

Top managers also need to "let go" some of the controls which they are used to and they need to delegate more.

Finally, even in the successful companies observed, a minority of people are not prepared to change. Some have to leave their jobs in order to unblock the way for others and to convince people that top management is serious about change.

INVOLVING PEOPLE IN UNDERSTANDING THE CHALLENGE

For a TQ process of change to be effective there must be a shared understanding of the business challenges the organisation faces.

Yet it is easy for senior managers to underestimate the gulf in perception and understanding between themselves and staff at all levels and assume there is shared understanding when none in fact exists. Top management will see competitor moves, customer changes or other industry trends and see the need for radical change; after months or years of looking forwards and outwards the case for change may seem overwhelming. Staff, on the other hand, may see statements of the need for change as just management assertion. They do not have access to the same information as top management nor do they have the same company-wide perspective. They may be cynical about the motives and abilities of senior management.

To develop shared understanding, top management must first be prepared to share sensitive information with staff. If employees are to feel trusted and empowered, they must have the same key information as management has, warts and all. For example, if costs are far too high to sustain a long-term competitive position, far better to share that problem with employees and seek their support than hide it and come forward later with apparently arbitrary cuts. If products and services are uncompetitive, say so. The truth will come out in time so it makes sense to win support among staff by trusting them with important information.

In Grundfos sensitive information is widely shared and employees are well informed. The group chief executive, Jorgen Madsen, devotes 30 days a year to sitting in seminars with all levels of managers sharing his views of the company's philosophy and strategy. The once a week briefings of every team include updates on the state of the business. In addition to weekly and monthly newsletters, management brief all workers formally three times a year on the financial performance of the business. A key reason for seeking to flatten the organisation structure even further (from two to one level of management between the factory manager and shopfloor workers) is to improve communications on key issues.

In ICL Product Distribution the general manager, David Palk, and his team pulled no punches in communicating the challenge that faced the company in 1988. Employees were told about the plan to move the division (only 30 out of 188 staff were to move to the new site) and that the unit "was about to die" unless it radically improved its performance. Nevertheless, service levels improved dramatically as people responded to the new leadership and the tackling of long festering problems. "People wanted to go out on a high," says David, "to show that they could do the job properly."

But what of the risk of valuable information leaking to competitors? The TQ companies trust their employees not to divulge information which would really be of value to competitors. They demonstrate commitment to their staff – by their training and development work, the benefits and facilities they provide, their employment policies – and they expect and receive commitment from their staff in return.

However, involving staff is much more than sharing sensitive information. It means organising processes in which staff explore for themselves the business challenges facing the company and allowing them to come to their own conclusions.

In Nissan Motors UK the management team collectively has spent years in Japan visiting different plants and seeing the standards and processes used by the leading car makers. The managers talked endlessly to the highly skilled production engineers who came across to the UK and still use the Japanese advisers as "walking encyclopedias" of information and ideas on best Japanese manufacturing practices. Repeatedly the British managers had to re-examine established ideas or practices, not because they were told to but because they could see the power of the alternatives they were seeing and talking about.

NMUK staff were surprised by what they saw. One manager says:

> It was not high tech as I had expected. The machines were largely the same as in British plants. The difference was all about philosophy, management, use of resources. I was dazzled by how simple the Japanese approach seemed.

Another way to involve people is by setting up benchmarking exercises (see Chapter 6). This can be particularly important where a quantum leap in performance is needed. Many companies comment on the radical challenges that have been thrown up by well designed and organised benchmarking and the galvanising effect on the managers involved in the benchmarking work. Staff see for themselves the superior processes employed by other companies and are fired up to apply the approaches in their own environments.

Involving people in understanding the business challenge may result in a more demanding assessment of those challenges than management had expected. In ICL Product Distribution staff were assigned to benchmark the PC service offerings of the company against best international practice. Managers came back not just with detailed suggestions for service improvements but a proposal for a new business unit based on 24 hour supply and customised software. The new instant service unit (ISU) was set up as a result.

To help people understand the challenge they face doubtful senior managers can be asked to participate in an improvement project on some aspect of the way in which they work. A carefully designed project will show managers the benefits of Total Quality; the time they give to the project will be a powerful signal of commitment to the rest of the organisation.

In the UK Post Office directors worked on a project to improve the effectiveness of their own management process. Forums for discussions were changed, agendas altered, the customer's perspective highlighted. The exercise showed top managers what the quality improvement process could achieve and gave them a better understanding of the challenges faced by their own managers working on Total Quality.

Both IBM and Rank Xerox comment on the change in attitudes when staff generally became aware that their once apparently invulnerable organisations faced intense competition. "We're in a sprint marathon," says Barry Morgans of IBM, "and our people know it. We have to throw away the history and work on a paradigm shift."

ENCOURAGING CHAMPIONS OF CHANGE

One of the most difficult challenges in TQ work is balancing the long-term vision with short-term action; knowing that you want everyone eventually to be involved and being realistic about who has the commitment and skill to make real progress now; keeping constantly in mind the sort of organisation you want to develop and being very practical about what you can do "on Monday morning" to move in the right direction.

If the change process is to be owned by those directly involved in implementation, top managers must foster and encourage work by their staff; only rarely should they direct, for example when core values or standards are at stake. Top managers should seek to identify the potential champions of change and then encourage and support them to do what they want to do. It is by these first participants' pioneering changes that they will learn how to bring them about. It is their early successes that will persuade other sceptics in the organisation to consider change. Much better to have real change in a few areas setting the pace for others than superficial change across the organisation that leaves even its advocates disillusioned.

In Grundfos the process of change which Finn Moller, the quality director, began in 1981 has been targeted step by step. There has been no attempt to bring everyone in at the same pace. The first stage of the process was to make quality in the factory more systematic. Then inspection was abolished and employees took on management of their own quality. Later systematic processes were introduced in product development.

In ICL Product Distribution, too, the pattern of change has been organic: change has spread from unit to unit, with the managers concerned gaining in confidence and skill as they achieved a step change in performance in one area after another. The impact of the formal quality programmes in place before the new management team began to assume control in 1988 was limited. The real change in approach and in performance happened as David Palk and his team were given responsibility successively for the four units within Product Distribution between 1988 and 1991.

TAKING ACCOUNT OF NATIONAL AND LOCAL CULTURES

The need to provoke but not impose change is at its greatest for those seeking to lead change in multinational companies across cultural differences. If staff in one region or country resist change which is imposed, how much more so will staff operating in a different language and culture.

Chapter 6 described the enabling (rather than prescriptive) role multinational corporate centres are taking in quality initiatives. The case studies provide examples of local teams taking ownership of change because they were allowed to shape the process of change.

- In Ciba-Geigy, Italy, there is a very strong sense of local responsibility for change. The Italian team was asked to participate in the international Dyestuffs Division initiative but it pre-empted this by starting its own company-wide effort and it has shaped the development of quality in the company ever since.
- In Nissan Motors UK the local team took responsibility for deciding how quality was implemented.

In contrast, in the case of Federal Express corporate management waited until too late (April 1991) to insist that change took place. Despite some changes the underlying pattern of behaviour in the UK company they had taken over remained the same. Too "softly, softly" an approach meant that quality standards and approaches which were second nature in the company's US operation were not implemented in the UK.

USA versus Europe

A number of managers in US multinationals commented on the difference in implementing TQ in Europe compared with the USA. Jim Havard of Rank Xerox says:

> There's more flag saluting in the USA. Commitment comes more slowly in Europe but is more real. You have to involve people more to get it.

"LETTING GO" CONTROLS

It is no good saying you trust people but then maintaining all the old detailed controls on spending, appointments and projects. Managers must "let go" so that staff are seen to have the authority to initiate the changes needed in their area. A common criticism of top managements was that they talked empowerment but still applied the old rules. For TQ to flourish this must change.

In ICL Product Distribution David Palk was enabled to break at least some of the corporate policies, so keen were his bosses to allow him to sort out the mess he had inherited. Quality activities which did not in fact help the customer were suspended and financial reporting reduced. "Everything is focused on the customer; it's as simple as that," says Palk.

It is not a question of abandoning controls. The successful companies studied have strong control systems. It is a matter of signalling a change of direction, of abolishing antique authority limits that require almost every decision to go to top management and of showing trust in staff.

SELECTIVE PEOPLE CHANGES

Nearly all the companies taking part in this study faced the need for a few individuals to leave in order for the change process to continue and flourish. Interestingly it was very rarely a large number or the majority. In the successful change processes most people in time became active supporters. But a few have been left behind, unable or unwilling to adapt to the new regime. Their departure became essential to the change process: they were blocking change and people would have questioned management's commitment to the process if they had not been forced out.

In NMUK three managers out of the original start-up team of 15 left within 18 months of joining. The other managers have remained together. Similarly, despite an elaborate and careful selection procedure, there are a few recruits who do not fit in. They leave within about three months. After that the workforce is extremely stable: labour turnover is 5 per cent.

SUMMARY

1. Involve people early in understanding the challenges the business faces.
2. Encourage the champions of change. Do not fool yourself that change will happen evenly across the company but support local experimentation and development.
3. Avoid excessive controls which would signal that staff were not trusted.
4. Be prepared, as the change process unfolds, to ask a few people to leave their jobs.

10 Integrating Quality Into The Business

Jorgen Madsen, group managing director of Grundfos, says he is often asked how to implement Total Quality:

I can't give one simple answer. It's a process. Be involved, be there. You have to do the lot. You can't improve profits without improving relationships with people. If you want to be a leader, you must do the lot.

Practitioners of Total Quality now see its integration into the running of businesses as the major challenge. Says Mike Grabiner, quality director of British Telecom:

In too many organisations TQ has become marginalised. We have to understand more about how to change behaviours so that TQ is integrated into the culture of companies. We also have to increase the credibility of TQ by demonstrating the results that flow from it.

Barry Morgans, quality director of IBM UK:

The need now is to embed quality in the day to day running of the business. My ultimate dream is to drop the word "quality". People would regard it simply as part of the normal way they do their jobs.

Jim Havard of Rank Xerox:

The penny has dropped in managers' minds: quality has to be linked now to business efficiency and business results.

How is this to be achieved? How can quality become part of the way businesses are run?

The lessons from the case study companies are clear. The ones which have been most successful in implementing the Total Quality principles – Nissan, Club Med and Grundfos – have woven together a pattern in which quality is part of a greater whole. What strikes the outsider when visiting them is the coherence and consistency of their approach. On the surface all is simplicity. Dig deeper and the effort and intelligence that has gone into developing these patterns is revealed. Like all good professionals, these companies have made something very difficult seem simple.

Each has found a way to quality that is distinctive and suits its history and culture. To extract any one item from the patterns and say that is the reason for quality would be misleading. The point about the successful formulae is that they are jigsaws; change any one piece and you must consider the impact on all the others. Nevertheless some common themes emerge.

- Measurement in these companies is different from the conventional UK or US company where financial measures have priority. Indicators of quality are seen by people at all levels, including senior management, as of central importance. Managers know they will be reviewed rigorously on quality as well as (not instead of) financial measures.
- The successful companies keep it simple. When they find problems with a management or people process they do not impose initiatives on top of existing systems and structures. They seek to redesign or improve their processes to align them with quality goals. They do not go around the management structures but make them work properly.
- The successful companies keep their feet on the ground and maintain a practical, action oriented approach. They do not fall into the trap of measuring improvement activities but are

concerned with outputs, quality delivered to the customer. It is fine to dream. These companies want results and they get them.

HOLISTIC APPROACH TO QUALITY

The case studies describe how Nissan, Club Med and Grundfos have an integrated approach.

- Since Nissan UK was started, the company has seen quality as dependent upon and reinforcing the other operating themes of flexibility and teamwork.
- In Club Med the passion for being "closest to the customer" goes hand in hand with the unique role of the *gentils organisateurs*, the view that the company has "members" not customers, and effective market segmentation.
- Grundfos has a highly distinctive philosophy and strategy, combining a passion for superior and innovative products, the drive for world leadership in its chosen market and a remarkable commitment to its people and their potential to learn.

NEW MEASURES

It is an old adage that what gets measured gets done. But measure what? Many companies are overburdened with measurement. New managements add variables they consider important but often neglect to remove some of the old ones. With so many indicators where are subordinates supposed to focus their attention?

The case study companies provide examples of measurement which goes beyond financial indicators but remains focused.

- In ICL Product Distribution the new management team which took over between 1988 and 1990 monitored both service reliability – the percentage of complete shipments delivered on time – and cost reduction with relentless determination.
- Managers and staff at Nissan UK know that product quality is a must; the Japanese parent will not continue to invest unless customer satisfaction with products reaches the level attained by products made in Japan.
- Club Med gives absolute priority to tracking customer satisfaction (and responding to their comments).

Measurements need to be integrated. One of the problems in many large companies is that functions have their own measurement systems so that effectively they follow functional priorities, rather than company-wide ones. IBM and Xerox both stress the importance of aligning measurement systems. "Otherwise companies have Chinese walls in their measurement systems," says Barry Morgans, "which prevent people from looking at the interests of the corporation as a whole."

Many of the companies studied are including figures for employee as well as customer satisfaction in their assessment of business performance. In Mercury Communications the results from six-monthly random surveys of employees and regular focus groups are used.

FedEx measures

Federal Express use the same eight dimensions of service quality worldwide: delivery service failure, missing or late POD, overages and shortages, abandoned calls, traces, complaints reopened, lost packages and damaged packages.

It evaluates employee performance regularly on its "employee calendars" which record any feedback, good or bad, day by day, that each person receives. The document acts as a guide to development needs and coaching during regular appraisals.

The process of working towards business results also needs to be measured. This is most clearly set out in *Kaizen*. Milestones are established for the activities required to lead towards the business result. By monitoring completion of these process steps, managers can be assured that the right efforts are being made to secure the business result, even if for reasons beyond the control of the people concerned the result itself is not achieved.

An example of a new "balanced scorecard" – allowing management, in a single report, to review progress from the perspective of shareholders, customers, innovation and learning and internal excellence – is given in Figure 10.1. Clearly each company needs its own scorecard, tailored to its own situation.

Figure 10.1 A new balanced storecard

Financial Perspective

GOALS	MEASURES
Survive	Cash flow
Succeed	Quarterly sales growth and operating income by division
Prosper	Increased market share and ROE

Customer Perspective

GOALS	MEASURES
New products	Percent of sales from new products
	Percent of sales from proprietary products
Responsive supply	On-time delivery (defined by customer)
Preferred supplier	Share of key accounts' purchases
	Ranking by key accounts
Customer partnership	Number of cooperative engineering efforts

Internal Business Perspective

GOALS	MEASURES
Technology capability	Manufacturing geometry vs. competition
Manufacturing excellence	Cycle time Unit cost Yield
Design productivity	Silicon efficiency Engineering efficiency
New product information	Actual introduction schedule vs. plan

Innovation and Learning Perspective

GOALS	MEASURES
Technology leadership	Time to develop next generation
Manufacturing learning	Process time to maturity
Product focus	Percent of products that equal 80% sales
Time to market	New product introduction vs. competition

Source: Robert S. Kaplan and David P. Hatton

ALIGNING REWARD SYSTEMS WITH THE NEW MEASURES

To be effective the new measures need to be carried through into the pay, promotion and other recognition systems which signal what the company expects from its staff. Many companies are only beginning to grapple with this issue; they say customer service or quality is a top priority but continue to reward on sales, profits or volume numbers alone.

One company which has changed its reward systems is Rank Xerox. Measurements of customer and employee satisfaction are now included – alongside return on assets and revenue growth – in the assessment of management bonuses (typically 30 per cent of base salaries). Xerox in the USA has gone one better: achievement of the improved customer satisfaction rating planned in a particular year is a "gate" or precondition to the payment of any management bonus. Failure to meet the customer satisfaction objective therefore means no management bonus at all.

Recognising excellence

Fred Smith, the founder and CEO of Federal Express, takes every opportunity to recognise commitment to quality. A driver in the UK who gave up his own time to ensure delivery of a number of parcels was surprised a few days after the event to find his wife waiting for him at the depot at the end of his shift. They were both put on a flight to the Federal Express headquarters in Memphis, Tennessee, to have lunch with Fred Smith and stay for a few days at the company's expense. It was Fred Smith's way of saying that service matters.

IBM Europe has identified four measures for assessment of managers' incentive schemes:

- customer satisfaction;
- market share;
- profitability;
- employee satisfaction.

In addition, as a pilot for the European operation as a whole, all employees in IBM UK are to receive a bonus if improved customer satisfaction ratings are achieved.

Caution from Dr Deming

Any system which links individual performance to company results will be attacked by Dr Deming. He argues that individuals will be punished or rewarded for chance variations of a process, which have nothing to do with the individual's contribution; for performance to improve it is the process as a whole that must be changed, not the work of any one individual.

KEEP IT SIMPLE

The most successful TQ companies have made the basic management structures and systems work to support quality; they have avoided the proliferation of initiatives and specialists that plagues many companies.

Take the key area of communication. The case studies describe how Nissan, Club Med, Federal Express and Grundfos have all worked hard to ensure that line managers communicate effectively with staff. They stress:

- simple informal communications (like the Nissan supervisor's morning meeting with his team);
- flat organisation structures;
- sharing of sensitive commercial information;
- giving first line managers the authority and support to enable them to be true leaders of their teams;
- listening to employees, reinforced by quick response to their comments.

There is nothing remarkable here; just the basics done very well.

It is also necessary to recognise quality efforts. The companies studied were critical of the US style hoopla and awards that accompanied many of the early Total Quality initiatives. They see them as contrary to the cultures of their countries and/or companies and therefore ineffective in motivating people to participate in quality efforts. They dislike the monetary element in awards, seeing it as divisive and likely to lead to game playing and internal politics. If there are to be awards for suggestions and outstanding contributions to quality, they would like teams to be singled out at least as much as individuals. They criticise the "horse race" aspect of awards where only one or a few can win. They prefer "marathons" in which everyone can win by reaching a given standard.

The logic of TQ runs contrary to giving special financial awards and prizes for quality work. One of the TQ assumptions is that people want to take pride in their work and do a good job. The task of top management is to liberate the natural energy and ability of staff, not to manipulate them.

IBM Europe has moved away from giving monetary rewards to individuals for quality achievement or seeking to relate rewards to the value of the project worked on. The "Chairman's Award" now goes to cross-functional teams responsible for "an outstanding piece of quality teamwork".

Milliken uses recognition and publicity to mark special contributions by employees. Photos of staff members who have made an outstanding effort adorn the walls of its plant in Wigan. An "employee of the month" has a parking place allotted to him or her (these are the only reserved spaces; there are none for senior managers or directors). One staff member who recently received the award had no car but was so proud of his achievement he parked his bicycle in the space.

Nissan Motors UK is a good example of this approach in practice. The company has no suggestion scheme but thousands of improvement ideas every year from employees; no separate quality circles but intensive work to continuously improve the quality of work done. From the start the company emphasised that continuous improvement (*Kaizen*) is part of the normal job and avoided any special incentive or reward which would have signalled that it was not.

Recognition is part, in NMUK's view, of normal good management and leadership. Extra incentives are not only not necessary; they would be counterproductive as they would run contrary to the core philosophy on which the business is run.

Jonathan Smilansky, formerly a general manager of VISA International, says:

> We learnt not to give presents for good ideas. It's the worst thing you can do. It represents putting the marketing of TQ ahead of the substance and leads to cynicism and posturing.

AVOID QUALITY DEPARTMENTS

The companies taking part in this study do not now have large quality functions. Instead they employ small numbers of managers, with line experience, to act as catalysts in helping the process of change. Their job is to encourage, to energise people in line positions, to provide ideas and expertise, always leaving the responsibility for action with divisional managers.

Joe Goasdoue, Director, Quality and Corporate Affairs of ICL, reorganised the central quality function when he joined the company from British Airways in 1988. He has reduced the number of professional staff from 20 to five. All are now experienced managers and are described as consultants, working with units that invite them in. "We achieve far more with the smaller team we now have than with the one we had five years ago," says Goasdoue.

In IBM Europe there are small quality staffs in Paris and in individual country firms. Barry Morgans, director of market driven quality, describes their role as "facilitating, cajoling, offering training, being passionate about quality". It is accepted that line managers must take responsibility for continuous improvement.

Sollac talks about the "artificial limb" of quality departments. The stronger the crutch or support from this limb, the weaker the muscle in line departments to deliver quality. Like it or not, the artificial limb needs to be thrown away before staff in the line will become skilled and confident in managing quality.

DRIVE FOR ACTION

Integration into the business also means a proper concern for action and for results. TQ is about long-term improvement but this does not mean that managers should neglect the need for short-term improvement, however small, nor fail to establish clear milestones to measure progress towards longer-term objectives. Without a drive to see tangible improvements in the quality and service delivered to customers, there is no objective test of quality efforts and no rigorous base for learning. Quality requires a long-term perspective and a concern for effective action here and now.

A good example of the drive for action is given in the case study on ICL Product Distribution. Says general manager David Palk: "We only do what the customer wants; the rest is a waste of time."

The Japanese approach of *Kaizen*, emphasising as it does small-scale, incremental improvement, places a high premium on action and experimentation. The logic is that you learn by doing. All the workshops and committees in the world are no substitute for taking action to make change, for trying to improve and then learning from what happens.

Peter Willats of the Kaizen Institute of Europe describes the approach:

> The question experienced Japanese managers ask of Western managers is: "What are you doing to improve performance?" Not: "What are you planning?" They know that in many large companies plans are political gestures. The Japanese advisers only have time for those who are genuine about seeking change.

SUMMARY

1. Work out your own way of weaving quality into the fabric of your organisation.

2. Include measures of quality and service, as seen by the customer, in the review of performance by management, starting at the top, and give them real priority.

3. Integrate performance measurement so that company priorities are followed, not just functional ones.

4. Demonstrate that the commitment to quality is genuine by including quality and service in the assessment of individual performance.

5. Keep it simple. Avoid multiple initiatives and work instead to ensure that key structures and systems are working properly.

6. Avoid US style hoopla; most European companies find it counterproductive. Find the style of reward and recognition that suits the culture of your company and country.

7. Do not have a separate quality department. Facilitators are usually needed but ensure everyone understands that the responsibility for quality rests with line departments.

8. Look for action and results; do not let them tell you TQ is only about the long term.

11   Learning By Doing

> *All the good maxims already exist in the world; we just fail to apply them.*
>
> Blaise Pascal

Chapter 3 described how one of the core TQ principles is the creation of a learning organisation. With continuous improvement goes continuous learning. Companies need to place a high value on individual and collective learning and to ensure that the development of people is an integral part of the job of management.

What have the more successful companies done to make a reality of these ideas? The answer is in three parts.

- They have sustained a major investment in training and education, whatever the pressures on sales or profits. They do so because they see investment in training and development as a precondition of business success, not out of wide eyed emotional commitment to education.
- They have organised training and education on a "just-in-time" basis, helping to provide skills and knowledge at the moment when they will be applied. They link education to the solving of real life problems and the advancement of the business. They have avoided "sheep dip" training.
- They recognise that real learning comes from experience. They have reorganised tasks and responsibilities and provided opportunities for experimentation and review so that learning takes place alongside doing. (This is another reason why the drive for action described in Chapter 10 is so important.)

SUSTAINED PRIORITY FOR TRAINING AND EDUCATION INVESTMENT

The most successful quality companies are investing in training and education at levels which many organisations would find extraordinary and they are sustaining that investment. For them it is expenditure which must be protected even in times of recession and declining profits.

In 1991 each of Nissan Motor UK's 3,000 employees received an average of 24 days' off-the-job training and manufacturing staff an additional 12 days of on-the-job training. Total training expenditure amounted to £6.5 mn. If the salaries of people being trained are included the figure rises to 14 per cent of the annual salaries bill.

Grundfos, too, demonstrates an extraordinary commitment to training and development. Over six years an operator may have 150 days of training. Education extends to subjects not directly linked to job skills. Even in the tough times expenditure on training and education is protected.

Federal Express spends $225 mn a year on training, equivalent to 3 per cent of its total costs. An interactive video network delivers job training and testing to 45,000 customer contact employees, couriers and ground operations people around the world. An electronic university network using personal computers provides college courses. A Leadership Institute grounds managers in the company's culture and philosophy. A Quality Academy helps build a common language and teaches numerous quality processes and tools. The company does not subject the training expenditure to its normal cost/benefit analysis.

Many of the front line staff in Club Med referred to the Club as a "school". As a consequence of both its formal training activities and its overall approach to managing in a service environment, it is recognised as an excellent grounding for a career elsewhere, particularly in the communications, hospitality or marketing sector.

Training in many of the TQ companies covers much more than immediate work skills. Milliken & Co has sent all its manufacturing associates on the Dale Carnegie courses to improve presentation and public speaking skills. It feels the self-confidence and the communication skills more than justify sending shopfloor staff on the training.

Similarly Rank Xerox is now giving particular attention to developing in managers the skills of the "new model manager"; that is, coaching, supporting, facilitating, as well as "management by fact".

"JUST-IN-TIME" TRAINING AND EDUCATION

The most successful companies link education closely to real life experience and tasks in the workplace. They recognise that the real learning happens when people come to apply new ideas and skills in their everyday work and when there is consistent support from managers to do so. Training and education is demand led: helping to provide the skills and knowledge that individuals need to do their jobs to a high standard and to progress within the company. Training has a very practical flavour in these organisations; it is not separate from the day to day job but part of it.

The integration of training into work starts with a careful process of induction of new workers, on which the companies place great emphasis. Every new Nissan trainee received in 1991 a staggering 61 days of off-the-job training. Many go to Japan and spend periods working in the Nissan plants within their first two years.

The centrepiece of the training effort in the factory is the ILUD charts which are displayed, recording the progress of each member of every work team in mastering all the different jobs in their part of the plant (see case study, pages 13–21).

In Grundfos the training starts as soon as people join the company with an overview of quality lasting four days. Everyone has a personal development plan. The discussion between manager and individual is held six months away from the time for salary review. Individuals propose their own objectives for the coming year. There is no rating. Instead the output is a carefully designed development plan for the individual which emphasises training and education.

Federal Express customer service people take five weeks of training before they begin work and the company says this will soon be six weeks. The preparatory training for couriers is being increased from three to four weeks. After that Federal Express's approach is different but still aimed strictly at linking training and education to day to day work. The company measures the knowledge of individuals every six months. If employees cannot pass the test, they cannot stay in a customer contact position. The company takes the view that it provides the resources and the tools for training and pays staff for test preparation time; it is then up to employees to take the training they need and to keep up.

When operations managers are appointed in FedEx they undergo a seven week development programme. They are seconded to a station where the station manager becomes their mentor for the period. Education includes both classroom and station based work.

In Club Med, upon promotion to village manager, each staff member attends a development course in Paris focused on leadership and communication.

Avoid "sheep dip" training

Chapter 5 examines the failure of programmes involving "sheep dip" training: putting everyone in an organisation through the same short courses. In the absence of widely agreed vision and objectives the training is seen as a tiresome distraction from day to day responsibilities. The quality of training is often diluted as the message is passed down the hierarchy. The continuing pattern of behaviour of managers contradicts the quality messages.

There is no effective follow-up to training events. Where these do raise the enthusiasm of staff, they go back to their ordinary jobs to find that "nothing has changed" and so become cynical about the programme. They know the words relating to quality but miss much of the understanding.

LEARNING BY DOING

Real learning comes from doing. It is not enough to read about new ideas or hear them in the classroom. Until you begin to apply them, to see what works in real life and what does not, you do not begin to internalise the ideas, to fix them in such a way that they are truly learnt.

Observation of the case study companies reveals that effective culture change, the learning of new patterns of behaviour, does not happen in culture change workshops. At best a workshop may cause people to rethink, to challenge existing assumptions. At worst it can seem like a tiresome interruption to real life responsibilities. The learning will only become firm when people try out the new ideas and find that they produce results. A cycle of planning, experimentation, review and learning is needed.

The best way to do this is to give people new tasks and responsibilities, to place them in new relationships aimed at solving here and now business problems. The problems – and the results as they begin to flow – provide the motivation to change.

In NMUK learning has happened in this way at several levels. The start-up team, appointed in 1984, had two years before the plant started operation to plan in detail how the new business would run. They worked long hours as a team planning the new operation from scratch and facing detailed cross-examination from their Japanese advisers. Participants describe it as an intense period of learning, throwing out old assumptions about the industry, management and organisation.

Once the new plant began to operate the crucial unit of organisation became the work teams of about 20 people grouped under a supervisor with full responsibility for their leadership. Individual staff members again describe the intensity of learning when they joined these teams. Fundamental assumptions about work and industry were changed.

In ICL Product Distribution there was an abrupt culture change when the new management came in, focusing everything on delivery reliability to the customer. Initially the forum for change in the first unit involved, Literature and Software Operation, was a daily meeting of supervisors and managers with the general manager, going through all late items. Pretty soon people got the message: customers were the priority and results in serving them were what mattered. An operation which had been complacent and internally oriented was transformed over months into an efficient, customer results driven business.

The shift in Grundfos when self-management of quality was introduced was less dramatic but still significant. Following careful preparation, training and investment in new measuring equipment, workers progressively assumed responsibility for inspecting their own quality. The culture was changed from "quality is their responsibility" to "quality is our responsibility". The move was a powerful boost to workers' self-esteem: management had demonstrated its confidence in them.

Task alignment

Michael Beer and his colleagues in their book *The Critical Path To Corporate Renewal* argue that the way to start an effective process of change is by giving people new roles, relationships and responsibilities; not by setting up programmes nor by establishing new formal structures. The new roles and relationships should be "aligned" to key business tasks to ensure people are motivated to work in them. By working in the new framework, people learn new skills.

Developing leaders

Another example of learning by doing is in the key area of developing managers capable of leading transformations. Companies need nurseries to develop these potential leaders, not courses in the classroom on leadership. The combination of qualities – forthrightness, listening, consistency, business understanding, determination – is hard to find. They can be developed only by the mix of doing and learning.

In ICL Product Distribution top management took a calculated risk. They put David Palk at age 30 in charge of a key part of their operation, with cost responsibility for £20 mn. Over four years Palk and his team have more than justified the confidence shown in them by transforming the performance of the unit.

SUMMARY

1. TQ requires a heavy and continued investment in education and training; do not allow recessionary or other pressures to undermine this commitment.
2. Link training and education closely to the performance of tasks in the workplace; make on-the-job training a reality, not an excuse for doing nothing.
3. Organise new responsibilities and relationships and provide for frequent review so that people can learn by doing.

12   Using Outside Consultants

Consultants are a necessary evil who can bring a vital objectivity.
                                                        Mike Dent, director of quality assurance, Forte plc

Total Quality as an identifiable subject started with the gurus and consultants. Around 1980, first in the USA and then in Europe, increasing numbers of companies looked at the ideas of the emerging or established quality gurus, particularly Phil Crosby, Dr Deming and Dr Juran.

With his talent for expressing the case for quality in dollars and cents and his striking phrases such as "Quality is Free", Phil Crosby took an early lead. Many of the large companies interviewed in Europe started their quality initiatives working with his consultancy firm. Dr Deming, by contrast, has a much more radical and challenging message and no consultancy firm to offer but is increasingly influential. Dr Juran has found supporters among those looking for a project based approach and an emphasis on the systematic management of quality. Around these and other gurus a small industry of consulting firms has grown up, seeking to guide companies towards the bright promise of a quality revolution.

Yet the reputation of the consultants with leading companies is now at best mixed (see box). Many companies which have worked with consultants are disillusioned. The problems they most often mention are as follows.

- Ironically, the poor quality of the work. Companies cite, for example, training packages which were poorly designed, badly produced and ineffectively delivered.
- Lack of in-depth understanding of TQ.
- Approaches developed for other companies which are transferred without regard for the specific situation and needs of the client.
- Failure of managers to take ownership of change because TQ is identified with the consultants.
- Consultants who may be fine on TQ tools and techniques but can give no practical help in managing or leading a process of change.
- Consultants unable to establish credibility with senior managers.
- Inability to work in different cultures and languages.
- Consultants who are eloquent on what TQ is but give no help when it comes to how to implement.

So is there still value in using consultants? And if so how should companies go about seeking it? Based on research for this report, there are three areas where companies can gain from outside support.

- There are valuable specialist roles which skilled consulting firms can play.
- Companies can tap into the growing series of networks between companies. A very strong value of sharing ideas and experience exists among the companies trying to apply TQ. Firms are remarkably open and helpful.
- Companies do benefit from outside challenge and facilitation: not experts who tell them what to do but sympathetic guides who act as catalysts, questioning the progress that has been made, making suggestions and supporting processes in which the company can learn more effectively.

What the clients think

The role of the consultant as a guide, facilitator, conscience is a valid one.
Libby Raper, TQ coordinator, IDV Ltd

There are too many consultants around and many are of doubtful value.
Jonson Cox, quality manager, Shell UK Oil

There's too much external advice; what's lacking are the internal resources to do TQ.
Brian Ellis, director of manufacturing, Anchor Foods

We use outsiders to help with team building. For the rest of it, we now know more than the consultants.
Gerald Bailey, quality manager, Motorola Communications

We don't need consultants now; our expertise is home grown
Jim Havard, quality director, Rank Xerox

Though it is criticised, Crosby was of great value in getting us started. Now we have our internal quality consultancy.
Peter Pring, director of customer and external relations, 3M UK

The survey of our customers by an outside consultant was a real eye opener. It changed our view of what is important to customers.
Dr Ibrahim, head of marketing international, Ciba-Geigy Dyestuffs and Chemicals

We've learnt the hard way to avoid some consultants. They should be used sparingly to ensure ownership is with line managers.
John Gage, business development manager, Manpower Ltd

SPECIALIST CONSULTANTS

The areas where specialist consultants can play a valuable role in supporting TQ work include the following.

Understanding customer needs and expectations. Research by a third party can bring a new objectivity and incisiveness to the understanding of customers. Ciba-Geigy is one of a number of companies which said their views of customer needs changed decisively following a survey by an outside consultant.

Surveying employee views. As with customers, a survey by an outsider can bring needed objectivity.

Benchmarking. As explained in Chapter 6, benchmarking is not easy. Support from a consultant can help identify the best firms to benchmark against and ensure that the process is done rigorously and with a view to learning how to do things better.

Self-assessment. A consultant can facilitate this process to make sure it is done effectively.

Organisation development. A consultant may be able to help with the OD issues that arise as TQ work proceeds.

Review of key processes. A consultant can bring understanding of how to map processes and how to identify key issues, particularly cross-functional ones.

Quality concepts. A consultant can help to introduce understanding of the TQ principles.

Quality systems. Help may be needed to teach and coach understanding of systems related to quality such as JIT, Total Productive Maintenance and Quality Function Deployment.

Leadership and teamwork skills. A consultant can help support the learning of these skills.

Problem solving tools and techniques. Training may be needed in selected tools and techniques.

Control of variability. Understanding of variability and of techniques such as statistical process control is still not common; consultants can help teach and coach.

New financial management. TQ implies a new approach to financial management; consultants can help introduce the new ideas.

COMPANY NETWORKS

One of the most striking characteristics of the TQ companies is their desire to share their experience with other companies. This stems partly from a wish to spread further the implementation of TQ and partly from a realisation that there is nearly always something to learn from others. Increasingly, too, companies are seeing the publicising of their work in TQ as a very effective "soft sell" of their organisation. Numbers of companies have described the benefits in reputation, senior management relationships and in customer understanding that come from telling others about their work in quality.

The European Foundation for Quality Management can be contacted at: Fellenoord 47A, 5612 AA Eindhoven, The Netherlands (Tel: (31) 40 461 075; Fax (31) 40 432 005).

CONSULTANTS AS PARTNERS IN LEARNING

The other type of support for which there is a need is in helping companies to learn. Rather than being positioned as the expert, the consultant acts as both a challenge and a catalyst, helping the company to think through what it wants to do, to become more aware of its true strengths and weaknesses and to learn more quickly and effectively from others and from its own experience. Support is given in such a way that individuals and organisations take ownership of change. The key to this support is the design of the process through which managers work.

For example, in one company studied middle managers were highly committed to the company and to quality but were unable to influence effectively the direction of change. Bringing them together in multi-functional teams unlocked a reservoir of energy and capability to improve the company's goods and services.

In another company a newly appointed top management was determined to push through change to make the organisation more customer responsive but failed to take account of the understanding and potential of people who had been in the organisation for many years. A process was needed, drawing in senior and some middle managers, to hammer out an agreed vision of what management was trying to achieve and how it would get there. Such a process would bring out into the open the real concerns and the strengths and weaknesses of both new and old managers and enable them to begin to work as an effective team.

In yet another company management was committed to change but failed, because of past success, to see the potential challenge from international competition. A process was needed to involve a broad group of managers in benchmarking best international practice. Visiting the benchmark companies together gave managers a much sharper understanding of the challenge they faced and helped mobilise both the energy and teamwork to begin to tackle that challenge.

QUALITY CONSULTANTS: A HEALTH WARNING

Companies usually turn to consultants to help them in the early days of TQ implementation and are often disappointed. The reason is not hard to find: there are few consultants who have participated in or helped companies achieve transformations; and even fewer who have the consulting skills to help others undergo fundamental change. Some of the traps to avoid include the following.

Going to the consultant you know from years back. You may have confidence in him or her but does he or she have the breadth of experience and understanding to help your organisation?

Consultants whose only qualification is past employment by a well known TQ company. How deep is their experience and understanding of TQ in that company? Can they stand back from what worked there and think in an open minded way about what may be right for your probably very different organisation?

Consultants selling a package. You need a process that fits your circumstances and that your people own. Hand-me-downs do not work.

Consultants who do not listen. Consultants often think they have the answer and can be more interested in pushing this at you than in attending to your problem. Make sure that they have really listened and understand your needs and wants.

Big name consultants that send the office junior to work on your project. Who exactly is going to work with you? Will you have the people with the real insight and experience?

Trainers posing as strategists. Many consultants would like to help shape the strategy of change but few have the experience and skill to do it well. If a consulting firm's experience is as a trainer by all means use it as that; do not let it stray into work it is not suited for.

Consultants who confuse quality assurance and TQ. ISO 9000 and other forms of quality assurance are only one part of the picture. What understanding and experience does the consultant have of the other aspects of TQ?

Consultants who know it all already. Continuous improvement applies to the consultants as well. If they know the answers already they probably do not have minds open enough to help you.

Consultants who can do everything. Consultants have their clear strengths and weaknesses. If you are not clear about what they do not do, you probably do not understand what they can do.

TEN QUESTIONS FOR QUALITY CONSULTANTS

1. What is your track record in helping TQ processes as a consultant or as a manager? Who have you helped and in what way? How far did that organisation really change? If so, in what way?
2. What are your definitions of quality and of Total Quality?
3. What is your approach in working with clients? Exactly what support to the process of change do you provide?
4. What are your particular strengths and skills as a consultant? What examples can you give of the application of these?
5. What do you not do? What are the areas of expertise which you cannot offer?
6. Who would work on our team with us? When will we meet him or her? What is their experience and background? Who will be responsible for the relationship with us? Who will actually do the work?
7. Which past or existing clients of yours can we talk to about your work?
8. What are your charges and what exactly do they cover?
9. When would your team be available to work with us?
10. How and when would we review the effectiveness of your support to us?

SUMMARY

1. Be wary of consultants. Many in the quality field have gained a reputation for taking too limited a view of TQ and for doing poor quality work. Avoid trainers and quality assurance consultants who claim to be able to help with the strategy of quality but cannot.
2. Do not rely on consultants. If real change is to happen your own people must own the change process.
3. Make full use of the networks of companies seeking to apply TQ, including EFQM.
4. Think through carefully what sort of help you need and shop around: there are many and very different sorts of help available.
5. Consider the use of a consultant as a partner in learning: not an expert but someone who can act as a catalyst and challenge, increasing the speed and effectiveness of your learning.

Part 5

Directory

Contents

Introduction

The directory has been compiled using the Economist Intelligence Unit's databases and the information available to the authors of the report. It is aimed at companies looking for consultants who work *at a strategic level*, helping top management and others with the implementation of the continuous improvement principles. There are many other, particularly smaller firms, who help with training or with implementation of ISO 9000 (BS 5750) but it is not possible in a volume of this size to include them.

The consultants have been listed alphabetically in the directory but Table 1 (page 146) lists them in three groups:

- **Change Consultants** – those who focus on helping clients to implement change and who see application of the quality principles as one way into change;
- **Quality Specialists** – firms whose main or sole practice is helping clients to implement quality;
- **Broad-Based Consultants** – those where quality is one of a number of types of work they do.

To help readers, the characteristics of each consultancy are first summarised using the following criteria:

Ownership
Cons = part of larger consultancy group
Ed = owned by educational trust or college
Ind = independent company or partnership
Sub = subsidiary of larger commercial firm

Size
Large = more than 20 partners or equivalent
Medium = between 4 and 20 partners or equivalent
Small = 3 partners or less

Approach
Part = seek learning *partnerships* with clients
Expert = rely mainly on expert role
Mix = mix of both roles

ISO 9000
Percentage of work concerned directly with implementation of ISO 9000.

Country
Country where operations are based or, in the case of larger firms, where head office is located.

Internationalism
I = frequently work across national boundaries

Fees
Premium = daily rates of more than £1,200
Medium = between £600 and £1,200 per day
Low = less than £600 per day

Symbols
– = not available/applicable
. . . = information not given

Table 1 Key data on Europe's leading quality consultants

CONSULTANT	OWNER-SHIP	SIZE	APPROACH	ISO 9000 %	COUNTRY	INTERNAT-IONALISM	FEES	COMMENTS
CHANGE CONSULTANTS								
Ashridge Consulting Group	Ed	Medium	Part	0	UK	I	Premium	Distinctive approach stresses client learning and ownership of change
Centre for Service Excellence	Sub	Small	Part	0	UK	I	...	Joint venture between Digital Equipment Corporation and John Humble
Harbridge Consulting Group	Cons	Large	Mix	Very little	US	I	...	Employee owned firm stressing management development
Hay Management Consultants	Cons	Large	Mix	Much	US	I	Medium	Strong people development, training and rewards consulting background
Laurie International	Ind	Medium	Mix	0	UK	I	Premium, but can vary across all ranges	Blue chip clients and strong links to leading business school academics
QUALITY SPECIALISTS								
Adaptation Limited	Ind	Medium	Mix	Much	UK	I	Medium	Has close relationship with Rank Xerox UK
Bekeart-Stanwick	Sub	Small	Mix	0	Belgium	I	...	Grown out of consultancy work in quality done for parent company. Bekeart SA
Crane Davies	Ind	Small	Mix	0	UK	–	Medium-premium	Quality Assurance advisers to the Department of Employment in UK
Philip Crosby Associates	Cons	Large	Expert	5	US	I	Medium, includes expenses	Helped start the quality initiatives in many leading companies in the 1980s but market share has fallen in recent years; now owned by the profit and productivity improvement firm, Alexander Proudfoot

CONSULTANT	OWNER-SHIP	SIZE	APPROACH	ISO 9000 %	COUNTRY	INTERNAT-IONALISM	FEES	COMMENTS
Develin & Partners	Ind	Medium	Expert	0	UK	I	Medium	
European Centre TQM – Univ. Bradford	Ed	Small	Mix	0	UK	I	...	
Gilbert Associates (Europe)	Cons	Medium	Mix	0	Switz	I	Medium	European arm of large US consultancy
David Hutchins Associates	Ind	Small	Mix	40	UK	I	...	
ICME International	Ind	Medium	Mix	0	Switz	I	...	Strong emphasis on training and coaching
Inter Consult (UK)	Ind	Small	Mix	30	UK	–	Low	Stresses facilitator and tutor roles
INVENTA Limited	Ind	Small	Mix	33	Czech	–	...	Seeks to apply Deming philosophy
Management-Newstyle	Ind	Small	Expert	0	UK	–	Medium	Seeks to apply teachings of Deming and of US mentor, Homer Sarasohn
Anthony Mitchell Associates	Ind	Small	Mix	0	UK	–	Medium	Particular experience of business process management and of the construction industry
MRA International	Ind	Small	Mix	5	UK	I	Medium-premium	Stresses need for ownership to be with client
Neville Clarke International	Ind	Medium	Mix	40	UK	I	Medium	
O & F Management Consultants	Ind	Medium	Expert	30	UK	I	Medium	Strong emphasis on quality systems; includes staff drawn from the European Centre for TQM at the University of Bradford
Prism Consultancy	Ind	Medium	Mix	0	UK	–	Medium	Leading advocate of the Deming philosophy
Process Management International	Cons	Medium	Mix	25	UK	–	Medium	Work is based on Deming philosophy
Profile Consulting Group	Ind	Medium	Mix	25	UK	–	Low	Emphasis on quality management systems
Promentor Management	Ind	Medium	Mix	50	Denmark	–	Premium	
Quality Management International	Ind	Medium	Mix	60	UK	I	Medium	

CONSULTANT	OWNER-SHIP	SIZE	APPROACH	ISO 9000 %	COUNTRY	INTERNAT-IONALISM	FEES	COMMENTS
Quality System Srl	Ind	Medium	Expert	50	Italy	–	...	Specialises in technical support to manufacturing companies
Quarto Consulting	Ind	Small	Mix	Little	UK	I	Medium	Done a great deal of work supporting UK Post Office TQ initiatives
Quest Quality Consulting	Ind	Medium	Part	0	UK	I	Medium	Emphasizes need for behavioural change in client organisations
REL Consultancy Group	Ind	Medium	Mix	0	UK	I	Medium	
Services Limited	Ind	Small	Mix	25	UK	I	Medium	Link to Nottingham Polytechnic
Strategic Quality Management Institute	Ed	Small	Part	0	Neth	I	Low-medium	Research-based organisation owned by the Erasmus University of Rotterdam
Total Quality Management International	Ind	Medium	Mix	5	UK	I	Medium	Experienced TQ consultants with record of working with leading companies
BROAD-BASED CONSULTANTS								
Arthur D Little	Cons	Large	Expert	0	US	I	...	Identifies Total Quality with all approaches needed for a "high performance business"
Brooks International	Cons	Large	Expert	0	US	I	Quote on project basis	Emphasises behavioural change needed for sustained improvement in company performance
Bywater	Ind	Medium	Expert	40	UK	–	Low	
Coopers & Lybrand	Cons	Large	Mix	10	UK	I	...	Stresses the range and depth of its involvement in TQ
Ernst Young	Cons	Large	Expert	20	UK	I	Medium	
Forum Europe	Cons	Small	Expert	0	US	I	Medium-premium	"The Customer-Driven Company – Moving From Talk to Action" written by vice chairman of the firm, Richard C. Whiteley

CONSULTANT	OWNER-SHIP	SIZE	APPROACH	ISO 9000 %	COUNTRY	INTERNAT-IONALISM	FEES	COMMENTS
Gramma	Ind	Medium	Mix	0	Italy	–	...	
Gruppo Galgano	Ind	Medium	Mix		Italy		Medium	
ISQ – Institute for Corporate Strategies and Quality	Ind	Small	Mixp	38	Germany	I	...	Multilingual services offered from offices in Austria, Switzerland, France and the USA as well as Germany
A T Kearney	Cons	Large	Expert	0	US	I	...	Views TQ not as a discrete product but as "a way of doing business"
Kepner-Tregoe	Sub	Medium	Mix	0	US	I	Premium	Strong emphasis on training and education
KPMG Management Consulting	Cons	Large	–	0	UK	I	Medium-premium	Investing heavily in effort to gain leading position in TQ consultancy
Matrix Srl	Sub	Medium	Mix	30	Italy	–	...	
ODI, Europe	Cons	Large	Mix	10	US	I	Premium	Recently established European offshoot of leading US firm
PA Consulting Group	Cons	Large	Expert	15	UK	I	...	
P-E Batalas	Cons	Large	Expert	90	UK	I	Low-medium	Focus on ISO 9000 (BS5750)
PERA International	Ind	Small	Expert	50	UK	–	Medium	Emphasises own TQ methodology
Price Waterhouse	Cons	Large	Mix	20	UK	I	...	
TMI A/SZ World Class International	Cons Ind	Large Medium	Mix Mix	50 5	Denmark UK	I I	Premium Medium	Stresses education and training Sees TQ as one aspect of world class operations as defined by Richard Schonberger

Adaptation Limited

Address:	Rathgar House, 237 Baring Road, Grove Park, London SE12 0BE, UK	**Telephone:** **Fax:** **Contact:**	(44) 081 8575907 (44) 081 8575907 Dr Colin Coulson-Thomas

Other offices: Operates internationally through modern/WAN links to global corporate networks, eg. TQM joint venture partner Rank Xerox UK has access to Rank Xerox/Xerox Corporation global networks

Ownership: Independent private company, but offers a range of implementation of total quality services through a strategic joint venture with Rank Xerox (UK) Ltd (established 1991)

Year established: 1987

Total turnover: First full year results not available for Adaptation/Rank Xerox UK joint venture

Number of assignments in last 2 years: 6 clients involved since start up of joint venture in autumn 1991

Billing practices: Time costs estimated to achieve milestone output objectives. Invoices issued as and when project output milestones are reached

Personnel: 20 consisting of 6 directors; 10 consultants; 4 support staff (core team)

Background and experience of professional staff: Most have had line experience at managing director or director level with blue chip companies. Their experience is relevant for a company that wants to be a world leader, but not for a company that wants only to satisfy the requirements for BS 5750/IS0 9000. All those fielded have practical transformation or process reengineering experience with major companies.

Areas of specialisation:

- Understanding Customer Needs and Expectations
- Quality Function Development
- Corporate Culture
- Quality Understanding and Awareness
- Employee Involvement and Teamworking
- Elimination of Waste and JIT (some capability)
- Total Productive Maintenance (some capability)
- Problem Solving Tools and Process Involvement Tools and Techniques
- Control of Variability (including Statistical Process Control)
- Measurement of Quality-Related Costs
- Quality Assurance (including ISO 9000)
- Supplier Partnerships
- New Financial Management (some capability)
- World Class Product Development (some capability)
- Others: Corporate transformation; identifying and overcoming implementation barriers

Most important industry sectors for TQ work:

Through joint venture with Rank Xerox, Adaptation works in a range of industry sectors

Definition of TQ: The creation and maintenance of the people, organisation, technology and process capability to – establish and sustain longer term relationships with customers; harness the maximum potential of people in understanding and delivering what constitutes value to customers; and learn/adapt as requirements/circumstances change

TQ work in training and implementation of ISO 9000: Most assignments involve a mixture of the two – the aim being to develop client staff while implementing TQM. The emphasis is upon moving beyond recognised quality standards as these of themselves are unlikely to give leadership in competitive markets.

Types of work not undertaken: Conflicts of interest

Other information: The arrangement with Rank Xerox UK is unique. In an Adaptation Limited survey of over 100 companies, Rank Xerox emerged as the "role model" company re TQM. Most other corporate TQM programmes were found to be achieving little in terms of changes of attitudes and behaviour. The joint venture is particularly strong in the areas of – policy deployment; business/management process reengineering; business/management process simplification; training for TQM; identifying and overcoming implementation barriers.

Rank Xerox have won nine national quality awards including the Deming Award in Japan and Baldrige Award in USA.

Examples of recent assignments:

Client/description: International management consultancy
Project description: Editing of a manual of techniques and tools that are used worldwide by consulting staff
Client contact title: Director and partner
Consultant name/title: Dr Colin Coulson-Thomas, chairman and project leader (plus input from other consultants)
Length of project: 1 year
End product: Manual used worldwide by up to 20,000 consultants

---

Client/description: UK government department
Project description: A package for directors and boards, which includes a module specifically concerned with identifying customer requirements and another concerned with implementation barriers
Client contact title: A representative of the steering group
Consultant name/title: Dr Colin Coulson-Thomas, chairman and project leader (plus input from other consultants)
Length of project: 6 months ongoing
End product: Drawing upon a programme of work that has already involved over 1,000 individual directors and around 20 boards. A multimedia action learning package for directors and boards of organisations that are of critical importance to the UK economy.

Client/description: Major multinational company (US owned, IT sector)
Project description: Ongoing exercise to determine and prioritise external opportunities/challenges and the actions in terms of people, organisation and process needed to respond
Client contact title: Managing director
Consultant name/title: Dr Colin Coulson-Thomas, chairman and project leader (plus input from other consultants)
Length of project: 5 years ongoing
End product: An organisation with the vision, values, goals, objectives, attitudes, approaches and commitment to continue to gain market share/build customer satisfaction in one of the world's most competitive business sectors

Arthur D Little Limited

Address: Berkeley Square House,   **Telephone:** (44) 071 4092277
Berkeley Square,   **Fax:** (44) 071 4918983
London W1X 6EY,   **Contact:** Dr Peter Scott-Morgan
UK

Other offices: Australia (1); Belgium (1); Brazil (1); Canada (1); Czechoslovakia (1); France (1); Germany (3); Italy (1); Japan (1); Mexico (1); Netherlands (1); Saudi Arabia (1); Singapore (1); Spain (1); Taiwan (1); UK (2); USA (7); Venezuela (1). USA head office (Cambridge, MA) – Contact: R Nayak, tel (617) 8645770.

Ownership: Arthur D Little Inc, USA (ESOP company). The UK company was established in 1963.

Year established: 1886

Total turnover: Worldwide management consultancy – 1991: $359 mn; 1990: $318 mn; 1989: $293 mn

Number of assignments in last 2 years: Several hundred worldwide (covering different aspects of definition as described below)

Billing practices: Time spent x billing rates of individuals involved

Personnel: Worldwide management consultancy – 2,066 consisting of 218 directors; 1,061 consultants; 787 support staff

Background and experience of professional staff: Various. Typically with strong industry experience and MBA.

Areas of specialisation:

- Understanding Customer Needs and Expectations
- Corporate Culture
- Quality Understanding and Awareness
- Supplier Partnerships
- World Class Product Development
- Others: Efficiency/effectiveness of key business processes; stakeholder needs/strategy; cross-functional TQ

Most important industry sectors for TQ work:

- Automotive
- Chemicals
- Consumer products
- Electronics
- Information
- Telecommunications
- Energy
- General engineering
- Manufacturing

Definition of TQ: All the approaches needed to be a high performance business (defined in company specific terms) – balancing strategies against needs of owners, customers, employees, suppliers and the community; benchmarking and continually improving performance in key business processes (eg. product creation); balancing all forms of resources (including information); harmonising organisation, motivation and corporate culture with desired behaviour

TQ work in training and implementation of ISO 9000: Very little of either. ADL considers ISO 9000 implementation a very "narrow" aspect of TQ and would subcontract

Types of work not undertaken: Conflicts of interest

Other information: –

Examples of recent assignments:

Client/description: Major electronics company
Project description: Improvement of the product creation process to increase the hit-rate of "right products at the right time"
Client contact title: Chief executive
Consultant name/title: Jean-Philippe Deschamps, vice president
Length of project: One year involving 15 consultants full-time; ongoing implementation is being handled internally by the client with follow-on work from ourselves
End product: Shorter lead times; improved cross-functional cooperation; clarified milestone structure; modified reward system/career paths; all resulting in substantially improved performance

---

Client/description: Major insurance organisation
Project description: Overhaul of firm's administration and service delivery plus adoption of enabling technologies
Client contact title: Chief executive
Consultant name/title: Larry Chaite, vice president
Length of project: 1 year ongoing (have had a continuous relationship with this client for many years on various projects)
End product: Redesigned business processes implemented via a detailed migration plan leading to significant reduction in administration cost base, new generation of planned systems and systems enhancements and firm ideas of how to achieve these objectives

---

Client/description: Computer peripherals company
Project description: Evaluation and removal of barriers to performance created by the unwritten "Rules of the Game" within the organisation
Client contact title: Managing director
Consultant name/title: Peter Scott-Morgan, associate director
Length of project: 6 months. Major changes in behaviour have already occurred and may be applied to other divisions.
End product: Improved cross-functional cooperation; willingness to change; longer term view; consistency of purpose; company-wide approach to quality

Ashridge Consulting Group

Address: Ashridge Management College,   **Telephone:** (44) 0442 843491
Berkhamsted,   **Fax:** (44) 0442 843584
Hertfordshire HP4 1NS,   **Contact:** Kate Charlton
UK

Other offices: Through subsidiaries of The Ashridge Trust – Ashridge Management College; Ashridge Management Research Group; Ashridge Strategic Management Centre; Independent Assessment and Research Centre; Ashridge International Institute for Organizational Change (based in France)

Ownership: The Ashridge Trust (established in 1959)

Year established: 1986

Total turnover: 1991: £1.6 mn; 1990: £1.6 mn; 1989: £1.3 mn

Number of assignments in last 2 years: 12, of which 50% are ongoing

Billing practices: Daily consultant's rate plus VAT and expenses billed monthly in arrears

Personnel: 41 consisting of 8 directors; 26 consultants; 7 support staff

Background and experience of professional staff: All have a minimum of 5 years' consulting experience across a range of industrial sectors (ACG do not have specialists in particular sectors as they believe that learning in different environments is essential for developing a broad perspective). All consultants also have wide prior experience in industry, either in senior line management or HR management positions.

Areas of specialisation:

- Understanding Customer Needs and Expectations
- Corporate Culture
- Quality Understanding and Awareness
- Employee Involvement and Teamworking
- Problem Solving Tools and Process Involvement Tools and Techniques
- Control of Variability (including Statistical Process Control)
- Supplier Partnerships
- Others: Working with boards to develop a strategic approach to implementing TQ

Most important industry sectors for TQ work:

Work across all industry sectors but recent work has been concentrated in:
- Financial services
- Pharmaceuticals
- Manufacturing
- Food and drink
- Public sector health care

Definition of TQ: TQ is about concentrating organisational and individual focus on customer requirements; designing internal processes that smoothly satisfy or exceed those requirements and, most important, believing in and releasing the potential in people and encouraging and empowering them to bring about continuous improvement

TQ work in training and implementation of ISO 9000:   None

Types of work not undertaken: If preferred by the client, ACG would not allow the same consulting team to work simultaneously with competing clients. In practice, they have had no problems and clients have, in fact, recommended them to other people in their industries.

Other information: –

Examples of recent assignments:

Client/description: Booker Farming
Project description: Work with the board and senior management team to help them to understand the ideas and concepts of TQ and how they should adapt them for their special environment, preparing them to implement TQ down to the "tractor seat"
Client contact title: Managing director
Consultant name/title: Colin Williams, business director
Length of project: 6 months ongoing

Client/description: Elida Gibbs
Project description: Work with the board, managers and TQ coordinators, to initiate and support TQ; the emphasis has now moved to specific groups/projects within the business and ACG works in partnership with the TQ and corporate affairs director to design interventions at several levels
Client contact title: TQ and corporate affairs director
Consultant name/title: Lynn Lilley, business director
Length of project: 4 years ongoing

Client/description: J & B Scotland
Project description: Work with the board to establish what form a TQ initiative should take; helping to establish the overall strategic approach and developing the initial project teams
Client contact title: Production director
Consultant name/title: Colin Williams, business director
Length of project: 1 year ongoing

Bekaert-Stanwick

Address: President Kennedypark 27D,   **Telephone:**   (32) 56 766000
8500 Kortrijk,   **Fax:**   (32) 56 767369
Belgium   **Contact:**   Jacques Declercq

Other offices: France (1); Spain (1); USA (1). France and Spain began operation in 1991 and USA in 1989–90. USA head office (Georgia) – Contact: J Vinyard, tel (404) 4218520.

Ownership: NV Bekaert SA (49%); Bekaert Engineering (48%); Bekaert International Trade (3%)

Year established: 1970

Total turnover: Belgium – 1991: BFr170.7 mn; 1990: BFr185.5 mn; 1989: BFr157 mn

Number of assignments in last 2 years: ...

Billing practices: Fee is calculated per consulting day

Personnel: Belgium – 40 consisting of 1 director, 29 consultants; 10 support staff. There are 16 staff in other countries.

Areas of specialisation:

- Understanding Customer Needs and Expectations
- Quality Function Development
- Corporate Culture
- Quality Understanding and Awareness
- Employee Involvement and Teamworking
- Elimination of Waste and JIT
- Total Productive Maintenance

- Problem Solving Tools and Process Involvement Tools and Techniques
- Control of Variability (including Statistical Process Control)
- Measurement of Quality-Related Costs
- Quality Assurance (including ISO 9000)
- Supplier Partnerships

Most important industry sectors for TQ work:

- Process industry

- Manufacturing and related services

Definition of TQ: TQ is the continuous improvement of everything we do throughout the whole organisation using well known systems and with the participation of everybody

TQ work in training and implementation of ISO 9000:   Training 20% (implementation, much wider than ISO 9000, 80%)

Types of work not undertaken: –

Other information: –

Examples of recent assignments:

Client/description: NV Bekaert SA
Project description: Decrease of overheads
Client contact title: Chief executive officer
Consultant name/title: M Caluwaerts, managing director
Length of project: 9 months
End product: Overheads decreased by more than 16%

Client/description: Sidmar
Project description: A wide range of activities in the TQ field, eg. action learning to team work, problem solving, SPC, etc
Client contact title: Head of the quality steering committee
Consultant name/title: N Peirs, support manager (International Unit)
Length of project: 2 years ongoing
End product: Productivity, customer satisfaction and motivation of the staff have been increased while costs were decreasing

---

Client/description: Continental Foods
Project description: Determination of the strategy by internal and external research and implementation of the strategy through management work teams
Client contact title: General manager
Consultant name/title: R Goorman, senior consultant
Length of project: 9 months
End product: Market share has been increased by 10%; return on investment by 20%; the quality system will be certified (ISO 9002)

Brooks International

Address: 211 Piccadilly, London W1V 9LD, UK

Telephone: (44) 081 8828837
Fax: (44) 081 8863061
Contact: John W Ermentrout

Other offices: USA head office (Florida) – Tel: (407) 6267117

Ownership: Brooks International, USA, established in 1960 (private)

Year established: 1986

Total turnover: ...

Number of assignments in last 2 years: Worldwide – 10, of which 6 are ongoing, Europe – 3, of which 2 are ongoing

Billing practices: Fixed fee contract plus expenses

Personnel: Worldwide – 175 consisting of 10 directors; 146 consultants; 19 support staff

Background and experience of professional staff: Advanced degree; average 10–15 years' industry/consulting experience; line management history; proven project implementation skills. A mix of academic training and experience in the following disciplines – accounting and finance; engineering; behavioural sciences; manufacturing; marketing; information technology; organisational development.

Areas of specialisation:

- Understanding Customer Needs and Expectations
- Quality Function Development
- Corporate Culture
- Quality Understanding and Awareness
- Employee Involvement and Teamworking
- Elimination of Waste and JIT
- Total Productive Maintenance
- Problem Solving Tools and Process Involvement Tools and Techniques
- Control of Variability (including Statistical Process Control)
- Measurement of Quality-Related Costs
- Quality Assurance (including ISO 9000)
- Supplier Partnerships
- World Class Product Development
- Others: Superior human performance; change management; sustainable competitive advantage; results-based change

Most important industry sectors for TQ work:

- Transport
- Utilities (electric, gas and telecommunications)
- Food industry
- Metals and mining
- Banking and financial services
- Publishing and broadcasting
- Insurance

Definition of TQ: Brooks defines total quality as having the following attributes – the optimal level of quality is determined by the customer (both internal and external); customer standards are met the first time and every time; there is visible top management commitment; goals are aligned and linked throughout the organisation; behavioural application; reward and recognition practices reflect importance and provide motivation; there is an ongoing process of continuous improvement

TQ work in training and implementation of ISO 9000: Implementation is the keystone of Brooks' business. Training is often a part of implementation. It is accurate to state that 100% of their TQ work is concerned with implementation.

Types of work not undertaken: When conditions are not suitable for measurable and sustainable results; where client desires to buy facilitation activity instead of results implementation

Other information: –

Examples of recent assignments:

Client/description: Largest sugar beet producer in the USA
Project description: Total quality implementation
Client contact title: President
Consultant name/title: Project manager
Length of project: 57 weeks
End product: Total quality system resulting in 28% improvement in unit cost and 40% increase in profitability

---

Client/description: 6th largest forest products company in the world (building products division)
Project description: Total quality implementation
Client contact title: Executive vice president
Consultant name/title: Project manager
Length of project: 30 weeks
End product: Implementation of total quality system; internalisation of behaviours associated with total quality; significant reduction in costs and improvement in quality of finished product

---

Client/description: A major gas and electric utility
Project description: Total quality implementation
Client contact title: President
Consultant name/title: Director
Length of project: 60 weeks
End product: Total quality behaviours; redesigned organisation; employee empowerment; $35–40 mn per annum in measurable improvement

Bywater PLC

Address: 119 Guildford Street,
Chertsey,
Surrey KT16 9AL,
UK

Telephone: (44) 0932 567866
Fax: (44) 0932 568157
Contact: V A Allum

Other offices: 49% stakeholding in Bywater Camac, Australia; strategic alliance with KPMG Peat Marwick operations internationally including: Canada (1); France (1); Ireland (1); Netherlands (1); New Zealand (1); Spain (1)

Ownership: Independent

Year established: 1982

Total turnover: 1991: £2.57 mn; 1990: £2.94 mn; 1989: £2.07 mn

Number of assignments in last 2 years: 100 of which 50% are ongoing

Billing practices: Daily rate plus expenses in respect of all with whom we have contact, clients and suppliers alike

Personnel: UK – 37 consisting of 3 directors; 22 consultants; 12 support staff

Background and experience of professional staff: Specific industry experienced and professionally qualified

Areas of specialisation:

- Understanding Customer Needs and Expectations
- Corporate Culture
- Quality Understanding and Awareness
- Employee Involvement and Teamworking
- Measurement of Quality-Related Costs
- Quality Assurance (including ISO 9000)
- Others: Managing by Business Process; TQM training; consultancy and video-based learning

Most important industry sectors for TQ work:

- Oil and gas
- Food
- Transport
- Engineering
- Electronics
- Service
- Chemicals

Definition of TQ: A management led approach to create and maintain a culture dedicated to continuous improvement in all aspects of the organisation with full regard to the needs and expectations of customers, shareholders, employees and the community

TQ work in training and implementation of ISO 9000: Training 57%; ISO 9000 40%

Types of work not undertaken: All types of work undertaken; confidentiality agreements used

Other information: –

Examples of recent assignments:

Client/description: Major food company
Project description: TQM/ISO 9000 implementation programme
Length of project: 18 months ongoing
End product: Multi-site ISO 9000 registration; culture change; quality improvement; quality cost reduction

---

Client/description: Major airline
Project description: TQM consultancy and training
Length of project: 2 years ongoing
End product: Culture change; quality improvement; quality cost reduction

---

Client/description: Major oil and gas company
Project description: Quality improvement programme
Length of project: 2 years ongoing
End product: Quality improvement, culture change, quality cost reduction

The Centre for Service Excellence

Address:　The Crescent,
Jays Close,
Basingstoke,
Hants RG22 4BS,
UK

Telephone:　(44) 0256 371204
Fax:　(44) 0256 371790
Contact:　David Jackson

Other offices:　Parent company operates worldwide. Services account for $6 bn of total $14 bn turnover.

Ownership:　Digital Equipment Corporation. Established as a joint venture between John Humble & Company and Digital.

Year established:　1991

Total turnover:　–

Number of assignments in last 2 years:　8 major assignments of which 6 are ongoing

Billing practices:　Fixed price or fee related to the value the client agrees has been brought to their organisation

Personnel:　20

Areas of specialisation:

- Understanding Customer Needs and Expectations
- Quality Function Development
- Corporate Culture
- Quality Understanding and Awareness
- Employee Involvement and Teamworking
- Problem Solving Tools and Process Involvement Tools and Techniques

- Measurement of Quality-Related Costs
- Quality Assurance (including ISO 9000)
- New Financial Management
- World Class Product Development
- Others: Developing customer focused strategies; reducing bureaucracy; fostering creativity

Most important industry sectors for TQ work:

- Consumer packaged goods
- Retail
- Health

- Financial services
- Packaging
- Government

Definition of TQ:　The Centre believes TQ is everything an organisation does profitably to secure, satisfy and hold customers better than the competition

TQ work in training and implementation of ISO 9000:　All work relates to building and sustaining customer focused organisations

Types of work not undertaken:　Will not work with a competing client without the first client's consent

Other information:　The Centre is a joint venture between John Humble, a leading international consultant, and Digital Equipment Corporation, a leading hi-tech manufacturer. The alliance brings together leading edge thinking and practical experience of managing a multi-billion dollar company.

Examples of recent assignments:

Client/description: Packaging company
Project description: Service leadership
Client contact title: President
Consultant name/title: Partner
Length of project: 6 months
End product: A company wide vision and action plan (currently being implemented) to achieve industry leadership of quality of service

---

Client/description: Specialist retailer
Project description: Service excellence
Client contact title: Chief executive officer
Consultant name/title: Partner
Length of project: 1 year
End product: Significant revenue and profit improvement from service focused action learning

---

Client/description: Brewery
Project description: Customer focused organisation
Client contact title: HR director
Consultant name/title: Senior consultant
Length of project: 3 months
End product: Organisation structure design

Coopers & Lybrand

Address:	Plumtree Court,	**Telephone:**	(44) 071 5835000
	London EC4A 4HT,	**Fax:**	(44) 071 8224652
	UK	**Contact:**	R M G Millar

Other offices: Coopers & Lybrand has 734 management consultancy offices 80 countries worldwide employing 65,000 partners and staff

Ownership: Partnership

Year established: 1946

Total turnover: Worldwide (management consultancy) – 1991: $952 mn; 1990: $815 mn. European (management consultancy) – 1991: $416 mn; 1990: $408 mn (approximate % of European turnover TQ = 6%).

Number of assignments in last 2 years: Europe – 25 ongoing; 35–50 one off

Billing practices: Subject to particular contract requirements

Personnel: Worldwide – 65,000 of whom approximately 7,000 are involved in management consultancy and approximately 500 in total quality

Background and experience of professional staff: Maturity in business; experience in a range of TQ tools (minimum 5 years); significant achievements for which they personally were responsible

Areas of specialisation:

- Total Quality; Implementation and Top Executive Team Support
- Understanding Customer Needs and Expectations
- Quality Function Deployment
- Corporate Culture
- Quality Understanding and Awareness
- Employee Involvement and Teamworking
- Elimination of Waste and JIT
- Total Productive Maintenance
- Problem Solving Tools and Process Involvement Tools and Techniques

- Control of Variability (including Statistical Process Control)
- Measurement of Quality-Related Costs
- Quality Assurance (including ISO 9000)
- Supplier Partnerships
- New Financial Management
- World Class Product Development
- Others: Policy deployment; task team establishment and facilitation; performance measurement; international multilingual assignment delivery

Most important industry sectors for TQ work:

All sectors. Current assignments cover:
- Automotive
- Pharmaceutical
- Food and drink
- Electronics
- Banks, insurance and building societies

- Law firms
- Local and central government
- Private healthcare
- Utilities and airlines (cargo operations)

Definition of TQ: TQ is the culture of an organisation where continuous improvement is integrated into all activities

TQ work in training and implementation of ISO 9000: C&L's approach to TQ is tailored and therefore varies from client to client. Education and training from boardroom to shopfloor constitutes around 50% of TQ work, ISO 9000 may be around 10% and the balance will be strategic, operational improvement and culture change.

Types of work not undertaken: Generally work would only be turned down where conflict of interest is identified. TQ work is avoided where the client is only looking for a campaign.

Other information: Coopers & Lybrand have published ten text books on the subject of total quality. Their senior staff are frequently called upon to present new ideas and concepts at major conferences worldwide. They have been instrumental in developing with the EFQM the recently announced European Quality Award for Excellence. The firm also has extensive experience of applying Baldrige quality award criteria to business solutions.

Examples of recent assignments:

Client/description: British Aerospace (Space Systems)
Project description: Strategic orientation; breakthrough team training; cost of quality development
Client contact title: Operations director
Consultant name/title: Stuart Daughters, partner
Length of project: 16 months
End product: Client well orientated to take the project forward

---

Client/description: British Airways (Cargo Division)
Project description: Quality improvement using classic total quality methodology
Client contact title: Managing director of division
Consultant name/title: A C Collins, partner
Length of project: Ongoing up to 18 months
End product: A substantially more quality-aware organisation with process improvement at its core

---

Client/description: MK Electric
Project description: Total quality
Client contact title: Operations director
Consultant name/title: R M G Millar, partner
Length of project: Ongoing up to 20 months
End product: Improved forward engineering and a process improvement culture

Crane Davies Limited

Address: The Manor House,
Park Road,
Stoke Poges SL2 4PG,
UK

Telephone: (44) 0753 646411
Fax: (44) 0753 646080
Contact: Steve Wilshire

Other offices: –

Ownership: Private limited company

Year established: 1986

Total turnover: 1991: £1.7 mn; 1990: £2.2 mn; 1989: £1.8 mn

Number of assignments in last 2 years: 11, of which 7 are ongoing

Billing practices: On a per diem basis agreed with the client in advance of commencing any TQM assignment

Personnel: 14 consisting of 2 directors; 8 consultants; 4 support staff

Background and experience of professional staff: All consultants have honours degrees (most have postgraduate qualifications), line management experience in senior positions and have worked for a major consultancy/strategy house before joining Crane Davies

Areas of specialisation:

- Understanding Customer Needs and Expectations
- Quality Function Development
- Corporate Culture
- Quality Understanding and Awareness
- Employee Involvement and Teamworking
- Problem Solving and Process Involvement Tools and Techniques
- Supplier Partnerships

Most important industry sectors for TQ work:

- Financial services
- Professional services
- Information technology and communications

Definition of TQ: Quality management – meeting or exceeding agreed customer needs (both externally and internally) at lowest cost, through the commitment of everyone in the organisation

TQ work in training and implementation of ISO 9000: 100% TQM related consultancy and training. Crane Davies do/will work with consultants who implement ISO 9000.

Types of work not undertaken: –

Other information: Appointed as Quality Assurance Consultants to the Employment Department for the Investors in People Initiative (since March 1992)

Examples of recent assignments:

Client/description: International software house
Project description: Corporate culture change programme
Client contact title: Quality director
Consultant name/title: Robin Davies, director and Steve Wilshire, principal consultant
Length of project: 3 years ongoing
End product: Fully implemented programme for delivery of business plan to quality standards established for product development, customer management and people management

---

Client/description: Leading firm of UK accountants
Project description: Improving business performance in an increasingly competitive environment through market/ organisational analysis; performance planning; training
Client contact title: Regional managing partner
Consultant name/title: Steve Wilshire, principal consultant and Nic Smith, senior consultant
Length of project: 2 years
End product: Improved office performance against targets; cost reductions; quality plans incorporated into business plans; quality culture

---

Client/description: Telecommunications (district organisation)
Project description: Part of TQM programme; strategy formulation; personnel systems; training; internal consultant development
Client contact title: Implementation support manager
Consultant name/title: Steve Wilshire, principal consultant
Length of project: 2 years
End product: Shift in quality ratings (continuous customer monitoring) which raised district from 21st position to 4th nationally within two years resulting in significant improvement in service, image and lowered engineering costs

Philip Crosby Associates

Address: Centenary House,   **Telephone:**   (44) 081 9488333
                5 Hill Street,   **Fax:**   (44) 081 9408299
                Richmond,   **Contact:**   A T Barnes
                Surrey TW9 1SP,
                UK

Other offices: Australia (1); Belgium (1); Brazil (1); Canada (1); France (1); Germany (1); Italy (1); Japan (1); Mexico (1); Netherlands (1); New Zealand (1); Puerto Rico (1); Singapore (1); Spain (1); Taiwan (1); UK (1); USA (13)

Ownership: Alexander Proudfoot plc, UK, established in 1946. PCA's UK operation started in 1985. PCA was acquired by Alexander Proudfoot in 1989.

Year established: 1979

Total turnover: PCA figures not available. Alexander Proudfoot plc worldwide – 1991: £176.4 mn; 1990: £178.5 mn; 1989: £143.4 mn

Number of assignments in last 2 years: Worldwide – approximately 400

Billing practices: Pay as you go

Personnel: ...

Background and experience of professional staff: All have held senior managerial positions in industry and/or commerce, many at managing director level

Areas of specialisation:

- Understanding Customer Needs and Expectations
- Corporate Culture
- Quality Understanding and Awareness
- Employee Involvement and Teamworking
- Elimination of Waste and JIT
- Problem Solving Tools and Process Involvement Tools and Techniques

- Measurement of Quality-Related Costs
- Quality Assurance (including ISO 9000)
- Supplier Partnerships
- Others: Installation of TQM

Most important industry sectors for TQ work:

- All sectors

Definition of TQ: Total quality is a company culture in which everyone is dedicated to managing and continuously improving processes to ensure that all the products and services provided always satisfy the customer, now and in the future

TQ work in training and implementation of ISO 9000:   Education and facilitation 60%; installation 35%; ISO 9000 5%

Types of work not undertaken: Any work in which the ethical and legal integrity of the company could be compromised or any work in which the principles of the Crosby Complete Quality Management System could be compromised

Other information: Philip Crosby Associates (PCA) is the world's largest consultancy specialising in TQM. With the acquisition by Alexander Proudfoot, PCA is now able to call on the expertise of specialist content consultants who work inside client companies to make quality happen.

Examples of recent assignments:

Client/description: Electricity Board (whole organisation)
Project description: Total quality management, education and facilitation
Client contact title: Chairman
Consultant name/title: Michael Hutton, vice president Europe
Length of project: 28 months ongoing
End product: Increased productivity and a reduction in wasted resources of £8 mn

---

Client/description: Civil and military manufacturer
Project description: Total quality management, education and implementation
Client contact title: Chairman and chief executive
Consultant name/title: John Hutchinson, client director
Length of project: 17 months ongoing
End product: Improved business performance with indebtedness to banks reduced by 85%

Client/description: Computer systems supplier
Project description: Total quality management, education and facilitation
Client contact title: Director of customer services and support
Consultant name/title: Dr David Lawson, client director
Length of project: 15 months ongoing
End product: Reduction in wasted resources of over £250,000

Develin & Partners

Address: 211 Piccadilly, London W1V 9LE, UK

Telephone: (44) 071 5489988
Fax: (44) 071 8951357
Contact: Max Hand

Other offices: –

Ownership: Independent

Year established: 1988

Total turnover: 1991: £1.3 mn; 1990: £900,000 1989: £600,000

Number of assignments in last 2 years: 8 ongoing for large blue chip organisations

Billing practices: Agreed fixed fee basis

Personnel: 18 consisting of 5 directors; 8 consultants; 5 support staff

Background and experience of professional staff: Degree; about 50% are MBAs. All have at least five years' (generally much more) line management experience prior to entering consultancy.

Areas of specialisation:

- Understanding Customer Needs and Expectations
- Corporate Culture
- Quality Understanding and Awareness
- Employee Involvement and Teamworking
- Elimination of Waste and JIT
- Problem Solving Tools and Process Involvement Tools and Techniques
- Control of Variability (including Statistical Process Control)
- Measurement of Quality-Related Costs
- New Financial Management
- Others: Information technology strategy; organisation strategy

Most important industry sectors for TQ work:

- Financial services
- Manufacturing
- Logistics
- Public sector

Definition of TQ: Delighting the customer by harnessing the commitment of everyone to continuous improvement in every job

TQ work in training and implementation of ISO 9000: Training 30%. ISO – nil

Types of work not undertaken: ISO 9000/BS 5750 accreditation. Only work for competing clients with the approval of our present clients.

Other information: –

Examples of recent assignments:

Client/description: Abbey Life Assurance
Project description: Review of head office efficiency/effectiveness through quality improvement
Client contact title: Managing director
Consultant name/title: Max Hand, director
Length of project: 4 months ongoing
End product: Major rebalancing of resources to allow work to be done right first time, major business process reengineering. Significant organisation change.

Client/description: SGS Thomson Microelectronics
Project description: Cascaded TQC education
Client contact title: Vice president, service and quality
Consultant name/title: Max Hand, director
Length of project: 7 months ongoing
End product: Top three management layers aware/committed to TQM, leading to launch of TQM processes in facilities across Europe, and in the USA, Asia and Japan

---

Client/description: Aspen Business Communications
Project description: TQM education/training for process improvement teams
Client contact title: Deputy managing director
Consultant name/title: Max Hand, director
Length of project: 6 weeks ongoing
End product: Four process improvement teams trained in TQM and basic quality improvement tools. All teams then analysed a process, recommended and implemented improvements.

Ernst & Young

Address:	Becket House,	**Telephone:**	(44) 071 9282000
	1 Lambeth Palace Road,	**Fax:**	(44) 071 9281345
	London SE1 7EU,	**Contact:**	John Truman
	UK		

Other offices: Ernst & Young operate from more than 670 cities in 100 countries worldwide. European head office (Brussels) – Contact: P Smith, tel (32) 2 7749111; USA head office (New York) – Contact: S L Yearout, tel (216) 8614966; Asia/Pacific head office (Hong Kong) – Contact Dr W Leininger, tel (852) 8469888

Ownership: Partnership. Ernst & Whinney and Arthur Young merged in 1989.

Year established: 1903

Total turnover: ...

Number of assignments in last 2 years: Worldwide – over 100, of which some 30 are ongoing

Billing practices: Time against fixed quotation plus expenses

Personnel: Worldwide consultancy – over 4,000 consisting of over 400 directors and 3,600 consultants (all fee earning) Worldwide TQ – over 250 consisting of 25 directors and 225 consultants

Background and experience of professional staff: Industry specific experience; also experienced change managers; facilitators

Areas of specialisation:

- Understanding Customer Needs and Expectations
- Corporate Culture
- Quality Understanding and Awareness
- Employee Involvement and Teamworking
- Elimination of Waste and JIT
- Problem Solving Tools and Process Involvement Tools and Techniques
- Control of Variability (including Statistical Process Control)

- Measurement of Quality-Related Costs
- Quality Assurance (including ISO 9000)
- Supplier Partnerships
- New Financial Management
- World Class Product Development
- Others: As a diagnostic service, E&Y offers benchmarking against the International Quality Study SM database; business process improvement and innovation

Most important industry sectors for TQ work:

- Manufacturing (discrete and process industries)
- Banking and financial services (including insurance)

- Oil and gas
- Healthcare

Definition of TQ: Quality is more than the traditional notion of quality in products and services. It also encompasses performance improvement, reducing costs and improving delivery, time-to-market and responsiveness to changes in the market place. Quality improvement is achieved through the people, processes and technology of an organisation.

TQ work in training and implementation of ISO 9000: 80% is involved with TQM training, implementation and international quality study; ISO 9000 20%

Types of work not undertaken: –

Other information: The International Quality Study SM is a comparative study of the management practices of over 550 organisations. The study included organisations with operations in Germany, Japan and North America. In May 1992 sector reports will be released on computing, automotive manufacturers and suppliers, banking and healthcare.

Examples of recent assignments:

Client/description: Cleaning equipment manufacturer
Project description: The company recently consolidated its operations onto one site and was anticipating significant growth. E&Y were requested to develop a blueprint for its operations including appropriate physical arrangement of the manufacturing facilities; philosophy of manufacture including reduced batch sizes and short set up time
Length of project: 1 year
End product: Implementation through workshops encouraging involvement and leading to commitment and ownership of the new concepts including the application of JIT. Benefits achieved included halving of inventory; factory lead time 4 weeks to 3 days; 6% increased productivity; 20% reduction in space required

---

Client/description: Defence equipment manufacturer
Project description: To remain competitive and improve profitability the company had to reduce its scrap levels and working capital. However, more challenging was to change the culture of the organisation. E&Y provide a series of TQM workshops to educate and train the personnel, identify and implement improvements
Length of project: 6 months
End product: Savings in the order of £1.5 mn were identified during the first 12 weeks; one recommendation lead to savings of £1,000 per day

---

Client/description: Supplier of equipment to oil industry
Project description: Company had long lead time from receipt of order to the despatch of goods. The initial phase involved specification and design work prior to the necessary materials and components being purchased. The major concern was not so much the long lead time, rather its variability and thus its impact upon promise dates. Through workshops, underpinned by TQM, the process was challenged to identify non-value activities and delays.
Length of project: 9 months
End product: Lead times were reduced by some 10 weeks and variability reduced

European Centre for TQM – University of Bradford Management Centre

Address: Emm Lane,
Bradford,
West Yorkshire BD9 4JL,
UK

Telephone: (44) 0274 384313
Fax: (44) 0274 546866
Contact: Professor John Oakland

Other offices: –

Ownership: Department of University of Bradford

Year established: 1986

Total turnover: 1991: £300,000; 1990: £250,000; 1989: £200,000

Number of assignments in last 2 years: 50 (including training and research projects) of which 80% are ongoing

Billing practices: Training fees for open courses; daily rates for seminars, etc; project or lectureship funding over a number of years

Personnel: 9 consisting of 1 Head of Centre; 4 academic staff; 4 support staff

Areas of specialisation:

- Understanding Customer Needs and Expectations
- Quality Function Deployment
- Corporate Culture
- Quality Understanding and Awareness
- Employee Involvement and Teamworking
- Elimination of Waste and JIT
- Problem Solving Tools and Process Improvement Tools and Techniques
- Control of Variability (including Statistical Process Control)
- Measurement of Quality-Related Costs Quality Assurance (including ISO 9000)
- Supplier Partnerships

Most important industry sectors for TQ work:

Chemical industry Service All other sectors

Definition of TQ: TQ is an approach to improving the effectiveness and flexibility of a business as a whole. It is a way of managing to involve the whole organisation through its internal and external customer/supplier chains and processes.

TQ work in training and implementation of ISO 9000:   100% TQ work; 0% implementing ISO 9000 although the system is integrated into our TQ model

Types of work not undertaken: –

Other information: The European Centre for TQM is unique in its funding structure and range of activities. It is based in one of the largest business schools in Europe and enjoys all the facilities of a fully integrated business centre.

Examples of recent assignments:

Client/description: Exxon Chemical International
Project description: Funding of Chair in TQM
Client contact title: Chairman and managing director
Consultant name/title: Professor John Oakland, Head of Centre
Length of project: Ongoing up to 10 years
End product: Support, training and advice in TQ and all related areas for the company; a great deal of change, savings and increases in efficiency; many people trained

---

Client/description: Unilever
Project description: Funding of lectureship in TQM – benchmarking the innovation process; measurement in TQM
Client contact title: Chairman of one of Unilever's Companies
Consultant name/title: Dr Mohamed Zairi, lecturer in TQM
Length of project: 18 months ongoing
End product: Reports on the research work carried out; changes in the practices of the companies involved; development of training and support

---

Client/description: BP Chemicals
Project description: Funding of lectureship in SPC (statistical process control)
Client contact title: Senior manager responsible for TQ implementation
Consultant name/title: Roland Caulcutt, lecturer in SPC
Length of project: Ongoing up to 5 years
End product: Implementation of SPC throughout the organisation; many savings and improvements in processes and efficiency; much training and support for SPC

Forum Europe Limited

Address:	Orion House,	**Telephone:**	(44) 071 4975555
	5 Upper St Martin's Lane,	**Fax:**	(44) 071 3799870
	London WC2H 9EA,	**Contact:**	Karen Blal
	UK		

Other offices: Canada (1); Czechoslovakia (1); USA (6). Affiliated offices – Kasanen Training Group BTC Forum, Helsinki, Finland; EuroForm Srl (Division of Ambrosetti), Milan, Italy; USA head office (Boston) – Contact: Ms J Mason, tel (617) 5237300; Asia head office (Hong Kong) – Contact Ms G Jeffrey, tel (852) 8489260

Ownership: The Forum Corporation, USA, established in 1971 which is privately held, employee-owned

Year established: 1986

Total turnover: Total corporate gross revenues worldwide were about $50 mn for year ending April 1992

Number of assignments in last 2 years: Worldwide – 475, of which 360 are ongoing (TQ); Forum Europe – 20 of which 10 are ongoing (TQ). However, for the fiscal years 1991 and 1992, The Forum Corporation was involved in training and consulting assignments for a total of 950 client organisations of which approximately 75% are ongoing.

Billing practices: Standard practices, including project fee, retainer fee and daily rate; training programmes are often billed per participant

Personnel: Worldwide – 320 including 175 executives/consultants; Forum Europe – 17 including 9 executives/consultants. In addition, Forum Europe maintains and manages its own Resource Network (RESNET) of 25 contract instructors who are trained and licensed to facilitate Forum's generic and tailor-made training and development programmes.

Background and experience of professional staff: In general, Forum consultants hold advances degrees (MBA, PhD) and have experience managing in large, complex business organisations.

Areas of specialisation:

- Understanding Customer Needs and Expectations
- Corporate Culture
- Quality Understanding and Awareness
- Employee Involvement and Teamworking
- Problem Solving Tools and Process Involvement Tools and Techniques
- Others: The services Forum provides in its TQM work with organisations falls into four categories:

1. Best practices research – ongoing identification of the behaviours, practices and policies that differentiate exemplary organisations from their peers, and, further, those practices that distinguish especially effective individuals within an organisation.
2. Assessment of organisational and individual effectiveness – Forum's diagnostic services help clients collect the data they need to identify and analyse critical problems and opportunities and understand their strengths and weaknesses from the view of customers, the organisation, individual employees and competition.
3. Consulting – Forum's consulting services help clients lay a firm foundation for creating an externally focused, internally aligned organisation, targeting the critical issues of executive alignment and team building, direction setting and education.
4. Training and education systems – Forum's training programmes help make individuals and organisations more effective, help employees connect their personal commitment and skills to the organisation's vision and values, and strengthen the client's competitive position and increase employees' contribution and satisfaction. Programmes are offered in the areas of: executive direction setting; developing leadership and management strengths; integrating quality methods and tools; building team effectiveness; optimising sales and service effectiveness.

Most important industry sectors for TQ work:

- Consumer products
- Financial services
- Hi-tech
- Telecommunications
- Transport
- Chemicals
- Pharmaceuticals

Definition of TQ: Total quality is a strategy that helps organisations meet or exceed customer expectations. Successful implementation of the strategy requires an organisation to become externally focused and internally aligned. This involves simultaneous action in three critical areas – customers, processes and people.

TQ work in training and implementation of ISO 9000: 50% of Forum Europe Limited's work is in the area of TQ; 50% of this is training; Forum do not implement ISO 9000

Types of work not undertaken: Statistical process control

Other information: Forum's vice chairman, Richard C Whiteley, is the author of the successful business book *The Customer-Driven Company, Moving from Talk to Action*, published by Century Business Press.

Examples of recent assignments:

Client/description: A large UK financial services firm
Project description: Helping implement customer-focused quality at local, regional and national levels. Pinpointing the expectations of the client's customers, assessing customer satisfaction with the client's performance and determining priorities for improvements
Client contact title: Director, training and organisational development
Consultant name/title: John Aves, consultant
Length of project: 3 years ongoing
End product: Assured consistent quality of services customers value most and greater senior manager alignment about which processes are not reliable and need improvement.

Client/description: Global packaged goods company
Project description: Worked with the client to develop an executive education project designed to help the top management team drive their TQM strategy. Worked with senior executives to assure their in-depth understanding of the tools needed to identify, analyse and improve key quality issues and processes.
Client contact title: Manager, research and total quality
Consultant name/title: Gary Ransom, senior vice president
Length of project: 2 years ongoing
End product: Initial results have been reduced cycle time, higher quality ratings by customers, greater inventory accuracy

---

Client/description: Major international airline (ground operations services)
Project description: Assisted client in its effort to become the world's most customer-focused airline. The assignment involved extensive changes in the client's vision, organisational structure and internal controls. A major service quality training programme at all levels of the company also was conducted.
Client contact title: Organisation and development manager
Consultant name/title: John Bray, Chairman, Forum Europe Limited
Length of project: 3 years ongoing
End product: Helped improve operating results (one training programme for supervisors of customer-contact personnel helped bring about a 15% increase in passenger throughput with no increase in headcount and a decrease in overtime); 25% reduction in complaints; 30% increase in unsolicited, written compliments during the same period. Today the client is one of the top-rated airlines in the world and is highly profitable.

Gilbert Associates (Europe) Limited

Address: Fraser House,   **Telephone:**   (44) 081 8914383
                    15 London Road,   **Fax:**   (44) 081 8915885
                    Twickenham TW1 3ST,   **Contact:**   J B Piggott
                    UK

Other offices: Egypt (1); USA (6)

Ownership: Gilbert Associates Inc, USA, established in 1906

Year established: 1981

Total turnover: Worldwide – 1991: $277.4 mn; 1990: $260.6 mn; 1989: $257.3 mn UK – 1991: £1.6 mn; 1990: £1.1 mn; 1989: £915,490

Number of assignments in last 2 years: Approximately 250

Billing practices: To suit client requirements

Personnel: Worldwide – 3,500 of which about 80% are professionals UK – 36 consisting of 6 directors; 20 consultants; 10 support staff

Areas of specialisation:

- Understanding Customer Needs and Expectations
- Corporate Culture
- Quality Understanding and Awareness
- Employee Involvement and Teamworking
- Elimination of Waste
- Problem Solving Tools and Process Improvement Tools and Techniques

- Control of Variability (including Statistical Process Control)
- Measurement of Quality-Related Costs
- Quality Assurance (including ISO 9000)
- Supplier Partnerships
- Others: Business process management; safety management

Most important industry sectors for TQ work:

- Health
- Automotive
- Oil
- Transport
- Power and nuclear

- Manufacturing
- Financial services
- Government
- Local authorities

Definition of TQ: Total – means everyone in the organisation; quality – means delighting the customer by continuously meeting and improving upon agreed requirements

TQ work in training and implementation of ISO 9000:   Training 50%, of which 75% is concerned with implementing ISO 9000

Types of work not undertaken: Conflicts of interest

Other information: –

Examples of recent assignments:

Client/description: Government department
Project description: Evaluation of current quality position and department recommendation of future action
End product: Presentation of report

Client/description: Major teaching hospital
Project description: Assessment and planning of a strategic quality plan to change the quality culture of the whole unit
End product: Phase 1 – assessment; phase 2 – strategic plan including the next steps

---

Client/description: International oil company
Project description: Assessment leading to senior management workshop and strategic TQ plan
End product: Phase 1 – assessment; phase 2 – strategic plan including the next steps

GRAMMA Management Consultants

Address: Via Conservatorio 17, 20122 Milan, Italy

Telephone: (39) 2 76004176
Fax: (39) 2 784992
Contact: Liliana Martellani

Other offices: Italy (3); subsidiary companies – Com Metodi; Dimensione Controllo; Executive Group; Productivity Italia

Ownership: Partnership

Year established: 1978

Total turnover: 1992: L12 bn (est); 1991: L8.6 bn; 1990: L7.4 bn; 1989: L4.9 bn

Number of assignments in last 2 years: 30–40 assignments for 10–15 clients of which 80% are ongoing

Billing practices: Forfait

Personnel: 59 consisting of 12 partners; 32 consultants; 15 support staff

Background and experience of professional staff: When entering – degree; MBA degree; 3 years' work experience. Professional staff in general have 5–7 years' management consulting experience

Areas of specialisation:

- Understanding Customer Needs and Expectations
- Quality Function Development
- Corporate Culture
- Quality Understanding and Awareness
- Employee Involvement and Teamworking
- Elimination of Waste and JIT
- Total Productive Maintenance
- Problem Solving Tools and Process Involvement Tools and Techniques

- Control of Variability (including Statistical Process Control)
- Measurement of Quality-Related Costs
- Supplier Partnerships
- World Class Product Development
- Others: TQ as competitive strategy

Most important industry sectors for TQ work:

- Wholesale and retail trade
- Transport and storage
- Financial

- Textiles
- Office equipment
- Telecommunication equipment

Definition of TQ: Being competitive in the global market through value for the customer, continuous improvement, constant innovation, productivity through people to get the right things done

TQ work in training and implementation of ISO 9000: Consulting and training: 100%; ISO 9000 – nil

Types of work not undertaken: Works not focused on GRAMMA competences

Other information: GRAMMA is a licensee of the Tom Peters Group (USA) and of Productivity Inc (USA). GRAMMA is a member of Eurocore Management Consultants.

Examples of recent assignments:

Client/description: Ciba-Geigy
Project description: Assist in conceiving and developing quality programme
Client contact title: Chief executive officer
Consultant name/title: Silvio Rubbia, Partner
Length of project: 30 months
End product: Ciba-Geigy Italia Quality program; Ciba-Geigy Italia Quality program as a pilot; Ciba-Geigy Corporation

---

Client/description: Alcantara (ENI) (microfibre textiles)
Project description: Assisting in conceiving, developing and leading TQ program
Client contact title: President
Consultant name/title: Liliana Martellani, partner
Length of project: 3 years ongoing
End product: Top performing company with value added and continuous improvement

---

Client/description: Ferrari Cars
Project description: CVC creating value for the customer (A Tom Peters Group Programme)
Client contact title: Marketing director
Consultant name/title: Filippo Bucarelli, senior consultant
Length of project: 18 months
End product: New partnership relations between the company and its dealers

Gruppo Galgano

Address:	Piazza IV Novembre 1, 20124 Milan, Italy	**Telephone:** **Fax:** **Contact:**	(39) 2 6709186 (39) 2 66981685 Bruno Susio

Other offices: Italy (5); joint venture with Coopers & Lybrand, Spain

Ownership: Partnership – Gruppo Galgano which consists of six subsidiaries: Galgano & Associati srl; Galgano Consulting; Galgano Sud; Galgano Formazione; Summit; Varriale Formazione

Year established: 1962

Total turnover: 1991: L30 bn; 1990: L27 bn; 1989: L18 bn

Number of assignments in last 2 years: 670, of which 200 are ongoing

Billing practices: Daily rate

Personnel: 170 consisting of 16 partners; 90 consultants; 64 support staff

Background and experience of professional staff: Mainly graduates in professional disciplines and 3–6 years' experience in manufacturing/services areas

Areas of specialisation:

- Understanding Customer Needs and Expectations
- Quality Function Development
- Corporate Culture
- Quality Understanding and Awareness
- Employee Involvement and Teamworking
- Elimination of Waste and JIT
- Total Productive Maintenance
- Problem Solving Tools and Process Involvement Tools and Techniques
- Control of Variability (including Statistical Process Control)
- Measurement of Quality-Related Costs
- Quality Assurance (including ISO 9000)
- Supplier Partnerships
- World Class Product Development
- Others: Total quality management; service quality

Most important industry sectors for TQ work:

70% industry, 30% services with no specific emphasis on a particular sector

Definition of TQ: Total quality or company-wide quality control is the most innovative and all-encompassing managerial approach and is the main strategy of any company committed to excel and become highly competitive

TQ work in training and implementation of ISO 9000: ...

Types of work not undertaken: Financial management; defence work; competing clients; mergers and acquisitions

Other information: –

Examples of recent assignments:

Client/description: International Italian based rubber products company
Project description: Total quality management
Client contact title: Top management
Consultant name/title: Partner
Length of project: 1 year ongoing (up to 3 years)
End product: ...

Client/description: Italian based leading motor vehicles and parts company
Project description: Design of products
Client contact title: Top management
Consultant name/title: Partner
Length of project: 2 years ongoing
End product: ...

Client/description: International banking company
Project description: Management culture change
Client contact title: Top management
Consultant name/title: Partner
Length of project: 6 months ongoing (up to 1 year)
End product: ...

Harbridge Consulting Group Ltd

Address: Harbridge House,
3 Hanover Square,
London W1R 9RD,
UK

Telephone: (44) 071 6296341
Fax: (44) 071 4081667
Contact: John Kind

Other offices: USA (5); associates in Finland; France; Germany; Italy; Netherlands; Sweden. USA head office (Boston) – Contact: J Millard, tel (617) 2676410.

Ownership: Harbridge House Inc, USA which was established in 1950 is independent and owned by its senior employees

Year established: 1962

Total turnover: Worldwide consultancy – 1991: $20 mn; 1990: $23 mn; 1989: $26 mn; worldwide TQ revenue – 1991: $4 mn; 1990: $4 mn; 1989: $1 mn

Number of assignments in last 2 years: 21, of which 10 are ongoing

Billing practices: Agreed in advance with the client; normally on the basis of consulting time and the level of seniority of the staff involved

Personnel: Worldwide consultancy – 150 consisting of 32 directors; 58 consultants; 60 support staff; plus 50 outside professionals. Worldwide TQ – 5 directors; 6 consultants; 5 support staff.

Background and experience of professional staff: All are graduates with either MBAs or PhDs. There is a substantial amount of business experience as well particularly in engineering, human resources, finance and marketing.

Areas of specialisation:

- Understanding Customer Needs and Expectations
- Quality Function Development
- Corporate Culture
- Quality Understanding and Awareness
- Employee Involvement and Teamworking
- Elimination of Waste and JIT
- Total Productive Maintenance
- Problem Solving Tools and Process Involvement Tools and Techniques
- Control of Variability (including Statistical Process Control)
- Measurement of Quality-Related Costs
- Quality Assurance (including ISO 9000)
- Supplier Partnerships
- New Financial Management
- World Class Product Development

Most important industry sectors for TQ work:

- Automotive
- Chemicals
- Aerospace
- Pharmaceuticals
- Financial services
- Transport

Definition of TQ: Harbridge follows the Deming philosophy in particular – Quality begins with delighting the customer. To quote Rafael Aguayo, "Quality is anything that enhances the product or service from the viewpoint of the customer."

TQ work in training and implementation of ISO 9000: Training is about 50–60%. Very little is concerned with the formal implementation of ISO 9000.

Types of work not undertaken: –

Other information: Harbridge House specialises in management development. The TQM/continuous improvement practice area represents about 20% of total revenues.

Examples of recent assignments:

Client/description: BAA plc
Project description: Introduction to the concepts of continuous improvement for directors and managers via a series of workshops
Client contact title: Management training manager
Consultant name/title: John Kind, partner
Length of project: 6 months
End product: A wide ranging series of process improvement initiatives at a number of BAA's airports including changes to organisational structure

---

Client/description: General Electric (Aircraft Engines)
Project description: Identifying and organising process improvement priorities and actually conducting process improvement projects
Client contact title: General manager of continuous improvement and customer satisfaction
Consultant name/title: Jamie Millard, partner
Length of project: 3½ years ongoing
End product: Significant improvements to key processes such as product development and inventory management

---

Client/description: Scudder, Stevens and Clark (Mutual Funds)
Project description: Customer focused process
Client contact title: Vice president – quality
Consultant name/title: Matt Nash, partner
Length of project: 6 months ongoing
End product: Specific improvements in customer service

Hay Management Consultants Ltd

Address: 52 Grosvenor Gardens,   **Telephone:**   (44) 071 7300833
                     London SW1W 0AU,   **Fax:**   (44) 071 7308193
                     UK   **Contact:**   Nick Boulter

Other offices: 76 offices worldwide. Subsidiary companies: Lifeskills Management Group; McBer. European head office (Brussels) – Contact: J Bomers, tel (32) 2 3323233; USA head office (Washington) – Contact: D McDaniel, tel (202) 6376600; Asia Pacific head office (Singapore) – Contact: C Drakeford, tel (65) 3391166

Ownership: Worldwide partnership. The Hay Group was established in the USA in 1943.

Year established: 1964

Total turnover: ...

Number of assignments in last 2 years: ...

Billing practices: Based on per diem calculation

Personnel: Worldwide – approximately 2,025 consisting of 125 directors; 900 consultants; 1,000 support staff. Europe – approximately 810 consisting of 50 directors; 360 consultants; 400 support staff

Background and experience of professional staff: Hay/Lifeskills recruit consultants in their early/mid 30s; they should be graduates who will have undertaken two or more management positions and therefore be experienced in management issues, human resources management and quality

Areas of specialisation:

- Understanding Customer Needs and Expectations
- Quality Function Deployment
- Corporate Culture
- Quality Understanding and Awareness
- Employee Involvement and Teamworking
- Others: Strategy clarification; leadership; management processes; people development and reward consulting

Most important industry sectors for TQ work:

All sectors

Definition of TQ: Hay accepts the nine criteria of the European Quality Award as representing their view of the quality goals to which organisations should strive – they work to introduce total quality services to organisations. Hay recognises that neither TQM nor customer care by themselves are sufficient – they have developed a total quality service approach to harness the best of these approaches and enable companies to focus on the quality of their products, the skills of their people, the features of their presentation and the customer friendliness of their processes.

TQ work in training and implementation of ISO 9000:   Training 50%; much is related to BS 5750/ISO 9000/European Quality Award and with companies that are seeking to achieve this or already have achieved this and now want to improve further

Types of work not undertaken: ...

Other information: The Hay Group undertakes total quality services consulting through Hay Management Consultants (who specialise in strategy and mission clarification and in developing people and processes); McBer (who concentrate in culture change and on people development); and Lifeskills (who specialise in top team workshops and in conducting large scale training programmes.

Examples of recent assignments:

Client/description: A major brewer
Project description: To introduce total quality service programme throughout
Client contact title: Personnel director
Consultant name/title: Mike Scally, Director (Hay/Lifeskills)
Length of project: 3 years ongoing
End product: Improvements in quality measures across all functional and business areas

_____

Client/description: The downstream arm of a major oil company
Project description: To increase the level of customer responsiveness at cashier level
Client contact title: Managing director
Consultant name/title: Barrie Hopson, managing director (Hay/Lifeskills)
Length of project: 1 year ongoing
End product: 250 station managers trained to run quality improvement group throughout the organisation

_____

Client/description: A major retailer
Project description: To increase customer contact skills at sales assistant level
Client contact title: Training manager
Consultant name/title: Barrie Hopson, Managing director (Hay/Lifeskills)
Length of project: 1 year
End product: Every supervisor took their workgroup through an eight session customer care training programme backed up by eight open learning modules resulting in a significant reduction in staff turnover, significant improvement in employees' attitudes and reduction in number of complaints

David Hutchins Associates Ltd

Address: 13–14 Hermitage Parade,   **Telephone:** (44) 0344 28712
                     High Street,   **Fax:**   (44) 0344 25968
                     Ascot,   **Contact:**   Warren Winslow
                     Berkshire SL5 7HE,
                     UK

Other offices: UK (1); strategic alliances in Africa; Australia; Brazil; Europe; Far East; USA

Ownership: David Hutchins International, UK (holding company)

Year established: 1979

Total turnover: 1991: £1.7 mn; 1990: £1.6 mn; £1.3 mn

Number of assignments in last 2 years: 63, of which 37 are ongoing

Billing practices: Against standard business costing and proposals; invoice within 14 days

Personnel: 15 consisting of 3 directors; 6 consultants; 6 support staff

Background and experience of professional staff: Substantial experience from industry in a TQ senior staff role; understanding of ISO 9000 and total quality concepts

Areas of specialisation:

- Understanding Customer Needs and Expectations
- Quality Function Development
- Corporate Culture
- Quality Understanding and Awareness
- Employee Involvement and Teamworking
- Elimination of Waste and JIT
- Problem Solving Tools and Process Involvement Tools and Techniques

- Control of Variability (including Statistical Process Control)
- Measurement of Quality-Related Costs
- Quality Assurance (including ISO 9000)
- Supplier Partnerships
- Others: Strategic policy management; managing critical processes

Most important industry sectors for TQ work:

- Government
- Manufacturing
- Petrochemicals

- Services (banks/hotels)
- Healthcare
- Retailing

Definition of TQ: Everything everyone in the business does to satisfy the total requirements of all customers, internal and external

TQ work in training and implementation of ISO 9000:   60% TQ activity; 40% ISO 9000

Types of work not undertaken: Implementing TQ in consultancies

Other information: –

Examples of recent assignments:

Client/description: Government agency
Project description: Implementation of TQ
Client contact title: Director of quality
Consultant name/title: W Winslow, chief executive officer
End product: Establish infrastructure and team work; financial benefits

---

Client/description: Major worldwide pharmaceutical company
Project description: Implementation of continuous improvement
Client contact title: Director and vice president
Consultant name/title: M Jones, operations director
End product: Implementation of TQ at all sites; early projects delivery

---

Client/description: International Space Organisation
Project description: ISO 9000
Client contact title: Safety, reliability & 2A division
Consultant name/title: Alan Medley, Senior consultant
Length of project: 6 months ongoing
End product: Achievement of ISO 9000

ICME International

Address:	Restelbergstrasse 49,	**Telephone:**	(41) 1 3665511
	8044 Zrich,	**Fax:**	(41) 1 3665500
	Switzerland	**Contact:**	Rolf Iff

Other offices: France (1); Germany (2); Switzerland (1); USA (1)

Ownership: Partnership

Year established: 1954

Total turnover: 1991: SFr24.1 mn; 1990: SFr17.6 mn; 1989: SFr14.9 mn (15% TQ)

Number of assignments in last 2 years: 14, of which 11 are ongoing

Billing practices: Global fee basis with competitive fee rates by country

Personnel: ICME overall – 100 consisting of 15 directors; 60 consultants; 25 support staff. TQ – 10 consisting of 1 director; 6 consultants; 3 support staff.

Background and experience of professional staff: Line experience in industry; technical or economics degree, many with advanced technical and/or management (MBA) degrees; average age of consultant is 41 years

Areas of specialisation:

- Understanding Customer Needs and Expectations
- Corporate Culture
- Quality Understanding and Awareness
- Employee Involvement and Teamworking
- Elimination of Waste and JIT
- Total Productive Maintenance
- Problem Solving Tools and Process Involvement Tools and Techniques

- Control of Variability (including Statistical Process Control)
- Measurement of Quality-Related Costs
- World Class Product Development
- Others: Management of change; business process management; people excellence process

Most important industry sectors for TQ work:

- Chemicals/petrochemicals
- Food industry and distribution
- Banking

- Transportation
- Consumer products

Definition of TQ: An organisational transformational process which starts with the customer, involves the whole organisation and aims at contributing to the improvement of people and systems in order to achieve a company's most important strategic objectives

TQ work in training and implementation of ISO 9000:   ICME coaches clients in TQ including how to approach ISO 9000, but they do not do certification work. Training and coaching represent 70% of TQM activities.

Types of work not undertaken: Public sector

Other information: –

Examples of recent assignments:

Client/description: Ralston Energy Systems Europe
Project description: TQM implementation
Client contact title: Quality director Europe
Consultant name/title: G Perruchot, associate director
Length of project: 16 months ongoing
End product: Developing a "Vision 2000"; employee survey; European customer satisfaction survey; management
 workshops; quality awareness training; business management

Client/description: Union Bank of Switzerland (USB)
Project description: Total quality management
Client contact title: Director of TQ taskforce
Consultant name/title: Rolf Iff, partner
Length of project: Ongoing up to 1 year
End product: TQ training modules (leadership and quality awareness); train-the-trainer workshops

---

Client/description: Union Carbide Industrial Gases Europe
Project description: "From vision to action" workshops
Client contact title: Quality director Europe
Consultant name/title: G Perruchot and J Vachette, associate directors
Length of project: 1 year
End product: Management workshops derived from the company's vision and goals; set of strategic business process
 improvement opportunities

Inter Consult (UK)

Address: East Selaby, Darlington DL2 3HE, UK

Telephone: (44) 0325 730993
Fax: (44) 0325 730993
Contact: John R Heptonstall

Other offices: Associate in Germany (v.Mengersen & Partner GmbH, Heidelberg)

Ownership: Independent (owned by director, Sally Bell)

Year established: 1990

Total turnover: 1991: £210,000; 1990: £80,000

Number of assignments in last 2 years: 7, of which 4 are ongoing (plus 6 ISO 9000 of which 3 are ongoing)

Billing practices: Project fee with man/day rate as basis

Personnel: 8 consisting of 1 director; 1 senior consultant; 3 principal consultants; 1 trainee consultant; 2 research assistants/secretaries (4 fee earning professionals)

Background and experience of professional staff: Good first degree (usually non-business); MBA; about 3 years' managerial industry experience

Areas of specialisation:

- Understanding Customer Needs and Expectations
- Quality Function Deployment
- Corporate Culture
- Quality Understanding and Awareness
- Problem Solving Tools and Process Involvement Tools and Techniques
- Control of Variability (including Statistical Process Control)
- Quality Assurance (including ISO 9000)
- Supplier Partnerships

Most important industry sectors for TQ work:

- Professional firms
- General manufacturing companies
- R&D departments

Definition of TQ: TQ is the successful management of the customer/supplier chain, as defined by TQM theory, in a company whose culture is based on constant and continuous improvement

TQ work in training and implementation of ISO 9000: In TQ consultancy 70–85% is education and training workshops. ISO 9000 is considered a separate entity with approximately 30% of assignments being ISO 9000 implementations.

Types of work not undertaken: Competing clients as long as project is current; work in SIC codes – 09, parts of 02 and parts of 20

Other information: Active regular associate of the European Foundation for Quality Management (EFQM) in Eindhoven, Netherlands

Examples of recent assignments:

Client/description: Chemical company
Project description: Baseline assessment and improvement of existing TQ system along the criteria and guidelines of the European Quality Award (TEQA)
Client contact title: Managing director
Consultant name/title: John R Heptonstall, senior consultant
Length of project: 7–9 months ongoing
End product: Achievement of approximately 600 points under TEQA guidelines

---

Client/description: Solicitor practice
Project description: Induction of partners to TQ theory and tools/implementation of TQ infrastructure and basic tools
Client contact title: Senior partner
Consultant name/title: John R Heptonstall, senior consultant
Length of project: 1 year ongoing
End product: Successful implementation of embryonic TQ system and culture

---

Client/description: Precision engineering firm
Project description: Quality function deployment
Client contact title: QA manager
Consultant name/title: C D v Mengersen, principal consultant
Length of project: 9 months
End product: Concept and theory of QFD well understood throughout the company; successful use of QFD

INVENTA Limited

Address:	Rehorova 14,	**Telephone:**	(42) 2 265475
	130 00 Prague 3,	**Fax:**	(42) 2 265435
	Czechoslovakia	**Contact:**	Mirek Smira

Other offices: –

Ownership: Independent, partner-owned. Managing partner – Dr Ondrej Landa.

Year established: 1989

Total turnover: INVENTA overall – 1991: $675,900; 1990: $413,800 INVENTA Consulting – 1991: $148,300; 1990: $17,500

Number of assignments in last 2 years: 23, of which 12 are ongoing

Billing practices: Daily rate of US$800 – 1,700 depending on the seniority of assigned consultants, plus expenses

Personnel: INVENTA personnel involved in TQ – 9 consisting of 2 directors; 5 consultants; 2 support staff

Background and experience of professional staff: Master's or PhD in various areas, mainly in business management organisational development and technical sciences. All senior staff have a minimum of 5 years' experience in management consulting with focus on organisational development and TQ. Partners have more than 10 years' experience in management consulting.

Areas of specialisation:

- Corporate Culture
- Quality Understanding and Awareness
- Employee Involvement and Teamworking
- Problem Solving Tools and Process Involvement Tools and Techniques
- Control of Variability (including Statistical Process Control)
- Quality Assurance (including ISO 9000)
- New Financial Management

Most important industry sectors for TQ work:

- Textiles
- Glass making
- Machinery
- Services

Definition of TQ: Total quality is a continuous improvement of management, services and production processes aiming to satisfy and exceed both internal and external customers' needs and wishes

TQ work in training and implementation of ISO 9000: Management training 60%; ISO 9000 33%

Types of work not undertaken: Competing clients; clients without top management commitment; clients without readiness for TQM implementation

Other information: Training and consulting teams of INVENTA operate in such fields as development of corporate strategy, strategic planning, financial management, marketing, HRM and HRD making it possible to provide customers with comprehensive service. INVENTA cooperates with leading international firms and schools such as PMI Inc and Incos (both USA); Synectics and Strathclyde Business School (both UK). Because of Inventa's involvement in the transformation of the Czechoslovak economy and due to the public positions of INVENTA's managing partner, Dr Ondrej Landa, Inventa provided pro bono consulting services to a number of governmental and international institutions in 1989–91. The total of these free consulting services can be valued at $100,000.

Examples of recent assignments:

Client/description: Merina Trencin
Project description: Transformation of management, service and production processes toward continuous quality improvement and implementation of innovative corporate culture
Client contact title: Director TQM
Consultant name/title: Ing Mirek Smira, senior TQM consultant
Length of project: 3 years ongoing
End product: Improved productivity, increased profits and a greater market share as well as greater customer satisfaction, improved employee morale, increased job satisfaction and better communication at all levels

---

Client/description: Podnik Vypocetni Techniky
Project description: Transformation of management and services processes towards continuous quality improvement in all 50 regional offices
Client contact title: TQM director
Consultant name/title: Dr Hana Tomasek, partner
Length of project: 3 years ongoing
End product: Improved service efficiency, greater customer satisfaction, improved employee morale, increased job satisfaction and better communication among regional offices

---

Client/description: Stasis Slavkov
Project description: Implementation of the quality system according to ISO 9001, followed by development of the ISO 9001 elements into a system based on TQM philosophy
Client contact title: Director of quality
Consultant name/title: Ing Ivan Miller, consultant
Length of project: 2½ years ongoing
End product: ISO 9001 certification and continuous quality improvement at all company levels

ISQ – Institute for Corporate Strategies and Quality

Address:	Dinkelbergstrasse 42,	**Telephone:**	(41) 61 671703
	4125 Riehen,	**Fax:**	(41) 61 674853
	Switzerland	**Contact:**	W Hungerbuhler

Other offices: Austria (1); France (1); Germany (1); USA (1). European head office (Germany) – Contact: B Lutzer, tel (49) 7621 87453

Ownership: Independent. Known as Institut fur Unternehmensstrategien und Qualiä in Austria, Germany and Switzerland (all established in 1989).

Year established: 1988

Total turnover: ...

Number of assignments in last 2 years: 34 (middle and long term projects) of which 19 are ongoing

Billing practices: Monthly/quarterly according to consultancy volume; lump sum (conditions for assurance of success depending on agreement)

Personnel: 15 consisting of 2 directors; 9 consultants; 4 support staff

Background and experience of professional staff: University degrees (engineering; chemistry; economics); engineering diploma (machine/electronics)

Areas of specialisation:

- Understanding Customer Needs and Expectations
- Quality Function Deployment
- Corporate Culture
- Quality Understanding and Awareness
- Employee Involvement and Teamworking
- Total Productive Maintenance

- Problem Solving Tools and Process Involvement Tools and Techniques
- Quality Assurance (including ISO 9000)
- World Class Product Development
- Others: Business process management; cycle time management; strategic leadership

Most important industry sectors for TQ work:

- Manufacturing
- Chemistry
- Paper
- Textiles
- Machine and electronics services

- Banks
- Insurance
- Software
- Engineering;
- Nuclear waste disposal

Definition of TQ: A management tool for continuous improvement of all performances towards even better customer orientation

TQ work in training and implementation of ISO 9000: 62% (workshops for top management and seminars "train the trainers" in TQ; 38% EN 29000=ISO 9000)

Types of work not undertaken: Head hunting; TQ for organisations with less than 10 employees

Other information: ISQ's consulting activities are offered in English; French; German; Italian; Portuguese

Examples of recent assignments:

Client/description: Ciba-Geigy Co (dyestuffs, pigments, additives, engineering etc)
Project description: Implementation of TQ in all levels of the organisation
Client contact title: Director
Consultant name/title: Hugo Tlach, consultant
Length of project: 30 months
End product: Higher motivation of employees; higher productivity; reduced cycle time

---

Client/description: Siemens Nixdorf (Switzerland)
Project description: Implementation of EN 29001 with certification
Client contact title: Director quality assurance
Consultant name/title: Dr Richard von Rutte, senior partner
Length of project: 2 years ongoing
End product: Certification according to EN 29001 (ISO 9001)

Client/description: Sulzer Thermtec
Project description: Training of top management in strategic leadership and TQ and EN 29000
Client contact title: Executive director
Consultant name/title: Peter Krebs, senior consultant
Length of project: 1 year ongoing
End product: All top managers know how to conceive and implement a quality system which is adapted to the specific needs of their organisations

A T Kearney Limited

Address: Stockley House,   **Telephone:**   (44) 071 8346886
130 Wilton Road,   **Fax:**   (44) 071 6306645
London SW1V 1LQ,   **Contact:**   Malcolm Graveling
UK

Other offices: Belgium (1); Canada (1); Czechoslovakia (1); Denmark (1); France (1); Germany (4); Hong Kong (1); Italy (1); Japan (1); Netherlands (1); Norway (1); Singapore (1): Spain (1); Sweden (2); USA (15). European head office (Germany) – Contact: P A Wagner, tel (49) 211 13770; USA head office (Chicago) – Contact: M Schiller, tel (312) 6480111; Asia/Pacific head office (Tokyo): Contact: W Best, tel (81) 355619155

Ownership: A T Kearney Inc, USA, privately held

Year established: 1926

Total turnover: Worldwide – 1991: $178 mn

Number of assignments in last 2 years: Over 100

Billing practices: Dependent on situation and client's needs

Personnel: Worldwide – 1,235 consisting of 770 directors/consultants; 465 support staff

Background and experience of professional staff: Graduate degree; line management experience in industry supported by a business degree

Areas of specialisation:

- Understanding Customer Needs and Expectations
- Quality Function Development
- Corporate Culture
- Quality Understanding and Awareness
- Employee Involvement and Teamworking
- Elimination of Waste and JIT
- Total Productive Maintenance
- Problem Solving Tools and Process Involvement Tools and Techniques
- Control of Variability (including Statistical Process Control)

- Measurement of Quality-Related Costs
- Quality Assurance (including ISO 9000)
- Supplier Partnerships
- New Financial Management (activity based costing/ throughput accounting)
- World Class Product Development (simultaneous engineering)
- Others: General management consultancy (eg. strategy, marketing, logistics, organisation effectiveness, manufacturing)

Most important industry sectors for TQ work:

- Manufacturing
- Financial services

- Energy and other service sectors, eg. IT distribution

Definition of TQ: Creating competitive advantage by focusing on what is important to the customer and by achieving superior performance at lower cost

TQ work in training and implementation of ISO 9000:   Training of some form is a part of every assignment to assist in the successful transfer of skills and knowledge to client personnel. "Training" and "ISO 9000" in isolation will not bring benefits to clients therefore A T Kearney does not undertake them individually.

Types of work not undertaken: A T Kearney will not undertake work which contravenes the code of ethics and standards of professional practice of the management consulting associations to which they belong or which they believe not to be in the interest of their clients

Other information: A T Kearney views TQ as a "way of doing business" not a discrete product. As such every situation differs and their work is tailored to recognise the specific stage of development of the client organisation. Internally, they practise what they preach. They have an internal programme worldwide, review client satisfaction after all projects and input their assessment of the work into the partner compensation process.

Examples of recent assignments:

Client/description: Food processing
Project description: Business process reengineering
Consultant name/title: Dale Marco, vice president
Length of project: 6 months ongoing
End product: Reduced costs; increased production; cultural change

---

Client/description: Fine chemical industry
Project description: Operations strategy reengineering
Consultant name/title: Antonio Ardit, vice president
Length of project: 1 year ongoing
End product: Drastic cost reduction; improved quality and service; simplification of organisation; cultural change

---

Client/description: Consumer goods manufacturer
Project description: Redesign of manufacturing business to improve quality and delivery, to reduce costs and to develop client personnel
Consultant name/title: Steve Young, vice president
Length of project: 18 months ongoing
End product: Improved quality; reduced stocks and workforce; significant cultural change; reduced investment programme

Kepner-Tregoe Limited

Address:	Bentley House,	**Telephone:**	(44) 0753 856716
	13–15 Victoria Street,	**Fax:**	(44) 0753 854929
	Windsor,	**Contact:**	Brian R Bentley
	Berks SL4 1HB,		
	UK		

Other offices: Australia (1); France (1); Germany (1); Japan (1); Malaysia (1); North America (2); Singapore (1); Switzerland (1); UK (1) Associated companies: Brazil (1); Denmark (1); Finland (1); Ireland (1); Italy (1); Mexico (1); Netherlands (1); Taiwan (1); Thailand (1); Venezuela (1). USA head office (Princetown, NJ) – Contact: Ms D Mather, tel (609) 9212806; Asia/Pacific head office (Sydney, Australia) – Contact: P Jordan, tel (61) 2 9091377.

Ownership: Kepner-Tregoe Inc, established in 1958, a wholly owned subsidiary of United States Fidelity and Guaranty Corporation, Baltimore, USA

Year established: 1965

Total turnover: Worldwide management consultancy – 1991: $37 mn; 1990: $35 mn; 1989: $33 mn; Europe – 1991: $7 mn; 1990: $6 mn; 1989: $5.2 mn UK – 1991: $2.9 mn; 1990: $2.8 mn; 1989: $2.2 mn

Number of assignments in last 2 years: Europe – total 25 of which 20 are ongoing, UK – 12 major and many smaller projects. As Kepner-Tregoe transfers ownership, all are ongoing with their support.

Billing practices: Project fee based on consulting days, training days, licensing of clients and training materials

Personnel: Worldwide – 300 consisting of 12 directors; 200 consultants; 88 support staff. Europe – 44 consisting of 4 directors; 30 consultants; 10 support staff. UK – 30 consisting of 3 directors; 21 consultants; 6 support staff. All consultants have a role to play in TQ.

Background and experience of professional staff: Minimum 5 years' relevant manufacturing business experience after graduation with line management experience

Areas of specialisation:

- Understanding Customer Needs and Expectations
- Quality Function Development
- Corporate Culture
- Quality Understanding and Awareness
- Employee Involvement and Teamworking
- Elimination of Waste and JIT
- Total Productive Maintenance

- Problem Solving Tools and Process Involvement Tools and Techniques
- Control of Variability (including Statistical Process Control)
- Measurement of Quality-Related Costs
- New Financial Management
- World Class Product Development

Most important industry sectors for TQ work:

- Transport
- Chemicals
- Pharmaceuticals
- Natural resources

- Hi-tech manufacturing
- Paper making
- Petrochemicals
- Financial services

Definition of TQ: Continuously satisfying customer requirements; achieving quality at the lowest cost; achieving total quality by involving everyone

TQ work in training and implementation of ISO 9000: Training 100%; ISO 9000 not directly

Other information: –

Examples of recent assignments:

Client/description: Aircraft maintenance in major international airline
Project description: Installing a TQM system and structure and training in skills for quality improvements
Client contact title: Chief maintenance engineer
Consultant name/title: William Hextall, director
Length of project: 2 years ongoing
End product: System and structure of TQM; skills for quality improvement

---

Client/description: ICI Agrochemicals
Project description: Provision and installation of "Tools for Quality" programme to drive the company wide TQM programme
Client contact title: Director of quality
Consultant name/title: G Edmondson, consultant
Length of project: 6 months ongoing
End product: Tools and skills for non-management and management staff

---

Client/description: Petroleum refinery
Project description: Structure, systems and skills for resolution of refinery incidents affecting production, quality and safety
Client contact title: Refinery manager, technical department
Consultant name/title: John Smith, consultant
Length of project: 9 months ongoing
End product: Client owned system for problem solving/problem prevention

KPMG Management Consulting

Address:	8 Salisbury Square,	**Telephone:**	(44) 071 2368000
	London EC4Y 8BB,	**Fax:**	(44) 071 8328513
	UK	**Contact:**	Owen Bull/Paul Mills

Other offices: KPMG operates in 125 countries worldwide

Ownership: Partnership

Year established: 1957

Total turnover: KPMG worldwide – 1991: $801.5 mn (management consultancy)

Number of assignments in last 2 years: –

Billing practices: Per diem plus expenses

Personnel: TQ (UK) – 1 partner; 1 managing consultant; 2 senior consultants in core team plus 6 fully trained consultants from other parts of the KPMG network. KPMG worldwide – 76,217 consisting of 6,042 partners; 52,628 professional; 17,546 other. KPMG worldwide management consultancy – 643 partners; 5,237 professionals. EC worldwide management consultancy – 232 partners; 2,245 professionals.

Areas of specialisation:

- Understanding Customer Needs and Expectations
- Corporate Culture
- Quality Understanding and Awareness
- Employee Involvement and Teamworking
- Elimination of Waste and JIT
- Problem Solving Tools and Process Involvement Tools and Techniques
- Control of Variability (including Statistical Process Control)
- Measurement of Quality-Related Costs
- Quality Assurance (including ISO 9000)
- Supplier Partnerships

Most important industry sectors for TQ work:

- Manufacturing
- Process
- Financial institutions

Definition of TQ: TQ is a means to an end, not an end in its own right. It may be shown thus – "Become the best: by maximising financial performance; by continuously matching then exceeding customer requirements; by adopting the practices of TQ management."

TQ work in training and implementation of ISO 9000:   Training forms a part of KPMG's approach – but not a large one. They believe training enables people, but does not empower them. KPMG does not really consider ISO work to be TQ (rather quality systems).

Types of work not undertaken: No specific categories except training in TQ as a stand alone

Other information: Original parts of the firm were established in 1914 and 1925. In 1957 management consultancy was established at Peat, Marwick, Mitchell & Co. On 1 January 1987, Peat Marwick International and Klynveld Main Goerdeler merged to form the international accountancy and management consultancy firm Klynveld Peat Marwick Goerdeler. The total quality consulting practice began work in 1991.

Examples of recent assignments:

Client/description: Specialist metal treatment company
Project description: Implementing a full TQ management process including identification of "Quality Success Factors" and use of successful pilot improvement projects to spread the change process across the organisation
Client contact title: Managing director
Length of project: 1 year ongoing

Client/description: Major UK clearing bank (strategic business unit)
Project description: Improving the skills and awareness of senior and middle managers regarding service quality including planning for quality and quality performance indicators, service-level agreements, new approaches for customer care, service delivery and complaints handling
Client contact title: General manager
Length of project: 2 years complete

Client/description: Large professional services firm
Project description: Provided advice and support to a large professional services firm in developing a quality culture throughout the organisation including providing training in quality techniques, establishment of quality improvement teams and facilitator training
Client contact title: Senior partner

Client/description: Major clothing manufacturer
Project description: Designed and implemented a programme of quality management activities aimed at generating improvements at every link in the service chain of activities to increase external customer satisfaction
Client contact title: Managing director

Laurie International Limited

Address: Cumberland House,   **Telephone:** (44) 071 9385400
1 Kensington Road,   **Fax:** (44) 071 9385454
London W8 5NX,   **Contact:** Donald L Laurie
UK

Other offices: USA (1) USA head office (Lexington, MA) – Contact: Ms M Braswell, tel: (617) 8631640

Ownership: Independent limited company

Year established: 1980

Total turnover: ...

Number of assignments in last 2 years: UK and USA – 8 of which 3 are ongoing

Billing practices: Consultants' time is charged at a daily rate and clients are billed for fees and expenses monthly

Personnel: UK and USA – 22 consisting of 4 directors; 12 consultants; 6 support staff

Background and experience of professional staff: They have experience as management academics, TQM professionals and former directors of quality, strategic management consultants with implementation experience, organisational learning, leadership and process management specialists and line managers with industry experience

Areas of specialisation:

- Understanding Customer Needs and Expectations
- Quality Function Development
- Corporate Culture
- Quality Understanding and Awareness
- Employee Involvement and Teamworking
- Problem Solving Tools and Process Involvement Tools and Techniques
- Measurement of Quality-Related Costs
- Supplier Partnerships
- Others: Creating a Learning Organisation; The Work of the Leader in Sustaining Continuous Improvement and Customer Responsiveness

Most important industry sectors for TQ work:

- Petroleum
- Telecommunications
- Office products
- Consumer electronics
- Airlines
- Travel and leisure
- Conglomerates and privatised utilities
- Public sector
- Specialise in working with medium and large size organisations

Definition of TQ: Total quality is the consistent, organisation-wide practice of continuously meeting customer requirements the first time at the least cost

TQ work in training and implementation of ISO 9000: Not directly concerned with implementing ISO 9000. In an overall TQM initiative, roughly 30–40% of work is training related.

Types of work not undertaken: Competing clients in the same industry

Other information: The consultancy has an ongoing commitment to research in management issues and has produced/is researching reports on:
- *The Work of the Leader in Creating Customer Responsiveness* (June 1992)
- *Management Training and Development Issues for the 1990s* (January 1991)
- *Best Practice Transfer Within Organisations* (July 1992)

Examples of recent assignments:

Client/description: British transport conglomerate with 23 subsidiaries worldwide
Project description: To effect turnaround from financially-driven environment to a customer-driven company. Development of comprehensive TQM process and group identity from analysis, diagnostics and top management workshops through to implementation to 10,000 staff
Client contact title: Chief executive
Consultant name/title: David Kohler, director
Length of project: 18 months (quality process is maintained within the company without the need for consultancy support)
End product: Documented diagnostics on cost of quality, listening to the customer and listening to employees; group executives made responsible for key issues to be resolved at group level; management system developed to measure progress through Quality First Council; group mission with supporting values and practices; roll-out to 10,000 employees through custom-designed tools

---

Client/description: Office products manufacturer/supplier
Project description: Five years into TQ initiative, client (a Malcolm Baldrige winner) identified a problem with managing customer losses. Worked to relate investment in customer service to financial performance by establishing the number of customers leaving, the resulting financial losses to the client, reasons for customer losses and, through a Quality Improvement Team, developed an implementation plan to reduce customer losses.
Client contact title: Managing director
Consultant name/title: Charles Constable, manager
Length of project: 1 year (Laurie is involved in rolling out the results in Europe and the US; follow-on work has focused on "best practice" transfer across the business)
End product: Analysis showed potential profit improvement of 15% over three years if action was taken to reduce customer losses; Quality Improvement Team developed specifications to reduce customer losses including a Losses Tracking System and Advance Warning System; implementation plan developed by Quality Improvement Team

---

Client/description: Petroleum company
Project description: Company launched a major culture change centred on creating customer responsiveness and building continuous improvement into the fabric of the business. Initial work involved conceptualising the framework to enable a structured approach to achieving customer responsiveness and jointly, with the client, building an implementation plan. Involved planning guidelines and "How-to" manuals for five businesses on five continents.
Client contact title: Executive vice president
Consultant name/title: Donald L Laurie, chief executive
Length of project: 1 year (Laurie are actively supporting parts of the business with implementation)
End product: Framework and implementation plan for making the organisation ultimately more customer responsive; work is ongoing

Management–Newstyle

Address:	Hill House, 20 Old Hill, Chislehurst, Kent BR7 5NB, UK	**Telephone:** **Fax:** **Contact:**	(44) 081 4671255 (44) 081 4671255 David Howard

Other offices: UK (3)

Ownership: Partnership

Year established: 1991

Total turnover: 1991: less than £100,000

Number of assignments in last 2 years: 1991: 8, of which 50% are ongoing

Billing practices: Day rate with man day target

Personnel: 5 consisting of 4 UK consultants and a US mentor and adviser (Homer Sarasohn)

Background and experience of professional staff: Extensive industrial and engineering backgrounds

Areas of specialisation:

- Understanding Customer Needs and Expectations
- Corporate Culture
- Quality Understanding and Awareness
- Employee Involvement and Teamworking
- Problem Solving Tools and Process Involvement Tools and Techniques
- Control of Variability (including Statistical Process Control – see "Types of work not undertaken" below)
- Others: Deming's System of Profound Knowledge; process mapping and added-value worktime mapping (for Kaizen)

Most important industry sectors for TQ work:

No pattern. No preference. Sector interest expanding rapidly.

Definition of TQ: Total quality is a corporate state of mind which drives towards sustained world class performance. It demands optimising the whole business activity to meet customer preferences and provide balanced stakeholder benefits.

TQ work in training and implementation of ISO 9000: 100% TQ; not involved with implementation of ISO 9000

Types of work not undertaken: "TQM fashion shows"; SPC without statistical thinking in the boardroom; ISO 9000 without commitment to continuous improvement

Other information: US mentor and adviser, Homer Sarasohn, is a professional engineer and began managing for quality in 1945 (on General MacArthur's staff) with the rebuilding of the Japanese communications industry. Over five years a dramatic turnaround was achieved to be continued by Dr Deming's arrival in 1950. Sarasohn retired as corporate director of IBM in 1977 and now speaks and counsels on all aspects of management.

Examples of recent assignments:

Client/description: Food company (own label supplies)
Project description: To reduce trade debtor days from 6 weeks to 3.5 weeks
Client contact title: Owner
Consultant name/title: David Howard, principal
Length of project: 6 months
End product: Improvement to 3.2 weeks by redesign of product distribution warehouse process through total team involvement; error in pallet assembly reduced from 4,100 ppm to 260 ppm over 18 months

---

Client/description: Utility company
Project description: Training middle/senior management about system approach to process improvement and use of suitable techniques
Client contact title: Quality programme coordinator
Consultant name/title: David Howard, principal
Length of project: 1 year ongoing
End product: Improved awareness of, and use of, process mapping techniques for use in improving performance of people, processes and problem solving

---

Client/description: IT division of an electric company
Project description: Stategic review
Client contact title: Quality cordinator, group
Consultant name/title: David Howard, principal
Length of project: 6 months
End product: Change of top management and restructuring of operation to better serve needs of group customer

Management-NewStyle

Managing for Quality, Productivity and Service Effectiveness

We specialise in the removal of wasted effort in business by mapping processes and reducing variation to increase added-value and reliability.

Management-NewStyle provides counselling, facilitation and training services dedicated to the long-term improvement of profitability by means of concentrating on cultural change and process management.

Our purpose : Continual improvement in the new economic age.

Our aim : Helping suppliers economically meet customers' preferences.

Our values : Knowledge, not rule-of thumb. Co-operation, not conflict. Sustainable development. Continual learning.

Our approach : Thinking in systems; working on processes.

Enquiries to:

David Howard   081 467 1255
Dr John Norrie   060124 603
Paul Hollingworth   0371 851122
Patrick Dolan   0747 52581

"Trying harder is not the answer."

"The chances of successfully improving our position in the future under the present system of management is non-existent."

"Management of a system is action based on prediction."

"Draw a flowchart for whatever you are doing. Until you do, you do not understand what you are doing. You just have a job."

Dr W Edwards Deming

Principal Address: Management-NewStyle Hill House 20 Old Hill Chislehurst Kent BR7 5NB

Matrix Srl

Address: Corso Moncalieri 69,   **Telephone:** (39) 11 6602242
10133 Turin,   **Fax:** (39) 11 6602067
Italy   **Contact:** Massimo Boario

Other offices: Through subsidiaries of Gruppo Poliedros – Poliedros Srl, Milan; Consulbank Srl, Milan; Consulnova Srl, Rome; Stratos Srl, Milan

Ownership: Gruppo Poliedros, Milan established in 1981

Year established: 1987

Total turnover: 1991: L2.25 bn; 1990: L1.95 mn; 1989: L1.4 mn

Number of assignments in last 2 years: Over 30, of which about 20 are ongoing

Billing practices: Fee by day of each consultant involved

Personnel: 18 consisting of 5 directors; 7 senior consultants; 2 junior consultants; 4 support staff

Background and experience of professional staff: Industry and service management; university teaching staff

Areas of specialisation:

- Corporate Culture
- Employee Involvement and Teamworking
- Elimination of Waste and JIT
- Problem Solving Tools and Process Involvement Tools and Techniques
- Quality Assurance (including ISO 9000)
- Others: Project management

Most important industry sectors for TQ work:

- Transport services (railways)
- Banking
- Manufacturing

Definition of TQ: Commitment by all employees at all levels to achieve customer satisfaction through continuous improvement in the quality of all products and services

TQ work in training and implementation of ISO 9000: Training 70%; ISO 9000 30%

Types of work not undertaken: –

Other information: –

Examples of recent assignments:

Client/description: Fiat – Auto
Project description: Improve front-line quality of dealers
Client contact title: Commercial manager
Consultant name/title: Massimo Boario, managing director
Length of project: 2 years ongoing
End product: Improved sales and service

Client/description: Ente Ferrovie Dello Stato
Project description: Development of continuous improvement of railways process
Client contact title: Quality function manager
Consultant name/title: Alberto Trivero, partner
Length of project: 1 year ongoing
End product: Commitment by employees to develop quality

Client/description: Banca CRT
Project description: Quality circles (building up and training on tools and techniques)
Client contact title: Human resources manager
Consultant name/title: Carlo Penati, partner
Length of project: 1 year
End product: Operating quality circles

Anthony Mitchell Associates

Address: "Aysgarth",
Horsham Road,
Cranleigh,
Surrey GU6 8DY,
UK

Telephone: (44) 0483 277894
Fax: (44) 0483 268529
Contact: Anthony Mitchell

Other offices: –

Ownership: Independent, part-time consultancy. Draws upon a network of Ashridge Management College tutors and consultants.

Year established: 1989

Total turnover: ...

Number of assignments in last 2 years: 2 major, both ongoing

Billing practices: Negotiable, different rates for development/consultancy and training; charges per day, fixed for one year, renewed on merit; terms 30 days

Personnel: 1 director; 1 support staff; up to 3 associates on any assignments

Background and experience of professional staff: Typically 10–20 years' industrial experience; all graduates; mixture of engineering, strategy, HRM and finance backgrounds

Areas of specialisation:

- Understanding Customer Needs and Expectations
- Corporate Culture
- Quality Understanding and Awareness
- Employee Involvement and Teamworking
- Problem Solving Tools and Process Involvement Tools and Techniques
- Others: Development of quality strategy and implementation plan to meet specific company needs

Most important industry sectors for TQ work:

- Petrochemical/engineering contracting
- Foods
- Toiletries

Definition of TQ: Creating a culture where customer (both internal and external) requirements are understood and met as effectively as possible throughout the organisation. The objective is to attract, retain and cross-sell to more customers than before thus increasing long term profitability.

TQ work in training and implementation of ISO 9000: Approximately 50–60% is tailored TQ training; the balance is consultancy, largely on TQ issues; ISO 9000 – nil

Types of work not undertaken: Training/consultancy work judged to compete with Ashridge – executive approval required. As a part-time consultancy, limited to two days per week.

Other information: –

Examples of recent assignments:

Client/description: Stone & Webster Engineering
Project description: Introduction of TQ
Client contact title: Personnel and administration manager
Consultant name/title: Anthony Mitchell, director
Length of project: 3 years ongoing
End product: Moving towards a quality culture; preferred supplier status to BP Chemicals (successful Grangemouth project – subject of European Construction Institute Report June 1991 and *FT* management article)

Client/description: Humphreys & Glasgow International
Project description: Introduction of TQ
Client contact title: Quality manager
Consultant name/title: Anthony Mitchell, director
Length of project: 2 years ongoing
End product: Moving towards TQ; current focus on cost of quality and TQ practice on client contracts

---

Client/description: Elida Gibbs (London and Leeds)
Project description: Initial training for TQ
Client contact title: Manager corporate quality
Consultant name/title: Anthony Mitchell, director (1989–91)
Length of project: 4 years ongoing
End product: TQ training on a company-wide basis (currently Ashridge Consulting Group client for other projects eg. process measurement/management)

MRA International

Address:	The Clock House,	**Telephone:**	(44) 0235 770067
	Grove Street,	**Fax:**	(44) 0235 771167
	Wantage,	**Contact:**	Mike Robson
	Oxon OX12 7AA,		
	UK		

Other offices: Associated offices in France (1); Ireland (1); Netherlands (1); USA (1)

Ownership: Independent limited company

Year established: 1981

Total turnover: 1991: £1.5 mn; 1991: £1.2 mn; 1989: £0.75 mn

Number of assignments in last 2 years: 50, of which 60% are ongoing

Billing practices: Daily fee rates plus expenses

Personnel: 24 consisting of 3 directors; 15 consultants; 6 support staff

Areas of specialisation:

- Understanding Customer Needs and Expectations
- Quality Function Deployment
- Corporate Culture
- Quality Understanding and Awareness
- Employee Involvement and Teamworking
- Elimination of Waste and JIT
- Total Productive Maintenance
- Problem Solving Tools and Process Involvement Tools and Techniques
- Control of Variability (including Statistical Process Control)
- Measurement of Quality-Related Costs
- Quality Assurance (including ISO 9000)
- Supplier Partnerships
- Others: Total quality management; management development; customer care

Most important industry sectors for TQ work:

- All industry
- Public and private sectors

Definition of TQ: Quality is meeting the agreed requirements of the customer now and in the future. Total quality, done properly, is a complete, integrated and coherent way of running an organisation as described in *The Journey to Excellence*.

TQ work in training and implementation of ISO 9000: Consultancy 70%; Training 25%; ISO 9000 5%

Types of work not undertaken: MRA will work in any field that is legal and, in their view, ethical

Other information: –

Examples of recent assignments:

Client/description: Llanelli Radiators
Project description: Introduction and maintenance of TQ
Client contact title: Managing director
Consultant name/title: Mike Robson, managing director
Length of project: 4 years
End product: Improved business performance (more than £1 mn); changed organisational culture; involvement of employees

---

Client/description: Blakemore (distribution)
Project description: Introduction and maintenance of TQ
Client contact title: Managing director
Consultant name/title: Ciaran Beary, operations manager
Length of project: 2 years ongoing
End product: Improved business performance; ongoing and widening application of TQ throughout the group

---

Client/description: Lothian & Edinburgh Enterprise
Project description: Introduction and maintenance of TQ
Client contact title: Chief executive
Consultant name/title: Jon Harvey, senior consultant
Length of project: 1 year ongoing
End product: Development of improved infrastructure; awareness of managerial behaviour; improved organisational performance

Neville Clarke International Limited

Address: Stratton Park House,   **Telephone:** (44) 0793 828222
Wanborough Road,   **Fax:** (44) 0793 828962
Stratton St Margaret,   **Contact:** Stuart Burnley
Swindon,
Wilts SN3 4JE,
UK

Other offices: Malaysia (1); Singapore (1); UK (1). Subsidiaries in UK: Miro Communications; Mastersearch; Culture Dynamics. Asia/Pacific head office (Malaysia) – Contact Dr B Mullock, tel (603) 2623501.

Ownership: Independent

Year established: 1979

Total turnover: 1991: £4 mn

Number of assignments in last 2 years: 65, of which 30 are ongoing

Billing practices: Daily rates

Personnel: 90 consisting of 8 directors; 60 consultants; 22 support staff

Background and experience of professional staff: Corporate culture change specialists; process consultants; software consultants

Areas of specialisation:

- Understanding Customer Needs and Expectations
- Quality Function Deployment
- Corporate Culture
- Quality Understanding and Awareness
- Employee Involvement and Teamworking
- Elimination of Waste and JIT
- Problem Solving Tools and Process Involvement Tools and Techniques

- Control of Variability (including Statistical Process Control)
- Measurement of Quality-Related Costs
- Quality Assurance (including ISO 9000)
- Others: Strategic culture change; cross-cultural team building; mergers and acquisitions; cross cultural synergy

Most important industry sectors for TQ work:

- Service sectors
- Government agencies

- Computer industry
- Mergers and acquisitions

Definition of TQ: Exceeding customer expectation profitably

TQ work in training and implementation of ISO 9000: Strategic culture change 60%; ISO 9000 40%

Types of work not undertaken: –

Other information: –

Examples of recent assignments:

Client/description: Japan Travel Bureau
Project description: Cross cultural team building (Japanese and European staff)
Client contact title: Chairman
Consultant name/title: Richard Sharpe, principal consultant
Length of project: 2 years ongoing
End product: Improved service to customers

Client/description: Thomas Cook
Project description: Culture change
Client contact title: Chairman
Consultant name/title: Philip Lloyd, principal consultant
Length of project: 2 years
End product: Improved service to customers ("Trust Thomas Cook")

Client/description: Yorkshire Electricity
Project description: Cultural transformation
Client contact title: Managing director
Consultant name/title: Richard Sharpe, principal consultant
Length of project: 1 year
End product: Customer service groups formulated; centralised site fully operational

ODI Europe

Address:
Apex Tower,
7 High Street,
New Malden,
Surrey KT3 4DQ,
UK

Telephone: (44) 081 3360022
Fax: (44) 081 3360246
Contact: Jon N Wilkie

Other offices: Australia (2); Canada (1); Denmark (1); Germany (1); Italy (2); Mexico (1); Netherlands (1); New Zealand (1); Norway (1); Spain (1); USA (20); Venezuela (1). USA head office (Burlington, MA) – Contact: T Varian, tel (617) 2728040.

Ownership: ODI (Organizational Dynamics Inc, USA) established in 1979

Year established: 1992

Total turnover: USA – $34 mn; Europe – $11 mn

Number of assignments in last 2 years: Europe – 40, of which 62% is ongoing

Billing practices: As per agreed quotations for consulting services (daily rate), materials and training workshops

Personnel: UK – 16 consisting of 1 managing director and chief executive officer of Europe; 1 director of training; 1 director of operations; 1 marketing director; 5 consultants; 4 support staff; 3 publishing staff. Europe – 78. Rest of the world – 310.

Background and experience of professional staff: Master's degrees; doctorates; business, teaching, marketing and executive management experience

Areas of specialisation:

- Understanding Customer Needs and Expectations
- Quality Function Deployment
- Corporate Culture
- Quality Understanding and Awareness
- Employee Involvement and Teamworking
- Elimination of Waste and JIT
- Problem Solving Tools and Process Involvement Tools and Techniques
- Control of Variability (including Statistical Process Control)

- Measurement of Quality-Related Costs
- Quality Assurance (including ISO 9000)
- Supplier Partnerships
- Others: Empowerment; strategic planning; Hoshin planning; senior management client conferences; Far East Seminar (Japan and North Korea); implementation consulting; senior manager education workshops and work conferences

Most important industry sectors for TQ work:

- Petroleum
- Petrochemicals
- Manufacturing
- Healthcare

- Information systems
- Banking
- Transport
- Service industries

Definition of TQ: Organisations practising TQ focus on customers and are driven by customer requirements; involve all of their employees in that goal; measure capability of work processes as well as measure results; align support systems; develop reward systems to align with these goals; and encourage continuous improvement movement

TQ work in training and implementation of ISO 9000: 90% training; 10% ISO 9000

Types of work not undertaken: –

Other information: –

Examples of recent assignments:

Client/description: Chevron UK
Project description: Total quality implementation (awareness workshops, quality action team training)
Client contact title: Quality director
Consultant name/title: Julie Soquet, director of training
Length of project: 18 months ongoing
End product: Process improvement

Client/description: Lufthansa
Project description: Total quality implementation (awareness workshops; quality action team training; facilitator training)
Client contact title: Quality director
Consultant name/title: Rob Evans, chief executive officer
Length of project: 3 years ongoing
End product: Process improvement

Client/description: Asea Brown Boveri
Project description: Total quality implementation (awareness workshops; quality action team training)
Client contact title: Quality manager, Eastern joint ventures
Consultant name/title: Jean Claude Simon, consultant
Length of project: 2 years ongoing
End product: Process improvement

O&F Quality Management Consultants Limited

Address:	Salts Mill, Victoria Road, Saltaire, Shipley, West Yorks BD18 3LB, UK	**Telephone:** **Fax:** **Contact:**	(44) 0274 597043 (44) 0274 581002 Professor John Oakland

Other offices: –

Ownership: Private

Year established: 1985

Total turnover: 1991: £1.2 mn; 1990: £800,000; 1989: £600,000

Number of assignments in last 2 years: Approximately 100, of which 80% are ongoing

Billing practices: Daily consultancy rates, or course/seminar fees, plus expenses and course materials/books

Personnel: 26 consisting of 3 directors; 15 consultants; 8 support staff

Background and experience of professional staff: Professional qualifications; degree level qualifications; experience in quality management at a high level – senior management or director level with several years' experience; average age 47

Areas of specialisation:

- Understanding Customer Needs and Expectations
- Quality Function Deployment
- Corporate Culture
- Quality Understanding and Awareness
- Employee Involvement and Teamworking
- Elimination of Waste and JIT
- Problem Solving Tools and Process Improvement Tools and Techniques
- Control of Variability (including Statistical Process Control)
- Measurement of Quality-Related Costs
- Quality Assurance (including ISO 9000)
- Supplier Partnerships

Most important industry sectors for TQ work:

- Process industries
- Polymers
- Packaging
- Services

Definition of TQ: TQ is an approach to improving the effectiveness and flexibility of a business as a whole. It is a way of managing to involve the whole organisation through its internal and external customer/supplier chain and process.

TQ work in training and implementation of ISO 9000: Training 60%; 30% is concerned with ISO 9000 implementation and audit training

Types of work not undertaken: –

Other information: –

Examples of recent assignments:

Client/description: British Gas – The Gas Business
Project description: Implementation of TQ
Client contact title: Director of quality and IS
Consultant name/title: Professor John Oakland, managing director
Length of project: 1 year ongoing
End product: Implementation plans for The Gas Business; senior management awareness of TQ; training and support materials for TQM; support of TQ team in client – customised for the client

---

Client/description: Tetrapack
Project description: Implementation of TQM
Client contact title: Quality director
Consultant name/title: Stephen Matthews, development director
Length of project: Ongoing up to 1 year
End product: TQM implementation programme; development of detailed training programme for teamwork development; training course material and seminars; TQ awareness and TQ project throughout company

---

Client/description: Field Packaging (Bradford)
Project description: Implementation of TQM
Client contact title: Managing director
Consultant name/title: John Glover, senior consultant
Length of project: Ongoing up to 2 years
End product: TQ well integrated into company; TQ projects based on teamwork very active and successful; savings in cost and increases in efficiency; TQ support and training materials/seminars

PA Consulting Group

Address:	123 Buckingham Palace Road, London SW1W 9SR, UK	**Telephone:** **Fax:** **Contact:**	(44) 071 7309000 (44) 071 3335050 David Cook

Other offices: 65 offices in 23 countries worldwide. USA head office (New Jersey) – Contact: A Robertson, tel (609) 4264700. Asia/Pacific head office (Sydney, Australia) – Contact: B Cooper, tel (61) 2 9642222. Scandinavia head office (Sweden) – Contact: M B Jensen, tel (46) 8 249020.

Ownership: PA Consulting Group, UK (shares held by Trust and employees)

Year established: 1943

Total turnover: PA worldwide – 1990: £172.6 mn; 1989: £155.6 mn; 1988: £122.6 mn. 1990 revenue split: Europe 65%; Scandinavia 20%; Asia Pacific 10%; North America 5%. TQM revenue worldwide – 1991: £12 mn; 1990: £9 mn; 1989: £7 mn

Number of assignments in last 2 years: Worldwide – 150, of which 70% are ongoing; Europe – 70 of which 70% are ongoing

Billing practices: PA bills against a proposal agreed with the client prior to the commencement of work and charge for time and the supply of books and training materials

Personnel: PA worldwide – total 2,630 consisting of 1,830 professional staff; 800 support staff. TQM worldwide – 189 consisting of 9 directors; 160 consultants; 20 support staff.

Background and experience of professional staff: TQM consultants, like all PA consultants, have to pass stringent entry requirements covering both capability and relevant experience. They will typically be 30–35 years of age, having demonstrated line management success before joining PA. An ability to effect change is paramount. Many are also qualified and experienced in some aspect of QA/QC/ISO 9000/SPC, etc.

Areas of specialisation:

- Understanding Customer Needs and Expectations
- Quality Function Deployment
- Corporate Culture
- Quality Understanding and Awareness
- Employee Involvement and Teamworking
- Elimination of Waste and JIT+
- Total Productive Maintenance+
- Problem Solving Tools and Process Re-engineering Tools and Techniques
- Control of Variability (including Statistical Process Control)

- Measurement of Quality-Related Costs
- Quality Assurance (including ISO 9000)
- Supplier Partnerships
- New Financial Management
- World Class Product Development+ (+Done by other parts of PA Consulting Group)
- Others: Corporate change based on TQM principles; strategic quality planning; policy deployment; seven new management and planning tools

Most important industry sectors for TQ work:

- Manufacturing
- Process industry
- Oil and gas
- Finance
- Defence

- Public sector
- Electronics
- Information industries
- Utilities

Definition of TQ: TQM is the mobilisation of the entire organisation to achieve quality continually and efficiently

TQ work in training and implementation of ISO 9000:   Training 40%; ISO 9000 15%; process consulting (planning, facilitating workshops, supporting projects, etc) 45%

Types of work not undertaken: Competing clients; quick fixes for people who do not understand the principles of TQM and the commitment required of top management

Other information: First TQM assignments were in 1985 following the initial development work in 1984. In 1989/90 PA spent £1 mn on the further development of the TQM/I ISO 9000 consulting services provided

Examples of recent assignments:

Client/description: Post Office Counters
Project description: Full implementation of TQM
Client contact title: Managing director
Consultant name/title: Chris Jackson, client director
Length of project: 3 years ongoing
End product: More customer focused organisation; changed internal culture and significant benefits

---

Client/description: British Steam Specialities UK Ltd
Project description: Full implementation of TQM
Client contact title: Managing director
Consultant name/title: Kevin Parker, client director
Length of project: 5 years ongoing
End product: Independent market research of customers 1991 rated BSS as the top supplier in their industry sector in all 18 categories of service identified as important by customers; full management commitment to the process; enthusiastic support amongst all staff; significant financial benefits; growth and profits up

---

Client/description: Rover Group
Project description: Full implementation of TQM
Client contact title: TQM Manager
Consultant name/title: Chris Jackson, client director
Length of project: 5 years ongoing
End product: Quality way of working now well established; many improvement projects yielding multi-million pound benefits

P-E Batalas Limited

Address: Batalas House,
Winchester Hill,
Romsey,
Hants SO51 7ND,
UK

Telephone: (44) 0794 524366
Fax: (44) 0794 517807
Contact: David Memmott

Other offices: Through parent company – Australia (1); France (1); Hong Kong (1); Hungary (1); Ireland (3); Netherlands (1); Nigeria (1); UK (9); USA (1)

Ownership: P-E International plc, UK, established in 1934. P-E Batalis was formed in 1991 as a result of the merger between P-E International and Batalas (formed in 1972).

Year established: 1991

Total turnover: P-E International worldwide – 1990: approximately £80 mn. P-E Batalas – 1991: £2.7 mn; 1990: £1.4 mn; 1989: £0.8 mn.

Number of assignments in last 2 years: 250–300, of which 150–200 are ongoing

Billing practices: Based on days of consulting input

Personnel: P-E International worldwide – approximately 850 including some 600 professionals. P-E Batalas (5 UK offices) – 54 consisting of 6 directors; 34 other consultants; 14 support staff.

Background and experience of professional staff: Line managers in manufacturing and service companies

Areas of specialisation:

- Understanding Customer Needs and Expectations
- Quality Function Development
- Quality Understanding and Awareness
- Employee Involvement and Teamworking
- Elimination of Waste and JIT
- Problem Solving Tools and Process Involvement Tools and Techniques

- Control of Variability (including Statistical Process Control)
- Measurement of Quality-Related Costs
- Quality Assurance (including ISO 9000)
- Supplier Partnerships
- Others: Consulting expertise; training courses

Most important industry sectors for TQ work:

- Engineering
- Financial
- Public health

- Services
- Public sector

Definition of TQ: A proven way of instituting and managing the practices, procedures and patterns of behaviour through which the combined efforts of all employees can be dedicated both to satisfying customer expectations and delivering profit objectives

TQ work in training and implementation of ISO 9000: Training 40%; ISO 9000 90% (these figures relate to P-E Batalas; some of the TQ work is done in conjunction with parent company)

Types of work not undertaken: –

Other information: P-E Batalas have assisted over 1,500 organisations towards BS 5750 registration

Examples of recent assignments:

Client/description: Bank
Project description: Implement TQM across all departments
Client contact title: Head of corporate quality
Consultant name/title: David Memmott, managing director
Length of project: 2 years
End product: Reported in *TQM Magazine*, October 1991

Client/description: Wire rope manufacturers
Project description: Implement TQM on 5 sites
Client contact title: Managing director
Consultant name/title: Gerald Bainbridge, principal consultant
Length of project: 18 months ongoing
End product: Major culture shift

Client/description: Government department
Project description: Implement quality assurance
Client contact title: Head of division
Consultant name/title: Jim McQueen, senior consultant
Length of project: 1 year
End product: BS 5750 plus cost savings

All these projects were completed under the name of the parent company

PERA International

Address: 54 Pall Mall, London SW1Y 5JH, UK

Telephone: (44) 071 8393666
Fax: (44) 071 8396737
Contact: Paul A Spenley

Other offices: UK (3). Paul Spenley is at the Swindon office Tel: 0793 772555.

Ownership: Independent

Year established: 1946

Total turnover: 1991: £2 mn; 1990 £0.5 mn; 1989: £0.5 mn

Number of assignments in last 2 years: 50 ongoing

Billing practices: Daily rate

Personnel: 30 consisting of 1 director; 25 consultants; 5 support staff

Background and experience of professional staff: All degree qualified and experienced in line roles in industry and commerce

Areas of specialisation:

- Understanding Customer Needs and Expectations
- Quality Function Deployment
- Corporate Culture
- Quality Understanding and Awareness
- Employee Involvement and Teamworking
- Elimination of Waste and JIT
- Problem Solving Tools and Process Involvement Tools and Techniques
- Control of Variability (including Statistical Process Control)
- Measurement of Quality-Related Costs
- Quality Assurance (including ISO 9000)
- Supplier Partnerships
- World Class Product Development
- Others: Business process analysis; marketing strategy; total safety management

Most important industry sectors for TQ work:

- Manufacturing
- Service industry

Definition of TQ: Meeting agreed requirements between internal and external customers

TQ work in training and implementation of ISO 9000: Training 50%; ISO 9000 50%

Types of work not undertaken: –

Other information: Director's book to be published in the UK and USA *World Class Performance Through Total Quality*

Examples of recent assignments:

Client/description: Multinational electronics company
Project description: Total quality
Client contact title: Managing director
Consultant name/title: Paul O'Reilly, managing consultant
Length of project: 1 year
End product: Senior manager education and training to implement total quality

---

Client/description: Aerospace business
Project description: Total quality
Client contact title: Managing director
Consultant name/title: Paul Spenley, director
Length of project: 18 months ongoing
End product: Manufacturing centre of excellence; improvement of teams at working level

---

Client/description: Major retailer
Project description: Total quality management
Client contact title: Director
Consultant name/title: Mike Woolley, managing consultant
Length of project: 18 months ongoing
End product: Totally restructured organisation in line with customer needs; improved performance and reduced costs

Price Waterhouse

Address:

Southwark Towers,
32 London Bridge Street,
London SE1 9SY,
UK

Telephone: (44) 071 9393000
Fax: (44) 071 6381358
Contact: R V Watkin

Other offices: 204 offices in 75 countries. USA headquarters (New York) – Tel: (212) 8195000 Contact for TQ in the USA: Bill Lehman Tel: (708) 5717250. Contact for TQ in the UK: R V Watkin Tel: (44) 0532 442044.

Ownership: Price Waterhouse. Individual partnerships coordinated on a worldwide basis through a World Board and a number of World Committees.

Year established: 1947

Total turnover: Management consultancy fee income – worldwide – 1991: £400.5 mn. UK TQ – 1991: £3 mn; 1990: £2 mn; 1989: £1.25 mn

Number of assignments in last 2 years: UK – 40, of which 25 are ongoing; Europe – 20, of which 10 are ongoing

Billing practices: Based on chargeable hours and cost of training materials

Personnel: Worldwide management consultancy – 7,262 consisting of 482 partners; 4,602 professional staff; 2,178 administrative staff. UK TQ consultancy – 25 consisting of 2 partners; 20 consultants; 3 support staff.

Background and experience of professional staff: Good degree or equivalent; relevant line management experience and/or substantial previous experience of implementing TQ

Areas of specialisation:

- Understanding Customer Needs and Expectations
- Corporate Culture
- Quality Understanding and Awareness
- Employee Involvement and Teamworking
- Elimination of Waste and JIT
- Total Productive Maintenance
- Problem Solving Tools and Process Involvement Tools and Techniques

- Control of Variability (including Statistical Process Control)
- Measurement of Quality-Related Costs
- Quality Assurance (including ISO 9000)
- Supplier Partnerships
- New Financial Management
- World Class Product Development
- Others: Implementation of total quality

Most important industry sectors for TQ work:

- Manufacturing and process industries
- Utilities

- Financial services
- Healthcare

Definition of TQ: A self-sustaining process of continuous improvement involving all employees with a focus on satisfying customers at least cost by doing the right things, right first time every time

TQ work in training and implementation of ISO 9000: Training 30%; ISO 9000 20%

Types of work not undertaken: Competing clients where a real conflict of interest exists

Other information: –

Examples of recent assignments:

Client/description: Power generating company
Project description: Implementation of total quality
Client contact title: Chief executive
Consultant name/title: Colin Hutchinson, managing consultant
Length of project: 18 months ongoing
End product: All employees participating in a wide range of process improvement projects

---

Client/description: Division of the ambulance service
Project description: Implementation of BS 5750/ISO 9000
Client contact title: Chief executive
Consultant name/title: Richard Dobson, managing consultant
Length of project: 18 months
End product: Successful accreditation; significant cost reduction; improved services to patients

---

Client/description: Automotive component manufacturer
Project description: Implementation of total quality
Client contact title: Managing director
Consultant name/title: Rob Garner, supervising consultant
Length of project: 2 years
End product: All employees participating in a wide range of quality cost reduction projects

Prism Consultancy Limited

Address: 10 Borrowdale Gardens,   **Telephone:**   (44) 0276 28101
Camberley,   **Fax:**   (44) 0276 62026
Surrey GU15 1QZ,   **Contact:**   Ian T Graham
UK

Other offices: –

Ownership: Independent limited company

Year established: 1989

Total turnover: 1991: £250,000; 1990: £200,000; 1989: £15,000

Number of assignments in last 2 years: 44, of which 13 are ongoing

Billing practices: Daily rate for seminars; daily rate for consultancy – varies according to level in client and seniority of consultant

Personnel: 13 consisting of 3 directors; 10 associates

Background and experience of professional staff: Senior line management experience; BSc/MSc/PhD; statistical knowledge to PhD level

Areas of specialisation:

- Understanding Customer Needs and Expectations
- Quality Function Deployment
- Corporate Culture
- Quality Understanding and Awareness
- Employee Involvement and Teamworking
- Elimination of Waste and JIT
- Problem Solving Tools and Process Improvement Tools and Techniques

- Control of Variability (including Statistical Process Control)
- Supplier Partnerships
- Others: Top management education and coaching; Taguchi methods; surveys; policy deployment (Hoshin Kanri), strategic deployment of improvement; team facilitation skills; experimental design (Taguchi methods)

Most important industry sectors for TQ work:

- Manufacturing

- Service

Definition of TQ: Total quality is a way of life – not a result. It is a philosophy of management that is totally committed to quality through continuous process improvement. It requires universal employee involvement and results in ever increasing customer delight.

TQ work in training and implementation of ISO 9000:   Training 50%; ISO 9000 – nil

Types of work not undertaken: –

Other information: The company also offers products – train the trainer kits for simulation training; process control charting software; training aids

Examples of recent assignments:

Client/description: Herman Miller Ltd
Project description: Study – listening to customers; better data used in a better way. Education/coaching.
Client contact title: Director, people and quality
Consultant name/title: Dr Peter Worthington, director
Length of project: 9 months ongoing
End product: Ongoing implementation – educated management working on their system; first areas for improvement identified; ongoing education/teamwork among designers

---

Client/description: Employment Service – Northern Region
Project description: Introduction of regionwide TQ – education; training; facilitation
Client contact title: Quality programme coordinator
Consultant name/title: Ian T Graham, director
Length of project: 15 months ongoing
End product: Ongoing implementation – education of top tiers of management (4,000 staff); top management coaching of use of data; pilot improvement teams trained and facilitated

---

Client/description: Medic-Aid Ltd
Project description: Consultancy support for full total quality implementation
Client contact title: Managing director
Consultant name/title: M Dickinson, director
Length of project: 8 months ongoing
End product: Educated top management team; developing strategies for implementation; facilitation of process improvement teams

Process Management International

Address:
The Manor,
Haseley Business Centre,
Warwick CV35 7LS,
UK

Telephone: (44) 0203 537000
Fax: (44) 0203 537028
Contact: Jan Gillett

Other offices: USA (3); USA head office (Minneapolis) – Contact: J Kirkpatrick, tel (612) 8930313

Ownership: Process Management Institute Inc, private limited company with extensive employee shareholding. UK office established January 1990.

Year established: 1984

Total turnover: Worldwide – 1991: $7.1 mn; 1990: $5.2 mn; 1989: $4.2 mn. Europe – 1991: $0.4 mn; 1990: $0.2 mn.

Number of assignments in last 2 years: Worldwide – 70 assignments of various sizes of which 54 are ongoing; Europe – 9 assignments of various sizes of which 4 are ongoing

Billing practices: Consulting – daily rates plus expenses at cost; in house training – price per course plus per participant

Personnel: Worldwide – 50 consisting of 6 directors; 30 consultants; 14 support staff. Europe – 3 directors and 4 active associate consultants; one administrator.

Background and experience of professional staff: Organisation development/psychology; industrial statisticians; general management; design and development of training

Areas of specialisation:

- Understanding Customer Needs and Expectations
- Quality Function Development
- Corporate Culture
- Quality Understanding and Awareness
- Employee Involvement and Teamworking
- Elimination of Waste

- Problem Solving Tools and Process Involvement Tools and Techniques
- Control of Variability (including Statistical Process Control)
- Quality Assurance (including ISO 9000) USA
- Others: Continual process improvement; training TQ facilitators/trainers

Most important industry sectors for TQ work:

- Automotive
- Oil/petrochemical
- Government
- Mining and refining

- Health
- Printing
- Electronic
- Food processing

Definition of TQ: Creating a corporate climate which leads to ever-widening and increasing involvement in and commitment to continual and systematic improvement of processes for the delight of customers

TQ work in training and implementation of ISO 9000: 45% TQ consulting; 45% TQ training (public and private; 2% ISO 9000 training and consulting in USA; 8% training materials and licences

Types of work not undertaken: ISO 9000 in Europe; high volume repetitive training (PMI trains client staff to do this)

Other information: PMI's work is based on the management philosophy of W Edwards Deming. They have good connections with TQ educators and consultants in Japan and their annual Japanese Study Mission is very popular. PMI aims for a balanced approach between culture change and the tools and techniques.

Examples of recent assignments:

Client/description: Pasminco Europe (Avonmouth, UK)
Project description: TQ transformation; attitude survey; customer and supplies survey; training of senior management and process improvement leaders; ongoing consulting
Client contact title: General manager and TQ manager
Consultant name/title: Colin Nichols, director (UK)
Length of project: Ongoing up to 2 years
End product: Too early for major results but there have been significant achievements in energy efficiency and stock reduction and many small benefits from process improvement

---

Client/description: Zytec Corporation (USA)
Project description: TQ organisation development including education and training on culture, tools and techniques of process management integrating Deming's principles
Client contact title: President
Consultant name/title: Sam Peckenham-Walsh, senior consultant
Length of project: 5 years
End product: Zytec awarded Malcolm Baldrige Award 1991; marked increase in sales and exports

---

Client/description: Three Icelandic fish and fish processing companies (Icelandic Government sponsored TQ pilot project for the industry) – Sildarvinnslan; Utgerdarfelag Akureyringa; Fiskiojusanilag Husavikur
Project description: Organised study mission to USA for management from three companies; ran training for management in philosophy/concepts and techniques of TQ; set up and coached steering and project teams; trained process improvement facilitators/trainers (3 weeks over 3 months)

Client/description: Managing directors and TQ coordinators
Consultant name/title: Alan Hodgson, senior consultant
Length of project: 20 months with some prospect of further work in autumn 1992
End product: Numerous examples of savings from process improvement; examples of major reorganisation; more work needed on culture and management process

Profile Consulting Group Limited

Address: Tabard Chambers,   **Telephone:** (44) 0452 525179
53 Northgate Street,   **Fax:**   (44) 0452 302180
Gloucester GL1 2AJ,   **Contact:**   David A Rolls
UK

Other offices: UK (2)

Ownership: Privately owned by directors and senior employees

Year established: 1983

Total turnover: 1991: £1.34 mn; 1990: £1.14 mn; 1989: £1.05 mn (includes non-TQ fee income)

Number of assignments in last 2 years: 6, of which 4 are ongoing

Billing practices: Monthly billing based on days worked, payable in 14 days

Personnel: 32 consisting of 6 directors; 8 consultants; 10 associate consultants; 8 support staff (24 fee earning professionals)

Background and experience of professional staff: Educated to degree level; members of Institute of Management Consultants; senior line management experience; at least 5 years' quality management/consulting experience

Areas of specialisation:

- Corporate Culture
- Quality Understanding and Awareness
- Employee Involvement and Teamworking
- Problem Solving Tools and Process Involvement Tools and Techniques

- Measurement of Quality-Related Costs
- Quality Assurance (including ISO 9000)
- World Class Product Development

Most important industry sectors for TQ work:

- Public sector (local authorities, health authorities and transport)

- Private sector (distribution/transport, construction and related industries)

Definition of TQ: A company-wide commitment to getting it right, first time, every time and continuously improving performance; based on systems which empower staff, tools which support them, and standards which challenge them

TQ work in training and implementation of ISO 9000:   Training represents 10% of consulting input; implementation of ISO 9000 represents 25% of TQ work

Types of work not undertaken: –

Other information: Profile firmly believes in implementing quality management systems as a foundation for sustained culture change and quality improvement. Profile is an IMC Registered Practice and has accredited certification to ISO 9001 for their entire management consultancy practice.

Examples of recent assignments:

Client/description: Parcel distribution company (UK and Europe)
Project description: Development and implementation of TQ throughout company starting with pilot depots/regional centres
Client contact title: General manager
Consultant name/title: M H C Buttery, regional director
Length of project: 18 months ongoing
End product: Planned – quality improvement teams in each location; quality assurance registration for entire company; reduced operating costs

---

Client/description: Building products manufacturer
Project description: Introduction of TQ at manufacturing location
Client contact title: Chief executive
Consultant name/title: J Barrett, senior consultant
Length of project: 8 months
End product: Reduced quality costs; increased sales; improved culture

---

Client/description: Health authority
Project description: Reinstallation of stagnant TQM programme, by introducing quality assurance systems to ISO 9000
Client contact title: Chief executive
Consultant name/title: A Wilkins, director
Length of project: 1 year
End product: Successful certification to ISO 9001; morale now high; TQ progress markedly improved

ProMentor Management A/S

Address:	Gl Bakkegaard,	**Telephone:**	(45) 43716400
	Klovtoftegade 46,	**Fax:**	(45) 43714565
	2630 Taastrup,	**Contact:**	Claus Thomsen
	Denmark		

Other offices: Danish regional office (Abyhoj) – Contact: P Drachmann tel (45) 86154200

Ownership: Partnership

Year established: 1984

Total turnover: Confidential but turnover more than doubled between 1989–90 and 1991–92

Number of assignments in last 2 years: Approximately 200, of which 50% are ongoing

Billing practices: Firm pricing based on budgeted resource allocation

Personnel: 35 consisting of 5 partners; 19 consultants; 11 support staff

Background and experience of professional staff: MBA; Master of Engineering; MA Econ

Areas of specialisation:

- Understanding Customer Needs and Expectations
- Corporate Culture
- Quality Understanding and Awareness
- Employee Involvement and Teamworking
- Elimination of Waste and JIT
- Problem Solving Tools and Process Involvement Tools and Techniques (train the trainer activities)

- Measurement of Quality-Related Costs
- Quality Assurance (including ISO 9000)
- Others: Top management involvement; quality related leadership development; internal marketing planning; TQM process design and planning

Most important industry sectors for TQ work:

- 50% service sectors (ie. banking; insurance; computers; transport; airlines; retail and wholesale chains, etc.)

- 50% production/manufacturing

Definition of TQ: TQM means determining, assuring, measuring and improving the entire quality of the company with the aim of achieving the highest possible levels of customer satisfaction, profitability and job satisfaction

TQ work in training and implementation of ISO 9000: 50% on workshops, seminars, conferences and train the trainer activities; 50% ISO 9000 (implementation of quality systems)

Types of work not undertaken: ...

Other information: –

Examples of recent assignments:

Client/description: International Service Systems – ISS (Linen Service division)
Project description: TQM process planning; sparring partner to the quality steering committee; training all managers and employees; follow-up activities such as measurement, results assessments etc.
Client contact title: Managing director
Consultant name/title: Claus Thomsen, general manager
Length of project: Ongoing up to 5 years
End product: Increased profitability; increased customer satisfaction; greater job satisfaction

---

Client/description: Lego and Lego Systems
Project description: Design and implementation of quality system according to ISO 9001 covering a total of 4,000 employees
Client contact title: General manager
Consultant name/title: Claus Toft Friis, chief consultant
Length of project: 2 years
End product: Achievement of the ISO 9001 certificate

Client/description: Statoil
Project description: Process planning for the different markets; sparring partner to the steering committee; management and employee training and follow-up activities
Client contact title: Managing director
Consultant name/title: Klaus Lund, managing director
Length of project: Ongoing up to 3 years
End product: Reduction of unnecessary costs; measurable increase in customer satisfaction

Quality Management International

Address: Quality Court,
The Precinct,
Egham,
Surrey TW20 9HN,
UK

Telephone: (44) 0784 472424
Fax: (44) 0784 471799
Contact: Michael J Kemp

Other offices: QMI (North Sea), Aberdeen, UK; QMI/Columbia, USA; QMI/Quest, Malaysia and Hong Kong. USA head office (Orefield, PA) – Contact: P Spence, tel (215) 3919596. Asia/Pacific head office (Malaysia) – Contact T Alcock, tel (603) 2931168.

Ownership: Limited liability company. Five main board directors of QMI plus director for each subsidiary.

Year established: 1986

Total turnover: 1991: £1.35 mn; 1990: £1.2 mn; 1989: £350,000

Number of assignments in last 2 years: 6, all of which are ongoing

Billing practices: Monthly in arrears

Personnel: 32 consisting of 5 directors; 19 consultants; 8 support staff Background and experience of professionals: Must have experience in – business comparisons and analytical surveys; global business strategy studies; teambuilding; process analysis; flowcharting

Areas of specialisation:

- Understanding Customer Needs and Expectations
- Quality Function Development
- Corporate Culture
- Quality Understanding and Awareness
- Employee Involvement and Teamworking
- Problem Solving Tools and Process Involvement Tools and Techniques

- Control of Variability (including Statistical Process Control)
- Measurement of Quality-Related Costs
- Quality Assurance (including ISO 9000)
- Supplier Partnerships
- Others: Strategic business planning; benchmarking; teambuilding

Most important industry sectors for TQ work:

- Manufacturing
- Construction

- Service sector

Definition of TQ: A style of business management which recognises that customer needs and corporate business goals are inseparable. Percentage of TQ work in the area of training and how much is concerned with implementing ISO 9000: 40% training; 60% ISO 9000.

Types of work not undertaken: Work undertaken in all areas of business, industry, commerce, etc. and in areas with strong economies and currencies

Other information: –

Examples of recent assignments:

Client/description: Tarmac Construction
Project description: To improve the systems attitudes of the company and sub-contractors in order to enter into long term partnerships with major clients
Client contact title: Quality systems director
Consultant name/title: J R Broomfield, project director
Length of project: 2 years initially, ongoing at present
End product: Third party certified to ISO 9001, at least one secure partnership and the progressive reduction of avoidable costs

---

Client/description: NK Fencing
Project description: To evaluate existing attitudes and internal and external perceptions, develop a 2–5 year business strategy and improve operational efficiency
Client contact title: Chief executive
Consultant name/title: Michael J Kemp, managing director
Length of project: 3 years ongoing
End product: Alignment of customer needs with business goals, highly motivated workforce, improved factory layout

---

Client/description: Through Transport Mutual Services
Project description: Quality awareness and attitude survey, policy generation, quality awareness and educational survey, process analysis and teambuilding
Client contact title: Director
Consultant name/title: D Coleman, managing consultant
Length of project: 18 months ongoing
End product: To move company focus from sales orientation to client satisfaction

---

► **STRATEGIC BUSINESS PLANNING**

► **BUSINESS PROCESS ANALYS1S**

► **ISO 9000 SYSTEM DEVELOPMENT**

► **TRAINING**

► **MANAGEMENT AUDIT**

► **BUSINESS IMPROVEMENT**

QUALITY MANAGEMENT INTERNATIONAL
Structuring Your Approach To Quality

Quality Court, The Precinct, Egham, TW20 9HN, England.
Telephone: 0784 472424 International Telephone: +44 784 472424
Fax: 0784 471799 International Fax: +44 784 471799

Quality System SrL

Address: Corso Giovanni Lanza 105,   **Telephone:** (39) 1 16601775
                10133 Turin,   **Fax:**   (39) 1 16601766
                Italy   **Contact:**   Pietro Gambino

Other offices: Spain (1)

Ownership: Limited company formed in 1990. Originally a partnership.

Year established: 1984

Total turnover: 1991: ECU1.1 mn; 1990: ECU0.86 mn; 1989: ECU0.65 mn

Number of assignments in last 2 years: 34 customers at present

Billing practices: Bills are calculated on the basis of a man/day price which depends on the type of activity not on the professionals involved, eg. training; audit; technical support; management support etc.)

Personnel: 18 consisting of 5 directors; 9 consultants; 4 support staff

Background and experience of professional staff: Quality System's policy is to work with professionals coming from real operational experience in their field of activity. They also hire a few young people in order that they can transfer the know-how from the "old" to the "young" and establish the basis for the future.

Areas of specialisation:

- Understanding Customer Needs and Expectations
- Quality Function Deployment
- Corporate Culture
- Quality Understanding and Awareness
- Employee Involvement and Teamworking
- Elimination of Waste and JIT
- Total Productive Maintenance

- Problem Solving Tools and Process Involvement Tools and Techniques
- Control of Variability (including Statistical Process Control)
- Measurement of Quality-Related Costs
- Quality Assurance (including ISO 9000)
- Supplier Partnerships
- Others: Value analysis; design of experiments

Most important industry sectors for TQ work:

- Automotive (both manufacturers of vehicles and components)
- Metal work

- Electromechanical
- Textiles
- Food industry

Definition of TQ: Quality System defines quality as the ratio between product or service performance and the customer expectations of them – a total quality system is a company system where the above concept is evaluated in a measurable way in the internal and external relationships among the departments

TQ work in training and implementation of ISO 9000:   The activity is not only orientated to implementation of ISO 9000 (where not more than 50% of professional time is spent) but to training (almost 25%) and development of advanced total quality systems (almost 25%)

Types of work not undertaken: –

Other information: –

Examples of recent assignments:

Client/description: Fiat Avio SpA
Project description: Structure and evaluation of a company total quality system
Client contact title: Quality general manager
Consultant name/title: Pietro Gambino, general manager
Length of project: 1 year ongoing
End product: Structure of TQS and relationship with the company chart; evaluation method of the TQS in a quantitative way; yearly quality plans, objectives and resources

---

Client/description: TRW Sipea
Project description: TQM – definition of suppliers, customers and exchange objects inside the company; measurements of quality level
Client contact title: Manager personnel and organisation
Consultant name/title: Fabrizio Colonna, president
Length of project: 2 years ongoing
End product: Set of indicators of the quality of the performance achieved by each company department; plan of continuous improvement with goals

---

Client/description: Miroglio Tessile
Project description: Involvement of the personnel in the quality system
Client contact title: General manager for personnel
Consultant name/title: Gianluigi Martani, partner
Length of project: 3 years ongoing
End product: Initial measurable results of the group activities; culture of quality spread throughout the company (different responsibilities, new way of managing human resources)

Quarto Consulting International

Address:
4 The Square,
Apsley Guise,
Milton Keynes MK17 8DF,
UK

Telephone: (44) 0908 235000
Fax: (44) 0908 281059
Contact: Paul Malyon

Other offices: Belgium (1)

Ownership: Partnership. Original firm Taba Midas formed 1984.

Year established: 1991

Total turnover: 1991: £3.4 mn; 1990: £2 mn; 1989: £1.5 mn

Number of assignments in last 2 years: 10–20, of which 6 are ongoing (sometimes more than one assignment for same client)

Billing practices: Agreed fees (project or per diem)

Personnel: 5 consisting of 4 partners; 1 support person

Background and experience of professional staff: Senior level business/senior academic experience; 1 graduate and 3 post graduate qualifications

Areas of specialisation:

- Understanding Customer Needs and Expectations
- Quality Function Development
- Corporate Culture
- Quality Understanding and Awareness
- Employee Involvement and Teamworking
- Problem Solving Tools and Process Involvement Tools and Techniques

- Measurement of Quality-Related Costs
- Quality Assurance (including ISO 9000)
- Supplier Partnerships
- Others: Organisation change; customer action teams

Most important industry sectors for TQ work:

- Distribution
- Fast moving consumer goods

- Services
- Communications

Definition of TQ: Quality means providing more perceived value to your customer than your competitor(s) are willing or able to provide. Quality is not what is left over when problems have been eliminated! Quarto sees total quality as a major challenge in change – the issues are of introducing radical change to the accepted definitions by which many organisations and companies operate. They do not see that total quality is common sense at all – it is a quite radical departure from previous concepts and processes involved in producing goods and services. At root they believe that total quality means – work organisation and production activity, including the work of managing, is structured, practised and measured in terms of the delivery of quality products and services.

TQ work in training and implementation of ISO 9000: Neither is a strong emphasis. Quarto tends implement quality, using training/workshops as required.

Types of work not undertaken: Competing clients except where competition is extensive (eg. have worked for two solicitors in different organisations and for BT and Post Office at the same time)

Other information: –

Examples of recent assignments:

Client/description: Colgate-Palmolive Europe
Project description: Implementation strategy/actions
Client contact title: European quality director
Consultant name/title: Paul Malyon, managing director
Length of project: 1 year ongoing
End product: Implementation strategy; support on initial actions; training/senior management workshops; support for Quality Improvement Teams

---

Client/description: The Post Office (Corporate and Parcelforce)
Project description: Implementation of Customer First
Client contact title: Chairman
Consultant name/title: Paul Malyon, managing director/Greg Schaffer, director
Length of project: 4 years ongoing
End product: Implementation strategy (document/education); director of quality for Parcelforce for 1 year; numerous actions (policy deployment/customer action teams)

Client/description: The Post office (Royal Mail)
Project description: Consulting support
Client contact title: Director of quality (Royal Mail)
Consultant name/title: Paul Malyon, managing director
Length of project: 4 years ongoing
End product: Implementation strategy; senior management training; training for consultancy skills for internal consulting; benchmarking

Quest Quality Consulting Limited

Address: Axis Centre,
3 Burlington Lane,
London W4 2TH,
UK

Telephone: (44) 081 7422532
Fax: (44) 081 7421990
Contact: Steve Smith

Other offices: Australia (1)

Ownership: Independent

Year established: 1988

Total turnover: 1991: £1.5 mn; 1990: £1.2 mn; 1989: £0.7 mn

Number of assignments in last 2 years: 35 assignments for approximately 15 distinct clients of which 15 are ongoing

Billing practices: Monthly on time used

Personnel: 19 consisting 3 directors; 12 consultants; 4 support staff (14 fee earning professionals)

Background and experience of professional staff: Hands-on TQ implementation experience; background from industry/commerce; prior line management and/or consulting experience

Areas of specialisation:

- Understanding Customer Needs and Expectations
- Quality Function Development
- Corporate Culture
- Quality Understanding and Awareness
- Employee Involvement and Teamworking
- Elimination of Waste and JIT
- Total Productive Maintenance
- Problem Solving Tools and Process Involvement Tools and Techniques
- Measurement of Quality-Related Costs

- Supplier Partnerships
- New Financial Management
- World Class Product Development
- Others: Policy deployment; quality maturity reviews; empowerment; world class management; implementation of TQ; business process management; benchmarking; study tours of best practice Note: Quest's primary focus is organisational improvement using total quality, therefore, the specialisations listed above are, to their mind subordinate to this

Most important industry sectors for TQ work:

All sectors and all regions. Significant sectors are:
- Financial services
- Consumer goods
- Engineering

- Research and transport
- Split between service/manufacturing applications is about 50/50

Definition of TQ: Accelerated organisational improvement

TQ work in training and implementation of ISO 9000: Training in the form of workshops/events/seminars is 40% of our engagement with a client. No ISO 9000 work.

Types of work not undertaken: Quality assurance; non-strategic input

Other information: Quest's primary focus is behavioural change in a client's organisation. As a result, they work with only a few clients at any one time and aim to develop a partnership relationship over a longer period of time. Quest operates in any country (about 40 since formation four years ago).

Examples of recent assignments:

Client/description: Unilever Personal Products Coordination
Project description: Strategic design and implementation support for advanced TQ for a £4 bn group of 40+ companies
worldwide
Client contact title: TQ coordinator PPC
Consultant name/title: Steve Smith, chairman
Length of project: 4 years ongoing
End product: Established common improvement language and process worldwide with resulting bottom line benefits

---

Client/description: Perkins Engines Group
Project description: Implementation of TQ across group
Client contact title: Group managing director
Consultant name/title: Gordon Foster, principal consultant
Length of project: 18 months ongoing
End product: TQ installed; bottom line benefits

Client/description: Legal & General
Project description: Implementation of TQ
Client contact title: Managing director
Consultant name/title: Gordon Foster, principal consultant
Length of project: 15 months ongoing
End product: Bottom line benefits

REL Consultancy Group Limited

Address: Park Gate,
21 Tothill Street,
London SW1H 9LL,
UK

Telephone: (44) 071 2221212
Fax: (44) 071 2330735
Contact: Christopher A Bielenberg

Other offices: France (1); Spain (1); UK (1); USA (2). USA head office (Harrison, NY) – Contact J E Cravenho, tel (914) 8353700.

Ownership: Independent

Year established: 1975

Total turnover: Worldwide – 1991: £8.05 mn; 1990: £7.6 mn; 1989: £5.1 mn Europe – 1991: £6 mn.

Number of assignments in last 2 years: 20, of which 12 are ongoing

Billing practices: On a project basis

Personnel: Worldwide – 160 consisting of 12 directors; 118 consultants; 30 support staff. Europe – 110.

Background and experience of professional staff: Graduates – 30% MBAs; 2–5 years' experience

Areas of specialisation:

- Understanding Customer Needs and Expectations
- Quality Function Deployment
- Corporate Culture
- Quality Understanding and Awareness
- Employee Involvement and Teamworking
- Elimination of Waste and JIT

- Problem Solving Tools and Process Involvement Tools and Techniques
- Measurement of Quality-Related Costs
- Supplier Partnerships
- New Financial Management

Most important industry sectors for TQ work:

- Financial services
- Technology

- Fast moving consumer goods

Definition of TQ: TQM is a managed change agent to move an organisation from a culture based on checking people, inspection and firefighting to a culture involving everyone in the organisation in total and continuous improvement

TQ work in training and implementation of ISO 9000: Training 50%; do not implement ISO 9000

Types of work not undertaken: –

Other information: –

Examples of recent assignments:

Client/description: Save and Prosper Group Limited
Project description: Total quality management process
Client contact title: Administration and development manager
Consultant name/title: Sarah Dawson, project manager
Length of project: 18 months ongoing
End product: Measurable gains in productivity, service standards and customer service; established working groups throughout the business concentrating on improvement and innovation in processes

---

Client/description: Prudential Assurance Co (Life Administration Division)
Project description: Total quality management
Client contact title: Quality initiative manager
Consultant name/title: Sarah Dawson, project manager
Length of project: 2 years (client managed)
End product: Savings in excess of £1 mn; 10%+ increase per annum in productivity; marked improvement in service standards; TQM also contributed to swift accreditation to BS 5750; over 300 improvement groups established

---

Client/description: St Helier NHS Trust
Project description: Total quality management
Client contact title: General manager
Consultant name/title: Judith Johnson, project manager
Length of project: 18 months ongoing
End product: All staff are focused on meeting requirements and systems have been established to allow staff at any level to highlight problems and receive help in identifying the root cause

Services Limited

Address:	Quality and Reliability House, 82 Trent Boulevard, West Bridgford, Nottingham NG2 5BL, UK	**Telephone:** **Fax:** **Contact:**	(44) 0602 455285 (44) 0602 817137 John M Kelly

Other offices: Through subsidiaries of parent company – Hong Kong (1); Scotland (1)

Ownership: Services (Holdings) Ltd

Year established: 1983

Total turnover: 1991–92: £400,000 (est); 1990–91: £303,529; 1989–90: £203,778

Number of assignments in last 2 years: 23, of which 9 are ongoing

Billing practices: Man day rate plus travel, subsistence and VAT

Personnel: 8 consisting of 1 director; 3 consultants; 4 support staff; plus 15 associates

Background and experience of professional staff: All engineering and business management professionals from industrial, production and academic backgrounds

Areas of specialisation:

- Understanding Customer Needs and Expectations
- Quality Function Deployment
- Corporate Culture
- Quality Understanding and Awareness
- Employee Involvement and Teamworking
- Elimination of Waste and JIT
- Problem Solving Tools and Process Improvement Tools and Techniques

- Control of Variability (including Statistical Process Control)
- Measurement of Quality-Related Costs
- Quality Assurance (including ISO 9000)
- Supplier Partnerships
- World Class Product Development
- Others: Design of experiments (Taguchi methodology)

Most important industry sectors for TQ work:

- Manufacturing

- Public services (health authority, MOD, etc.)

Definition of TQ: A self improving organisation, ie. continuous improvement is the normal or "rest position" for the organisation

TQ work in training and implementation of ISO 9000: Training 40%; ISO 9000 25%

Types of work not undertaken: –

Other information: –

Examples of recent assignments:

Client/description: Architectural masonry/building products manufacturer
Project description: Total quality management
Client contact title: Total quality coordinator
Consultant name/title: John M Kelly, director
Length of project: 18 months ongoing
End product: An initial 1,500 improvement suggestions received; cost savings of £200,000 within 12 months from commencement; 200 personnel trained in TQ approach and simple tools of quality; SPC introduced into production areas

---

Client/description: Garment manufacturer
Project description: Total quality management
Client contact title: Chief executive
Consultant name/title: John M Kelly, director
Length of project: 2 years ongoing
End product: Cost of quality (failure costs) identified and reduced; savings of several £'000s; approach and design analysed and improved leading to shorter time to market; internal procedures written and audited by internal, trained auditors

---

Client/description: Publishing company based in London
Project description: Total quality management
Client contact title: Publishing director
Consultant name/title: Professor Tony Bendell, chief associate consultant
Length of project: 1 year ongoing
End product: Roles and responsibilities defined and documented for creative functions; workshops held for all senior personnel; internal functions proceduralised

Strategic Quality Management Institute

Address:	Faculty of Economics,	**Telephone:**	(31) 10 4081353
	Erasmus University of Rotterdam,	**Fax:**	(31) 10 4526094
	PO Box 1738,	**Contact:**	Professor A R T Williams
	3000 DR Rotterdam,		
	Netherlands		

Other offices: –

Ownership: Erasmus University, established in 1913

Year established: 1988

Total turnover: –

Number of assignments in last 2 years: 6, of which 3 are ongoing

Billing practices: Project budgets

Personnel: 7 consisting of 5 directors; 2 consultants

Background and experience of professional staff: Business economics; psychology; engineering

Areas of specialisation:

- Understanding Customer Needs and Expectations
- Quality Function Deployment
- Quality Understanding and Awareness
- Employee Involvement and Teamworking
- Elimination of Waste and JIT
- Total Productive Maintenance
- Problem Solving Tools and Process Involvement Tools and Techniques
- Control of Variability (including Statistical Process Control)

- Measurement of Quality-Related Costs
- Quality Assurance (including ISO 9000)
- Supplier Partnerships
- New Financial Management
- World Class Product Development
- Others: Managing the quality improvement process over the long term

Most important industry sectors for TQ work:

- Financial/transport services

- Electronics

Definition of TQ: TQ is a philosophy and operating toolbox for making the best of what you have at the lowest consumption of resources aimed at improving profits and satisfaction of chosen customers

TQ work in training and implementation of ISO 9000: None

Types of work not undertaken: Long term training programmes; ISO 9000 training

Other information: SQMI is mainly a research organisation and they regularly visit leading edge TQM companies in the USA, Far East and Europe to see how they manage TQM

Examples of recent assignments:

Client/description: Bank
Project description: Developing self audit tools
Consultant name/title: A van der Wiele/J G Timmers
Length of project: 1 year
End product: Audit tools completed and being complemented

Client/description: Medical equipment firm
Project description: Total restructuring of one business unit from R&D to S&S
Consultant name/title: Professor A R T Williams
Length of project: 1 year
End product: Management team restructuring; analysis of development projects; design of core business processes

---

Client/description: Electronics company
Project description: Improving new product development performance
Consultant name/title: H B Bertsch
Length of project: 2 years ongoing
End product: Presentations, report and training

TMI A/S

Address:	Huginsvej 8, 3400 Hillerod, Denmark	**Telephone:** **Fax:** **Contact:**	(45) 42262688 (45) 42265455 Claus Munck Birch

Other offices: 29 offices in 26 countries worldwide Jalcos (a subsidiary of Japan Airlines) is licensed to represent TMI in Japan; Manager Service (partly owned by TMI) is licensed to represent TMI in Russia. The TMI Group operates worldwide. TMI A/S is the parent company. Some clients are serviced directly by the parent company; others are serviced by their subsidiaries or "partners" (licensees) which operate using the TMI name.

Ownership: Private

Year established: 1975

Total turnover: ...

Number of assignments in last 2 years: More than 100, of which more than 50 are presently ongoing

Billing practices: Daily fee per consultant

Personnel: The TMI Group employs about 450 staff including 147 consultants, most of whom work with TQ and other issues. Total hours for TQ work would equal 35 consultants.

Background and experience of professional staff: Generally have academic and managerial experience

Areas of specialisation:

- Understanding Customer Needs and Expectations
- Corporate Culture
- Quality Understanding and Awareness

- Employee Involvement and Teamworking
- Quality Assurance (including ISO 9000)

Most important industry sectors for TQ work:

Varies very much depending on geographical market

Definition of TQ: Meeting the criteria of the European Quality Award as stated by EFQM

TQ work in training and implementation of ISO 9000:   65% is in training, some of the training is concerned with implementing ISO 9000; 50% is concerned with implementing ISO 9000, some of the ISO work includes training

Types of work not undertaken: In principle none – in practice it varies depending on geographical market

Other information: TMI works within the areas of training and education, publishing and consultancy. They have 3 general "product lines": activities to help organisations and individuals increase productivity, activities to help them improve relations, activities to help them enhance quality. Most work is done within all three product lines, but under the "heading" of one of them.

Consultants and trainers are monitored, educated, trained and certified at a central training and education centre. Internal quality-assurance systems monitor and maintain high standard products, methodologies and performance.

Examples of recent assignments:

Client/description: Telecom
Project description: Redefining and implementing quality at all levels
Client contact title: Chief executive officer
Consultant name/title: Claus Munck Birch
Length of project: 2 years
End product: TQ commitment; increased customer satisfaction; bottom-line improvements

---

Client/description: Plastic manufacturer
Project description: Redefine Japanese TQM strategies for use in western Europe and implementing TQM in European subsidiary
Client contact title: Chief executive officer
Consultant name/title: S Winther
Length of project: 30 months ongoing
End product: Model for expansion in western hemisphere

Client/description: International organisation
Project description: Define and implement market-oriented TQ thinking and systems
Client contact title: Politician responsible and head of secretariat
Consultant name/title: S Schneider
Length of project: 18 months
End product: Flexibility, adaptability and "speed" increased dramatically throughout the organisation

Total Quality Management International Limited

Address: The Stables,   **Telephone:** (44) 0928 39191
                     Tarvin Road,   **Fax:**   (44) 0928 39496
                     Frodsham,   **Contact:**   G P Hillman
                     Cheshire WA6 6XN,
                     UK

Other offices: UK (1); defined associations in the Caribbean and Hungary

Ownership: Private limited company

Year established: 1987

Total turnover: 1991: £1.2mn; 1990: £800,000; 1989: £600,000

Number of assignments in last 2 years: 20 ongoing; 42 one-off

Billing practices: Based on time, materials and expenses

Personnel: 17 consisting of 5 directors; 9 consultants: 3 support staff

Background and experience of professional staff: Line management experience; professional qualifications in their specific fields; experience of TQM implementation

Areas of specialisation:

- Understanding Customer Needs and Expectations
- Quality Function Development
- Corporate Culture
- Quality Understanding and Awareness
- Employee Involvement and Teamworking
- Elimination of Waste and JIT
- Problem Solving Tools and Process Involvement Tools and Techniques

- Control of Variability (including Statistical Process Control)
- Measurement of Quality-Related Costs
- Quality Assurance (including ISO 9000)
- Supplier Partnership
- Others: Design and development of TQM processes for clients' facilitator training

Most important industry sectors for TQ work:

- Finance
- Telecommunications
- Process and chemical industries
- Packaging
- Manufacturing industry

- Construction and contracting industry
- Energy generation and supply
- Service
- Public sector

Definition of TQ: Continuously meeting agreed customer requirements at the lowest cost of releasing the potential of all employees

TQ work in training and implementation of ISO 9000:   Training 20%; ISO 9000 5%

Types of work not undertaken: Competing clients where specifically requested not to by client

Other information: –

Examples of recent assignments:

Client/description: Photographic manufacturer
Project description: Design, development and implementation of TQM into total organisation
Client contact title: Chief executive
Consultant name/title: G P Hillman, director
Length of project: 2 years
End product: Significant culture change and major cost benefits; improved speed of introduction of new products; improved quality of products; increased customer satisfaction – result increased profit and market share

---

Client/description: Packaging supplier
Project description: Support to implement TQM
Client contact title: Divisional director
Consultant name/title: L Bradley, director
Length of project: 1 year
End product: Improved speed of changeover, significant cost savings; culture change; high degree of employee involvement; improved customer satisfaction

---

Client/description: Telecommunications company
Project description: Diagnosis of current situation; design of TQM process and implementation support
Client contact title: Managing director
Consultant name/title: P R Davies, director
Length of project: 3 years ongoing
End product: Improved market share and profitability; improved employee involvement

World Class International Limited

Address: Technology House,
Parklands Business Park,
Forest Road,
Denmead,
Hampshire PO7 6XP,
UK

Telephone: (44) 0705 268133
Fax: (44) 0705 268160
Contact: Alistair Duncan

Other offices: Ireland (1); USA (1)

Ownership: Limited company owned by two joint managing directors – Alistair J Duncan and Paul E Collins. Originally established in 1986 as JIT Technology and expanded to become World Class International Ltd in 1989.

Year established: 1989

Total turnover: 1991: £1.5 mn; 1990: £1.1 mn; 1989: £1 mn

Number of assignments in last 2 years: 10, of which 50% are ongoing

Billing practices: Day rate mostly; some costed projects (10%)

Personnel: 25 consisting of 3 directors; 17 consultants; 5 support staff

Background and experience of professional staff: All are qualified professionals plus experienced practitioners from industry who have personally "done it"

Areas of specialisation:

- Understanding Customer Needs and Expectations
- Quality Function Development
- Corporate Culture
- Quality Understanding and Awareness
- Employee Involvement and Teamworking
- Elimination of Waste and JIT
- Total Productive Maintenance
- Problem Solving Tools and Process Involvement Tools and Techniques

- Control of Variability (including Statistical Process Control)
- Measurement of Quality-Related Costs
- Supplier Partnerships
- New Financial Management
- World Class Product Development
- Others: Business process management; structured management

Most important industry sectors for TQ work:

- Manufacturing and distribution
- Pharmaceuticals
- Healthcare

- Service industry
- Financial sector

Definition of TQ: World class – being the best in your industry as perceived by the customer, through waste elimination and right first time methodologies and cultures

TQ work in training and implementation of ISO 9000: Training 15%; ISO 9000 5%

Types of work not undertaken: –

Other information: Dr Richard Schonberger, the guru of World Class techniques, is a director of WCI. He is based in their US office in Portland, Oregon.

Examples of recent assignments:

Client/description: Philips Radio Communications Business Unit
Project description: Total company culture change including operational reengineering
Client contact title: Managing director
Consultant name/title: Alistair Duncan, Managing director
Length of project: 2 years
End product: Service levels improved; costs reduced; inventory reduced; company survived possible disaster

---

Client/description: Amtico
Project description: Production process improvements
Client contact title: Production director
Consultant name/title: Philip Stride, principal consultant
Length of project: 18 months ongoing
End product: Leadtime to quality improved; costs down; process simplified; culture changed

---

Client/description: Wrangler
Project description: Production and distribution operational reengineering
Client contact title: UK general manager
Consultant name/title: Adrian Reeve, principal consultant
Length of project: 1 year
End product: Inventories reduced; leadtime reduced; costs down; service levels increased

Appendix

BEST BOOKS ON TOTAL QUALITY: A BUSY MANAGER'S GUIDE

This chapter offers a few words on some 20 key books on total quality and related themes. The books are presented by author surname for ease of reference and because it is not possible to list them under different theme headings as each book on the list intermeshes all the ideas. Total Quality is an integrative theme.

Aguayo, R. (1990). *Dr. Deming; the Man who Taught the Japanese about Quality.* London. Mercury Books.

One of the best books on Total Quality as a management philosophy and practical way of life. It is strongly concerned with business success: "as quality improves, costs go down and productivity goes up". It sees loyal customers as "the engine which produces increased market share, higher profit margins, higher profits, higher share prices, a secure and satisfied work force, and more jobs". And loyal customers are created by quality which meets and exceeds customer expectations.

Aguayo gives a splendid summary of Deming's 14 points, without being obsequious to the veteran guru. Particularly his warnings about trying to run a business on visible numbers only (VNO) are timely; he gives good illustrations of the way in which meeting numerical quotas can destroy quality in the effort to get the quantity out of the door. Also he explains how individual merit payments can be divisive and almost impossible to administer fairly. They then make it more difficult to run a company on a cooperative team basis.

He explains how you can't blame the shop floor workers for most of the quality problems which arise, because they are largely systemic and require management decisions. So management by shouting at or sloganising the workers just creates adversarial relationships to no good effect. The removal of fear from worker/management relationships is a significant factor in quality outcomes, because it paves the way for commitment and ownership.

The same principle of working together is applied to the relationships of suppliers and customers, and even in many circumstances, of competitors. Better to expand the whole market, rather than just one's own market share, contrary to the received wisdom. Competition doesn't mean trying to create losers. Competition is seen by Aguayo as part of the challenge to continuous improvement, which is of the essence of the quality movement. Everyone keeps everyone else up to scratch, or they will go to the wall; but this is different from the "dog eat dog" approach. The focus should be the customer and then profitable results will follow.

Atkinson, P.E. (1990). *Creating Culture Change: the Key to Successful Total Quality Management.* Bedford. IFS.

Atkinson stresses that Total Quality Management is essentially about changing the culture of an organisation. TQ is not something that can be created by an accreditation system; it has to be owned by everyone in the organisation. "Quality is both thinking why something is done, and why it is done that way; when thinking differently to improve it" (Toyota chairman). It is about a collective and individual attitude pervading every part of a company, including the indirect and support functions. It concerns the way everything is tackled at every level in an organisation. It is a never ending mission to improve everything and it is rooted in thinking people through whom any culture flows.

These general principles are made to stick by a wealth of easy to absorb detail, summarised at the end of every short chapter in clear bullet points. To flick through these at any time will keep the whole book memorable.

Specific processes are highlighted as well as strategic issues; how total quality is a money-saver rather than a cost-increaser; leadership which creates a sense of ownership in everyone; working together in largely self-directed teams; a passion for learning, rather than merely training. All these are essential to quality.

The customer is the purpose of it all, the next in line in any activity, as well the ultimate consumer; this helps to cut out mass inspection and encourages mutual control by cooperation. Communication is fundamental and the book gives simple recipes to make sure that all these concepts can be turned into action.

Carlisle, J.A. and Parker, R.C. (1989). *Beyond Negotiation; Redeeming Customer Supplier Relationships.* Chichester. John Wiley & Sons.

This book shows how to get customer/supplier relationships out of the adversarial mode, so that both benefit by a joint effort to provide the final consumer with products or services which will contribute to a high quality of life. As one section heading puts it "competing through cooperating"! Particularly, suppliers and manufacturers are independent and both will lose by trying to score at the others' expense. If each customer in the supplier/customer chain is satisfied with the results of the suppliers' efforts, then the end consumer who finally pays the bill is going to be satisfied as well. There is a chain of satisfaction to which all contribute. Their interaction is based on continuous collaborative negotiation in which everyone wins.

Negotiation of this kind is a process for developing relationships; when parties meet it is to solve shared problems and seize joint opportunities; they will also be taking a long term perspective rather than trying merely to get the best in the short term. This book supports the Deming theme of keeping the number of external suppliers to the minimum so that close and long term relationships can be built up.

The book is well illustrated with examples, pictures, charts and checklists. Readers will never again to be able to engage in confrontational debate with suppliers without experiencing considerable unease. The recollection of its message will stop them in their tracks.

Collard, R. (1989). *Total Quality; Success Through People.* Wimbledon. Institute of Personnel Management.

A wonderfully concise summary, which covers all the main TQ issues, from the views of the gurus to how to train teams in statistical process control (SPC) and problem solving. Quality is presented essentially as a people development matter.

Part one defines quality and highlights its importance. Part two concerns implementation of a total quality programme, how to bring quality improvement to the forefront in everything done, how to revive the old spirit of craftsmanship even in a modern factory, and how to do away with elitism and restore pride in work, which will result in satisfied customers.

As you would expect in an IPM book there is a lot of very practical guidance on how to communicate throughout the whole organisation and ensure that everyone is trained to play their full part. Very clear guidelines are given which are easy to follow, though they will only succeed if commitment is total.

Crosby, P.B. (1979). *Quality is Free.* New York. New American Library.

Many lively anecdotes and mini novels to back a clear expression of the basic TQ principles. Crosby advocates zero defects in all business activity. By this he means that what the customer ultimately gets conforms absolutely to requirements.

Zero Defect (ZD) days and the tendency to sloganise may not suit all companies, and may not be appropriate where the problems are beyond the control of the individual or team. But, Crosby has a lot of successes. For many he is the introduction to the new philosophy, by his practical and down to earth approach, though many go on to absorb the deeper perceptions of Deming and Juran.

He is very good on the cost of quality and on the cost of not having it. Cut out failure and rework costs, reduce inspections costs drastically and spend money on prevention and overall costs will be substantially down.

Crosby has 14 steps, which in six or so pages gives a complete programme for action, that companies can easily adapt the programme to their own needs.

He has also written *Quality Without Tears* and *The Eternally Successful Organisation*, both published by McGraw-Hill. More stories to make the lessons stick and more exposition of the fourteen steps and the four absolutes which are his hallmark.

Dale, B.G. & Plunkett, J.J. (Ed) (1990). *Managing Quality.* London. Philip Allan

24 articles by various authors, with case studies on companies such as Nissan, Rank Xerox, Lucas and Goodyear. There are guidelines for implementation with a good account of specific techniques such as quality function deployment, reliability assessment and statistical process control.

Quality costs are particularly addressed in several articles. The authors believe that quality should not be made dependent on cost reduction even though this will often happen. The key factor must be customer requirement and this will include recognition of the hidden costs of lost customers, not only cost of rework. The cost of a bad reputation is beyond computation.

This book does not inspire, but it has practical value for those who have already been inspired to action.

Deming, W.E. (1986). *Out of the Crisis.* Cambridge University Press.

A classic. Written in a discursive way, yet very easy to find what you want. Loads of good little sorties to illustrate every point. Hammers home some of his basic themes expressed in the famous Deming 14 points. He explains the idea of operational definitions, by which generalised requirements are seen as inadequate; specific descriptions which can be tested in action are essential in establishing quality.

The theme of variation is clarified; it divides departures from plan into those which derive from specific wrong actions and those which are random fluctuations. The former can be dealt with quite often by the workers involved; the latter are systems issues, which can be improved only by management attention. Yet, so often the workers are blamed for all variations.

Everyone concerned with TQM should have this book on their shelves. Both basic philosophy for transforming a business and specific techniques vie for attention in the guru's testament.

Garvin, D.A. (1988). *Managing Quality; the Strategic and Competitive Edge.* London. Collier Macmillan.

Harvard teacher challenges the failure of USA to live up to the quality mythology through a comparison of Japanese and American firms, particularly in the air conditioning industry. Continuous improvement is superior to AQL (acceptable quality levels) and stable internal standards in winning customers.

The stance of this book is strategic: positioning total quality is fundamental to attaining competitive advantage. The contrast is drawn between leaving quality to the quality department and seeing it as everyone's responsibility. The third chapter is a useful comparison of the different emphasis in a range of definitions of quality.

Hakes, C. (Ed) (1991). *Total Quality Improvement; the Key to Business Improvement.* London. Chapman & Hall.

A PERA International executive briefing. It's probably the quickest way for a newcomer to get to grips with total quality management.

Six key concepts, including customer primacy, never-ending improvement, preventive management and teamwork, are the foundation of the book. Then there are six management elements; and six implementation stages. The book is full of good diagrams and tables.

There is a 100 page "dictionary" of all the main quality issues: B is for BS5750; C is for cause and effect diagram; C is for Crosby; P is for Pareto analysis; Q is for quality costs; S is for statistical process control. You would go a long way to find such a wide range of information in so short a compass.

Finally there are some brief case studies, including Gwent Health Authority, Hewlett Packard, National Westminster Bank, Nissan, Sony, IBM, Cossor Electronics.

Heskett, J.L., Jr, W.E., Hart, C.W.L. (1990). *Service Breakthroughs.* Oxford. Maxwell Macmillan International.

This book is concerned with quality in service industries where certain companies have changed the rules of competition, by setting new standards in consistently meeting or exceeding customer needs and expectations.

It helps understanding of the costs involved in poor quality service, well beyond rework, warranties and system audit. There is help on recovering the customer when things go wrong. The service concept is defined in terms of results achieved for the customer rather than the services performed.

Direct links are shown between quality perceived in this way and customer satisfaction and retention, and also between increased sales and profits and employee retention. The book has many examples from companies such as McDonald's and Federal Express.

Hutchins, D. (1990). *In Pursuit of Quality.* London, Pitman.

An update of the earlier Quality Circles Handbook puts quality circles and the responsibility of all employees in the context of quality and culture change.

The book is workmanlike though not at the expense of an overall concept, illustrated in a chapter heading: "development of a people based philosophy". It gives detailed guidance on running quality circles, including 152 questions and answers. Quality circles are not presented as a whole, though the commitment and widespread involvement of staff they create are seen as crucial.

Quality is defined as everything an organisation does, in the eyes of its customers, to enable them to perceive it as one of the best. The distinction is made between the Western approach which sees systems and procedures as the key to quality and the Japanese which relies more on the training, development and involvement of all its people.

Imai Masaaki (1986). *Kaizen; the Key to Japan's Competitive Success.* New York. Random House.

This is the standard text on continuous improvement as the umbrella under which all the quality concepts can be viewed. Emphasis is on doing little things better, with specific examples. System improvement, not error correction is the true *Kaizen* areas. Innovation is the larger scale, long term change.

Kaizen is an emphatic sort of word to describe never-ending improvement in every part of a business, involving everyone all the time. This book calls it the secret of Japan's competitive success, with total quality as the high road to the wider aim of continuous improvement.

The only index of company success is offering the customer quality of product or service. All other indices are internal measurements. Quality has to come before profit, though it will inevitably follow. From the obsession with continuous improvement come such competition-beating concepts as flexible manufacturing and competing in time, which meet rapidly changing customer and market requirements.

The book is a handbook which can be used when enthusing a company with this concept, which is even wider than total quality management.

Ishikawa, K. (1985). *What is Total Quality Control?* London. Prentice Hall.

One of the Japanese gurus surveys the whole quality scene and stresses that people have more ability than they are given credit for and want to do a good job if given the chance. The approaches and tools of enablement are described, but the people involvement is central.

The Japanese style of total quality is presented as a thought revolution in management. Ishikawa sees the cooperation needed to achieve quality as ultimately creating companies which can share their profits with consumers, employees, shareholders and society in general. They thereby become instruments for enhancing the quality of life of all peoples, and in this way bring peace to the world!

Such lofty sentiments are found in a book which gets down to detail on how to create this quality cooperation within the company in a very practical way, such as concentration on removing the cause of errors and not just the symptoms. While total quality is about respect for humanity it deals in hard facts and not just ideals.

Juran, J.M. (1989). *Juran on Leadership for Quality.* London. Collier Macmillan.

Detailed, but easy to find your way around. The Juran trilogy made clear: quality planning; quality control and quality improvement.

The emphasis is that a total quality approach will be the key to competitive advantage. This means sound leadership from executives with a clear plan which is practical in its details. Juran applies the concepts of business planning and control to quality leadership.

He proposes a step by step approach using project teams and a quality council drawn from the most senior managers. Juran is very management orientated, but like Deming, believes that there must be maximum delegation to the work force, who are well informed on the detail and need to be liberated to make a full contribution.

There is quite a large amount of technical information in the book but even where it is being factual, it is underpinned by an attitude of mind which has to pervade an organisation.

Macdonald, J & Piggott, J. (1990). *Global Quality; the New Management Culture.* London. Mercury Books.

This is a valuable survey of the whole quality scene; all the gurus are there, the cultural context and the techniques and attitudes necessary for success. It is thorough without being too technical. It stresses that TQM means managing in a different way throughout the organisation.

"Make goods or provide services which consistently delight the customer and your reputation will soar; make goods which fall below customer expectation and your customers will flock elsewhere."

This book makes a particularly smooth read for the busy manager. Yet it does not ignore the techniques of statistical process control which give tools to every level of an organisation to own quality. There is a sense of urgency running through the book. Total quality is not an option; it is a matter of survival.

The summaries of the views of the gurus are among the best in print. The charts and checklists are very practical, not least the one which gives the six stages of quality improvement. Highly recommended to develop a "new management culture" which will give a competitive edge to those who take its message seriously.

Mann, N. (1989). *The Keys to Excellence.* London. Mercury.

Very readable story of how Deming's thinking developed, with a good summary of the 14 Points as a new way to manage business. All the key issues are covered in a mere, and eminently readable, 130 pages.

The book lays to rest the idea that it is just Japanese culture that enables them to follow the quality route so effectively. The principles of statistical process control become implicit as part of the wider transformation crusade. Communication, cooperation, collaboration and even collaborative competition are key words in the philosophy expounded in this book.

It is an excellent exercise in "imagineering" thinking what a system would be if it were working perfectly and then comparing this concept of perfection with reality. This creative vision is to be shared in total quality management from the top to every level and area in a business. And it's not just an idealistic concept. It's actually happening in many companies, though still not enough.

Neave, H. (1990). *The Deming Dimension.* Knoxville, SPC Press.

If we are getting rather a lot of Deming in our book list this is no doubt because his followers have been so fired with enthusiasm and see his teachings as a message which can transform companies, and even the way the business world works. Juran and Crosby and Deming agree in more matters than they disagree, though being robust individuals, they might not agree that they do! They are all concerned with total transformation of business and probably society, by knock-on effect.

Neave's book deals with the major issues very powerfully. He helps understanding of the statistical issues as effectively as any writer, using a simple and chatty style. This is viewed in the context of the overall management. People urged to do their best, without the tools and systems needed is fruitless.

Neave moves on to one of Demings latest themes: "joy in work" as something which we should not be embarrassed by, but rather embrace enthusiastically. This is an antidote to the cynical tendencies of our self-deprecating attitudes. "Win-win" for everyone is another theme which receives emphatic coverage.

The role of education in all this is also emphasised, with the reply to someone who claimed to have "installed quality control": "you did NOT! you can install a piece of equipment, but you cannot install knowledge". Another challenging saying is "the first step in learning is curiosity", which takes us back to the theme of continuous improvement.

Oakland, J.S. (1989). *Total Quality Management.* London. Butterworth Heinemann.

A thorough how-to-do-it handbook, which covers most of the practical ground with less of the philosophy and context than some. Good for those who want facts rather than inspiration. Strong on simple statistics.

The fact that it is not following a particular guru's pet themes, makes this book a valuable corrective to riding on the crest of any particular wave. Most managers are probably at first a little put off by the enthusiasms of the gurus and may therefore welcome the lower key of this book. To have six acceptable statements of quality policy in different companies, all focusing on essentially the same objectives, but expressing them differently is somewhat reassuring.

A variety of methods of organising the company for quality are also offered, along with practical measuring approaches and detailed planning proposals. Quality is also taken back into the design process, which lies at the root of all else. How to build a system which links quality into every action of a company is followed by a chapter which describes how everyone can acquire a capability for quality, using statistical techniques, which are very clearly expressed, as well as the enthusiasm that teamwork can generate.

I came back to this book after being enthused by the gurus and valued its down-to-earth help in some practical consultancy in which I was engaged for various organisations.

Popplewell, B. and Wildsmith, A. (1988). *Becoming the Best; How to Gain Company Wide Commitment to Total Quality.* Aldershot Gower.

A novel which I couldn't put down. The TQ truths gradually dawn on everyone in this company. Plenty of memorable discoveries, like "everybody who is doing the job is the expert"; "everybody is a supplier and a customer"; "there's always a better way".

Anyone who has met the problems of invoices going out to the wrong customers will appreciate the story of the major customer who nearly broke off relationships after being refused credit, because he had not paid for an order he had not made and which had not arrived anyway. This illustrates the fact that quality is not only involved in the product or main service, but in everything the company does.

The people issues flow as practical business concerns and not just as a matter of being nice. The essential of success emerged as one of "improving the whole organisation, everybody, everywhere". The story is of a whole organisation turned upside down in a very positive way. It became essential to enable everyone in the company to see where their bit of the action fitted into the whole company purpose. The chain of suppliers and customers, internal as well as external, was also discovered out of necessity.

There is an emphasis on the need to have people working face to face and not merely pushing pieces of paper about. People would also keep their own scores on public notice boards instead of relying on formal reports. In the story, trust and shared information are seen as creating transformation. There was a move from previous protocol in the way of doing things, even, for example, in bringing together unions who had always met separately.

A major realisation was that the top executives who thought they were in charge couldn't possibly do such a job. They could issue edicts, but less senior people could always find ways around them. So why not make people responsible for more of the action as part of the internal supplier/customer chain of people who supplied each other with the results of their labours. The bosses certainly couldn't have stopped that half eaten pork pie from getting into a consignment of electronic goods to an important customer.

An interesting meeting is described where a definition of quality was agreed: "Quality is the degree of excellence by which we satisfy our customer".

Price, F. (1990). *Right Every Time*. Aldershot. Gower.

An entertaining presentation of Deming's 14 points with interesting examples. Deals with the cultural climate in which quality tools are put to work. Not just "how to do it", but "how to understand what you are doing".

The flexibility required by TQM is made clear, so that there is not much store set by rigid job descriptions or rating appraisals. The theme is to get more out of the workers by controlling them less, resulting in a pride in their work which will deliver quality.

There is a piece of fiction running through the book, in nine instalments called the "Idiot's Tale", which while making the book easy to read on a plane or train journey, does not detract from its serious purpose.

Continuous improvement is highlighted with a Welsh proverb "It is not good if it could be better". Price also suggests that when introducing a total quality approach it is not good to get hung up on any one ideology, but let them all come together in the thinking which is relevant to your company. And as to consultants, see them all and who knows you might end up like the man Price talks about. He called in a number of contract garden tractor suppliers. He asked them each for a demonstration and as a result was able to defer his decision for a year!

Rosander, A.C. (1989). *The Quest for Quality in Services*. Ailwaukee. American Society for Quality Control.

A quality veteran applies it all to the services area, distinguishing it from manufacturing. While believing in market research, he accepts subjective judgments of customer reaction as useful. He provides plenty of checklists, case studies, tables and charts. A valuable 570 pages.

He defines the cost of quality as getting rid of non-quality, and stresses that in services quality standards have often to be absolute, eg. you can't have a store assistants who is polite 90% of the time. There can be no acceptable levels of rudeness. So, if there is argument about the meaning of zero defects in products there can be none about services, because "services involve human reliability much more than product reliability".

In service organisations or the service part of any company, the customer deals mainly face to face with the front line employees not with the managers behind the scene. It is therefore essential to train them to act as the full representatives of the company with authority to exercise the flexibility the situation requires.

The kind of errors which can occur in the services are clearly analysed. There is guidance on how to measure these and use the measurement as the basis of improvement. How to motivate staff to provide good service is discussed along with what the gurus have said about services quality specifically. The detail to help the development of quality programmes in service industries is considerable. This book is a must for those concerned in this arena.

Scholtes, P.R. (1988). *The Team Handbook; How to Use Teams to Improve Quality.* Madison, Joiner Associates Inc.

A splendid spiral bound guide with details, methods and techniques for running successful self-directed teams. It is well (and often amusingly) illustrated. Any company seeking to organise its employees into service unit or production teams should issue the guide to the team leaders. No quality circles should be without one. Project teams and task forces will also find it invaluable.

The first two chapters provide as good a summary of the quality approach as you will meet in such a short compass. They include an array of problem solving tools. There are guidelines for running productive meetings and help in building an improvement plan.

There is a wide range of suggestions on how a team can take specific steps to enable it to grow together and work together, including how to win over problem members. Details on how to warm up at the first meeting and how to build up a team on practical and clearly expressed. In fact, it could be read with profit by anyone who has to work and to hold meetings with groups of other people, not least perhaps the boards of companies.

The diagrams and flow charts provided are a valuable contribution to turning the advice into action.

Schonberger, R.J. (1982). *Japanese Manufacturing Techniques.* London. Collier Macmillan.

This applies a whole range of Japanese methods to the operational activity of Western manufacturing (American in particular). Total quality is linked particularly with the Just In Time methods of keeping down inventory by having materials delivered exactly when required. How these can be developed and fitted together are dealt with in detail. The use of Kanban cards are shown to be a very powerful means of communication, contributing to the development of the chain of suppliers and customers within companies.

The book presents nine lessons, based on the fact that management technology is a very transportable commodity. A company-wide habit of improvement is shown to be the basis of success and the adoption of the methods is not culture-dependent. It is not a question of it being appropriate for the Japanese, but not for us.

Much of it is a matter of introducing techniques, but against a background of a cooperative relationship in all parts of the company. Flexible manufacturing is discussed as enabling the minority customers to buy for their particular needs, instead of having to put up with what mass production pours out. Long runs are no longer required and the workforce is multi-skilled. Conveyor belt working is minimised. The key thoughts throughout are of commitment, flexibility and simplicity.

Schonberger, R.J. (1990). *Building a Chain of Customers.* London. Business Books.

As the blurb says of the supplier/customer chain he "shows how the universal adoption of this simple yet fundamental principle can replace destructive interpersonal and interdepartmental wrangling with a powerful and profitable synergy". Every part of a company is united into being a cohesive learning organisation.

It may be difficult for the different parts of a company to imagine what a customer really means, if it is thought of mainly in terms of the ultimate customer. If however, they think in terms of the next person in line inside the company, who is waiting for the results of their labours, then the idea comes alive. And they communicate directly and therefore at each stage of the flow of action there is the opportunity to see that things are right, instead of waiting to the end when the product should be read to go off to the customer. At so late a stage it is then a question of expensive reworking.

Many sacred principles are queried in this book. Why not lump direct and indirect labour together in costing, as direct labour is often only a small part of the whole; ensure you have the true costs of making a product, instead of much of it being an arbitrary overhead; let these things be looked after by operators, gain greater accuracy with less work. And the chain concept enables the aggregation of information to pass with the flow of work, and to be used as it passes.

In everything it is a matter of serve the customer, internal and external, and involve the employee, who may be both a customer and a supplier.

Wellins, R.S., Byham, W.C., Wilson, J.M. (1991). *Empowered Teams.* Oxford. Jossey Bass.

About the clearest book on teams that from the start have been designed to be self-directed and to consist of all the people doing a particular job as a group. Its recipe is detailed and capable of specific application.

"A self-directed work team is an intact group of employees who are responsible for a whole work process or segment that delivers a product or service to an internal or external customer." They work together to improve operating methods, to handle day-to-day operations; they plan and control their work. They are self-managing. They all stand in for each other, instead of sticking rigidly in specific compartments, and the leaders work alongside their colleagues.

They are empowered; that is they have passed to them responsibility and authority which was previously vested only in bosses. They achieve discipline by peer pressure rather than by superior edicts.

Within the company as a whole they may be interlinked, so that the group leader of one may be a member of another, or a function expert on one work team may also be a member of a functional team, thus ensuring a good flow of information back to the operational team.

There are tips in this book for setting up the team, for training a new team and ensuring a spread of critical skills.

Womack, J.P., Jones, D.T. & Roos, D. (1990). *The Machine that Changed the World.* Oxford. Maxwell Macmillan.

Based on in-depth study of the auto industry, lean production emerges as the way to mass customisation instead of mass production. It requires the total quality approach for its success.

The book is applicable to other industries, wherever multiskilled workers use highly flexible and increasingly automated practices to produce high volume in enormous quantity. It avoids the high cost of craft production and the rigidity of mass production. It makes life at work less boring. It requires a workforce to use its mind.

The book illuminates lean production by telling the story of how mass production developed and how it came to outlive its usefulness. The principle of sharing information, instead of holding it back, is crucial to lean production which requires an environment where all the workers are committed to quality and continuous improvement. Its rise is due to the rapidity with which consumer demand now changes, meaning that flexibility and speed of introduction of new product becomes vital.

The authors give detailed guidance of what it all means for running the factory and for the design process. The supplier chain is radically affected by the lean production concept. And cooperation is of the essence. It is no exaggeration to say that this is a seminal work, providing a wider context to total quality management.

British Deming Association (1989–1991). *Deming's 14 Points for Management and Other Pamphlets.* Salisbury. British Deming Association.

About a dozen pamphlets of 20 pages each, covering most of the issues in the 14 points. The Association also stocks technical literature on statistical process control, five of them written or co-authored by Donald J. Wheeler.

Edgar Wille

Index

Bold numbers refer to directory entry